CARING LIKE A STATE

CARING LIKE A STATE

The Politics of Russia's Demographic Crisis

Inna Leykin

INDIANA UNIVERSITY PRESS

This book is a publication of

Indiana University Press
Office of Scholarly Publishing
Herman B Wells Library 350
1320 East 10th Street
Bloomington, Indiana 47405 USA

iupress.org

This book was published with the support of the Israel Science Foundation.

First Printing 2025

Cataloging information is available from the Library of Congress.

ISBN 978-0-253-07350-1 (hardcover)
ISBN 978-0-253-07351-8 (paperback)
ISBN 978-0-253-07352-5 (PDF)
ISBN 978-0-253-07353-2 (ebook)

In memory of my father
Roman Leykin (1936–2002)

CONTENTS

ACKNOWLEDGMENTS

THIS BOOK MATURED SLOWLY, AS BOOKS OFTEN DO. In many ways, it is the product of hundreds of conversations with people on two different continents whom I encountered and who cared for me and my ideas. I feel privileged to acknowledge their kindness, trust, and intellectual curiosity—in other words, their care.

First and foremost, my debt of gratitude goes to the many women and men in Russia who shared their personal and professional lives with me. Most of them will not read their names in this book because of my commitment to confidentiality, but I am deeply grateful for their time and for entrusting me with their stories and life experiences. I am indebted to women in Yekaterinburg who shared with me their stories about experiences of familial care and support. I owe special thanks to the social science institute's researchers for generously allowing me to follow their research and teaching routines. They were patient of my ignorance and kind enough to guide me through the ins and outs of conducting demographic research in Russia. In Yekaterinburg, Lara Petrova offered me intellectual support and friendship. She and her family helped me get settled and made my fieldwork experience joyful and pleasurable. I am eternally grateful for their lifelong friendship.

The book benefited from the intellectual community and friendships I gained over the years. I am immensely grateful for the unfailing support of Michal Kravel-Tovi and Anat Rosenthal, both of whom have read and talked with me through multiple drafts. I am also thankful to Michal Kravel-Tovi for suggesting the title of the book as she read one of the book's many iterations. I have profited from the unparalleled intellectual generosity of Michele Rivkin-Fish, who read the entire manuscript and provided valuable advice. I wish to thank my collaborator Anastasia Gorodzeisky, whose outstanding professionalism has been an inspiration to me and who protected my time so I could finish the manuscript.

Many colleagues and friends read and commented on parts of the book, while others participated in remarkably useful conversations about it. For their intellectual support and for thinking with me about the project throughout its gestation, I would like to thank the following people, listed in no particular order: Caroline Humphrey, Larisa Kurtović, Tomas Matza, Jeremy Morris, Serguei Oushakine, Doug Rogers, Nitsan Chorev, Igal Halfin, Xenia Cherkaev, Alice Elliot, Sohini Kar, Yagmur Nuhrat, Susan Ellison, Andrea Flores, Julia Lerner, Galia Plotkin-Amrami, Dina Moyal, Naor Ben-Yehoyada, Iddo Tavory, Tama Halfin, Anna Temkina, Elena Zdavomyslova, Bianca Dahl, Linda Cook, Lara Petrova, Elena Trubina, Nikolai Ssorin-Chaikov, Jeanne Kormina, Zhanna Chernova, Dominic Martin, Michał Murawski, Peter Meylakhs, Erica Weiss, Dan Rabinowitz, Tamar El-Or, Ofra Goldstein-Gidoni, Tom Pessah, Yifat Gutman, Guy Shalev, Ori Mautner and Tuya Shagdar. I am thankful for their much-appreciated and insightful feedback, which helped me articulate my ideas with more clarity. I am also indebted to the support and friendship of the brilliant scholar Sonja Luehrmann, who sadly passed away before the book was accepted for publication. I am grateful to Janet Christensen, who edited all the chapters with great care and professionalism.

The seeds for the book were sown many years ago at Brown University, and it could not have existed without the dedicated mentorship of Daniel Jordan Smith, Cathy Lutz, and Keith Brown. My utmost gratitude goes to Daniel Jordan Smith—a true mensch—for his superb mentorship skills, extreme intellectual generosity, and unfailing patience. Cathy Lutz has been a true source of personal and professional inspiration, teaching me to think more imaginatively. Long conversations with Keith Brown, his brilliant comments, and wonderful sense of humor played an invaluable role in the development of this project. I am also thankful to Jessa Leinaweaver and Paja Faudree for their scholarly and writing advice. Time spent at the Population Studies and Training Center was invaluable to my research and intellectual development. It taught me how to think and speak across disciplines.

The development of the project was also shaped by conversations with friends and colleagues, and I thank them for making my intellectual journey at Brown a socially significant experience: Yagmur Nuhrat, Kristin Skrabut, Kendra Ferher, Sohini Kar, Susan Ellison, Stacey Vanderhurst, James Doyle, Laura Vares, Andrea Flores, Sarah Newman, Yana Stainova, Katie Rhine, Andrea Mazzarino, Harris Solomon, Jen Ashley, Kathleen Millar, Trille Loft, and Gabriela Sanches-Soto.

The Open University of Israel has been a supportive and stimulating place to work. I am deeply grateful to my colleagues in the Department of Sociology, Political Science, and Communication and wish to thank Dafna Hirsch, Andy Rosenhek, Motty Regev, Dana Kaplan, Anat Ben-David, Eran

Fisher, Gal Levy, Bashir Bashir, Sara Kahn-Nisser, Reut Itzkovitch-Malka, Oren Shlomo, Yagil Levy, and Denis Sharbit for their support and guidance. Thank you also to Rafi Tsirkin-Sadan and Dani Szpruch for the many conversations about socialism, and to Varda Wasserman for her support during the final stages of the writing.

Parts of the book have been presented in conferences, workshops, and seminars to engaged audiences who shared with me an appreciation for healthy debate and heated arguments. I would like to thank the audiences at each of these places: the Working Group on Anthropology and Population, Brown University; *Soyuz*, the Postsocialist Cultural Studies Network Conference; American Anthropological Association Meeting; German Israeli Foundation Young Scientists' Meeting, Potsdam, Germany; Association for Slavic, East European, and Eurasian Studies Annual Conference; departmental seminars at the Department of Sociology and Anthropology, Hebrew University of Jerusalem, and at Ben-Gurion University of the Negev; the Israeli Inter-University Academic Partnership in Russian and Eastern-European Studies Seminar; Anthropology Workshop at the Department of Sociology and Anthropology, Tel Aviv University; Interdisciplinary Seminar on Russia and Eastern Europe, Centre d'études de relations internationals (CERI), Sciences Po, Paris, France; Saint Petersburg's Center for Independent Social Research International Conference, Saint Petersburg, Russia; the Cohn Institute for the History and Philosophy of Science and Ideas' Weekly Research Seminar and the Edmond J. Safra Center for Ethics' Weekly Seminar, both at Tel Aviv University; and Mongolia and Inner Asia Studies Unit Series, Department of Social Anthropology, University of Cambridge.

The Mongolia and Inner Asia Studies Unit in the Department of Social Anthropology, University of Cambridge, has been a supportive place to finish writing this book. Very special thanks to Caroline Humphrey and David Sneath for hosting me at a crucial time in the writing.

This research would not have been possible without funding to develop the project, conduct fieldwork, and write the book. Research and writing have been generously supported by the National Science Foundation's Doctoral Dissertation Improvement Grant; the Andrew Mellon Program in Anthropological Demography, Population Studies and Training Center and Department of Anthropology at Brown University; Career Development Grant from the Open University of Israel; and the Open University of Israel's Gender Equality and Publication Grants. I also gratefully acknowledge the contribution of the Israel Science Foundation toward the publication of this book.

Sections of chapter 1 first appeared in *Slavic Review* (2019) 78 (1), and a version of chapter 3 was first published in *JRAI* (2020) 26 (1). All texts and excerpts are reproduced here with permission from Cambridge University Press and John Wiley and Sons.

At Indiana University Press, Jennika Baines endorsed this project early on and then passed the baton to Bethany Mowry, whose support and professional integrity were exemplary as she guided this project toward completion. I am grateful to two anonymous readers for comments that significantly improved and sharpened the manuscript. I am grateful to Sophia Hebert, Allison Gudenau, and Nancy Lila Lightfoot for their assistance with all aspects of book production. I also thank Alex Trotter, who did the index, and Judith Robey for her superb proofreading skills.

I am grateful to my friends and family who supported me in this endeavor. Thank you to Palina Hariton, Sergey 'Ginger' Solovyev, Michael Ustinov, Ola and Boris Groisman, Annuska Evseeva, Nina Gofman, Masha Dukhovny-Harrary, and Yagmur Nuhrat for our lifelong friendship and for being there for me no matter what. My cousin Ida's family and the Medvedev family were the closest to me during my fieldwork and supported me in innumerable ways.

I thank my mother, Zina, and my brother Jenia's family—Ira, Sonia, Amit, Sharon, and Ronen—for teaching me my first lessons in care and unconditional love. I would like to thank my in-laws Amira and Dov Rabinovitch, the real unsung heroes of this project; without their everyday help and care, filled with humility and kindness, I could not have carried on.

Last but certainly not least, I owe my deepest gratitude to my partner, Oded Rabinovitch, and our two objectively wonderful children, Romi and Ilay. I have been lucky to live in a world brightened by their love, generous spirit, and boundless care. None of it would have meaning without them.

I dedicate this book to the loving memory of my father, Roman, whose frankness, sense of humor, and courage to ask difficult questions I always admired.

NOTE ON TRANSLITERATION, TRANSLATION, IMAGES, AND NAMES

THROUGHOUT THE BOOK, I USE THE LIBRARY OF Congress system of transliteration, with the exception of proper names recognized through alternative spellings (e.g., Yekaterinburg, Bolotnaya Square, Boris Yeltsin, Alexei Navalny, etc.). All translations from Russian into English are my own unless otherwise specified.

Photographs in the book are my own unless otherwise mentioned.

I only use the real names of publicly known figures whose published work I analyze in the book or who were acting in easily identifiable official capacities. The rest of the ethnographic subjects are anonymized.

ABBREVIATIONS

ANKh	Akademiia narodnogo khoziaistva
GosKomStat	Gosudarstvennyi komitet po statistike
Gosplan	Gosudarstvennyi planovyi komitet
IKSI	Institut konkretnykh sotsial'nykh issledovanii
ISI	Institut sotsiologicheskii issledovanii
MGU	Moskovskii gosudarstvennyi universitet
RAGS	Rossiiskaia akademiia gosudarstvennoi sluzhby
Sovnarkom	Sovet narodnykh komissarov
TsDU	Tsentral'nyi dom uchenykh
TsSU	Tsentral'noe statisticheskoe upravlenie
TsUNKhU	Tsentral'noe upravlenie narodnokhoziaistvennogo ucheta
VPSH	Vysshaia partiinaia shkola

CARING LIKE A STATE

INTRODUCTION

Demographic Anxiety

WAITING OUTSIDE THE KOLTSOVO AIRPORT FOR A TAXI to Yekaterinburg in August 2009, I struck up a conversation with Nikolai, who was also waiting for a ride home. A Yekaterinburg native in his mid-fifties, Nikolai worked as a manual laborer by day and a cab driver by night. Years before Uber launched, he, like many Russians, was using his private vehicle as a taxi to supplement his monthly income. When Nikolai asked me about the purpose of my visit, I gave him my well-rehearsed answer: "I'm here to study the demographic crisis [*demograficheskii krizis*]." He looked concerned. "Ha, yes, of course. Russia's dying out. We're dying out," he said earnestly, then paused. "But frankly, I think that in the situation we live in right now, if someone decides to have children, they should be given a medal, no less, but the state doesn't care about that [*gosudarstvo eto ne zabotit*]." He told me that his daughter had been waiting for over a year to place her son in municipal day care, an increasingly scarce service with a long wait list. In the meantime, without day care, his daughter could not go back to work, although her eighteen-month paid maternity leave was nearly over. Nikolai and his wife were helping their daughter as much as they could. "What's to be done [*a chto delat'*]?" he concluded rhetorically.

Olga Shevchenko (2009) has convincingly argued that in post-Soviet Russia the rhetoric of omnipresent crisis has been a ubiquitous framework for describing social reality.[1] The routinization of this framework has made it an important part of public discourse and a resource by which different social actors interpret and act on social reality (Shevchenko 2009). Indeed, the demographic crisis has occupied Russia's social imagination since the fall of the Soviet Union, and dramatic headlines about looming population catastrophe have been familiar to Russian citizens since the 1990s. Low fertility and high mortality rates, persistent over many years, have led to steep population decline, validating the concerns (Parsons 2014; Rivkin-Fish 2003, 2006). However, as Nikolai's reaction demonstrated, in Russia's *demographic crisis*, the fear of having too few people collides with concerns about having more.

My interlocutors' reactions certainly captured these demographic anxieties. Nikolai's sentiment, for example, was not very different from that of population expert Ivan Borisovich Alexandrov,[2] one of my main interlocutors during my year of fieldwork. Like Nikolai, he lamented, "Things are not looking good [*vse plokho*]. The Russian people are dying out [*Russkii narod vymiraet*]. People still can't afford to have more children, but the state doesn't care [*a gosudarstvo eto ne zabotit*]." Both spoke about their fear of the nation's disappearance—"we're dying out"—and, by extension, their fear of the collapse of the state. Both addressed the existential burden of pronatalism, which, without state intervention, can be very taxing on people's lives. Not having children poses a threat to the future of Russia, but having them is a daunting prospect for people concerned about the future of their families.

During my research, these conflicting concerns were almost always punctuated by narratives about state care or lack thereof. In these narratives, the state appeared as main arbiter and main culprit, carelessly asking women to have more children while depriving citizens of the means to take care of them. This pervasive fear of population implosion and the power attributed to a reified notion of state care prompted my interest in the national fascination with the question of population and demography. The demographic crisis seemed to be not only a fear of numerical decline and its implications for a dying nation. It was also a marker of and catalyst for another layer of crisis traversing the social fabric: the crisis of care, and specifically, the crisis of state care.

This book is an ethnographic exploration of the post-Soviet Russian state's aspirations and failures to care for its population. It traces cultural ideas, social actors, and institutional connections through which the country's demographic reality came to be conceived as a grave national problem in need of urgent intervention. As the Russian state increased efforts to reverse the steep decline in birthrates, production and dissemination of socio-demographic knowledge took central stage. Concepts and categories produced by post-Soviet demographic science gradually became a new interpretive framework shaping cultural narratives about state care and its effects on people's lives and aspirations. Demography shaped ideas about, to paraphrase James Scott (1998), how to "care like a state"—about who becomes a deserving subject of care and under what conditions. As vernacular indexing the state's efforts to care for its population, demography has not only shaped the forms of biopolitical care the Russian state exercises but also informed practices of relational care Russian citizens employ in their everyday lives.

Exploring the dynamics between biopolitical forms of state care and mundane care practices, the book argues that the ways in which knowledge about the population problem has been produced, circulated, and translated into political statements and pronatalist policies have impacted social imaginaries about self, normative families, and the Russian state as a fickle caregiver. The state's continued attempts to showcase itself as the most reliable caregiver through pronatalist policies all while privatizing a variety of social services reveal the existential burden of pronatalism. The state's pronatalist aspirations have situated Russian citizens at the crossroads of contradictory structural forces that both encourage and deter them from having more children. The state's ultimate failure to provide Russian families with adequate social conditions in which to comfortably raise their children compelled them to rely on cultural and material networks of support outside state models of care. This failure, thus, elucidated the effects of the state on existing cultural models of self and kinship care in Russia.

The Contradictions of State Care

The fear of population implosion culminated in 2006, when President Vladimir Putin, then in his second term in office, delivered a passionate statement about the country's dire demographic situation in his annual address to the Federal Assembly. "Let's talk about the most important thing [*o samom glavnom*]," he said. "That's right, the Ministry of Defense knows what is of the most importance to us," Putin said jokingly, indexing the threat to Russia's national sovereignty and security. He then drew a rhetorical line from the problem of security to the intimate and socially significant nature of the demographic problem, announcing, "We're going to talk about love, women, and children. About families. And about the most acute problem facing contemporary Russia—about demography" (Kremlin.ru 2006).

As a solution to the problem of declining population, Putin introduced an idea inspired by renowned author Alexander Solzhenitsyn, which he suggested should become a new national ideology: "the state care for the nation" (*sberezhenie naroda*).[3] *Sberezhenie*, the term with which Putin identified the state's commitment to its people, is a polysemic word loaded with different and at times conflicting connotations. It might mean protecting, preserving, or taking care of something or someone, but it can also mean saving, saving up, or economizing. Its plural, *sberezheniia*, exclusively means savings, as in a bank savings account. The singular *sberezhenie* in tandem with people (*narod*) is best translated as protecting, preserving, or taking care of people.

Synonyms for *sberezhenie*, such as protection (*zashchita*) and safeguard (*okhrana*), are no less confusing and shift meaning based on context. As a popular Russian joke goes: "Russian is a difficult language. For example, the nouns *safeguard* [*okhrana*] and *protection* [*zashchita*] are synonyms, but the adjectives *rights* in the context of safeguarding [agencies] [*pravookhranitel'nye*; literally, law enforcement agencies] and *rights* in the context of protecting [organizations] [*pravozashchitnye*; literally, human rights organizations] are antonyms" (Anekdot.ru 2010). Both adjectives combine *rights* (*pravo*) and a variation on *protection*, but as the punchline of the joke points out, although both supposedly denote some form of lawful protection of rights, their meanings clash in contemporary Russian reality. Law enforcement agencies, denoted by the adjective *pravookhranitel'nye*, are associated with the restriction of civil rights, working against national and international human rights organizations, denoted by the adjective *pravozashchitnye*. Highlighting these linguistic contradictions, the joke underscores the unstable meaning of care and protection, which can have pernicious and repressive effects despite the positive connotations of *care*.

The idiom of care and protection (*sberezhenie*) has a tenacious presence in post-Soviet political discourse. According to Boris Yeltsin's son-in-law and adviser, Valentin Yumashev, when Yeltsin announced his retirement on December 31, 1999, and named Vladimir Putin his successor, he asked Putin for one and one thing only: "Take care of Russia [*beregite Rossiiu*]" (*BBC News* 2019). During Putin's second term as president, the rhetoric of care came to even greater prominence; centralization of the state as a main source of care and benevolence became one of the regime's central political strategies.[4] Alongside neoliberal policies that outsourced the provision of social services to nonprofit and for-profit organizations, the Russian state under Putin worked hard to assert its role as primary provider in charge of both distributing and withholding care (Bindman 2017).

The annual Direct Line with Vladimir Putin is a notable example of how the regime generates and reproduces its image of a benevolent but fickle giver, providing and as easily withdrawing care.[5] Once a year, for three to four hours, Putin receives carefully curated messages and phone calls from ordinary citizens residing in Russia and the Commonwealth of Independent States, known as the near abroad.[6] In many of these calls, citizens complain about local injustices or social and infrastructural problems, asking Putin to personally intervene. The dramaturgy of "Direct Line" casts Putin in the role of benefactor with singular authority to intervene where local officials fail (Gorham 2014, 152–56). Famously, in many of these cases, Putin performatively scolds local officials for not fulfilling their duties and then, in some cases, personally follows up to ensure the problem's resolution (Gorham 2014; Mukhametshina and Bocharova 2019).

The rhetoric of state care, personified in Putin's image as a just and benevolent distributor and provider of care, guided the post-Soviet state's ambition to influence the reproduction of a seemingly dying nation. Social, welfare, and demographic policies were bundled under the banner of state care for the nation (*sberezhenie natsii*) (Goncharenko 2011; Lebedev 2007; Morozov 2009; Pyatigorskaya 2019; Shkel 2006; Zavrazhin, Kuksin, and Kuzmin 2017). State programs aimed at improving population dynamics were referred to as part of a "government strategy for taking care of the people" (*strategiia sberezheniia naroda*) (Morozov 2009). Inspired by Solzhenitsyn's idea that taking care of its people should be the country's national ideology, a new social conservative movement called For Protecting/Taking Care of the People (*Za sberezhenie naroda)* was established in 2009. Its stated mission was to improve the quality of life in Russia and monitor the state's chief mission of taking care of its population (Dashkov 2009; Zasn.ru 2009).

In 2007, the construction of the state as primary caregiver preserving the dying nation was operationalized in a new national monetary policy intended to stimulate fertility. Putin's address to the nation identified falling birthrates as the core of the problem and the main target of state intervention. Following the address, the government launched a high priority (*prioritetnaia*) pronatalist policy built almost exclusively around facilitating birthrates through monetary incentives. Called Maternity Capital (Materinskii Kapital), the new policy mandated the payment of a one-time lump sum of money with monthly inflation adjustment (250,00 RUB in 2007 and 693,144 RUB in 2022) to women who gave birth to a second or subsequent child after December 31, 2006 (see fig. 0.1). The money was initially paid to a woman when her child turned three and could be used for three purposes: the mortgage, the child's education, and the mother's retirement plan. Of the three, improving the family's living conditions via home mortgage has been the most popular (Borozdina et al. 2016).

Since its launch in 2007, the policy has been amended several times, becoming an important state instrument for accommodating crises. In

Figure 0.1. The Maternity Capital advertisement banner. 2010. "343,378 RUB for the child's education, the mortgage, and the mother's retirement plan. When your child turns three it is time to turn in a request!" Photo by the author.

2013, after the Maternity Capital policy had been running for several years, rumors began to crop up that the Ministry of Finance was lobbying the government to end the policy after its initial term in 2018 (Aptekar 2017; Baklanov 2014). Instead, it was reinstated for ten more years in 2013; in early 2020, before the onset of the global pandemic and with birthrates plummeting, President Putin announced an update on the policy, offering 466,617 RUB for the birth of a *first* child and another 150,000 RUB for the birth of a second child (Kremlin.ru 2020).[7] In late 2022, almost a year after the invasion of Ukraine and with the Russian economy in shambles, a proposal to allow the use of Maternity Capital for paying utility bills emerged. The proposal had little to do with the initial motivation of stimulating birthrates and focused on the Maternity Capital's capacity to alleviate the economic burden of growing inflation and rising prices (Dubrovina 2023; *RBK Life* 2023).[8]

The Maternity Capital policy, embedded in the state's pronatalist ideology, is a form of biopolitical care in which the Russian state is presented as a rational actor, providing its citizens with necessary support and allowing them to fulfill their desire to reproduce. State care offered by the Maternity

Capital policy is founded on a direct monetary transaction between the state and citizens. In this disenchanted model of care, state and citizens are imagined as two rational actors conducting a market exchange driven by a cost-benefit analysis of respective needs. In this sense, the meaning of state care offered by the Maternity Capital policy falls closer to the economic meaning of the word *sberezhenie* than to a meaning of care that implies an indirect and socially significant mutuality of relations between the state and its citizens.

Following the introduction of the policy, information about the problem of population delivered by experts, political contenders, and the general public produced conflicting interpretations of the care offered by the state. Optimistic political statements about rising fertility rates nurtured by the new economic incentives (Andreev 2014) were challenged by statistics showing that direct monetary incentives rarely produce positive effects on population growth in the long run (Timakov and Tokarev 2014; Vishnevsky 2010). Many of my interlocutors, young mothers who were not experts in demography but rather potential targets of the policy, voiced similar skepticism with a different set of ethical justifications. When speaking about their own reproductive choices, they rejected the self-interest implied in the Maternity Capital policy. "People have children because they want them, not because the state pays them to have them," they would say. Even if the policy played a part in their reproductive decisions—and perhaps it did—distancing themselves from transactional relations of care with the state allowed them to protect the symbolic order in which parents make responsible decisions about and for their children, outside state interests. In this symbolic order, relations of care are bound in mutuality, and care appears as an impartial and socially significant act.

The full-scale Russian military invasion of Ukraine in February 2022 intensified the rendering of the state as a benevolent caregiver and savior of the shrinking national body. While mortality rates for men have been growing, most likely due to war casualties (*Mediazona* 2023a; *Meduza* and *Mediazona* 2023; *Meduza* 2024a, 2024b, 2024c), Putin continues to identify the problem of birthrates and the state's commitment to preserving the nation as a main objective (*TASS* 2024a). Since the beginning of the full-scale invasion, policy proposals in the name of population care have been introduced on the federal level. Some offer monetary incentives to women and men, encouraging them to reproduce (Nabatkina 2023; *TASS* 2024a); others promote more repressive means, such as restricting women's rights to abortion (Chernova 2023; Preobrazhensky 2023). On the regional legislative level, short of a full ban on abortion, restrictions have been introduced, and several private clinics are outright refusing to provide abortions (Strel'nikov 2023; *Mediazona* 2023b).

The annexation of Crimea in 2014 and the invasion of Ukraine in 2022 have altered the contours of population understood as that which the Russian state should care for and protect. If in 2006, when the alarm about the demographic situation peaked, the problem of population was exclusively circumscribed by the borders of the Russian Federation, in 2014 the idea of state care for population began to expand beyond the borders of the nation-state, echoing nationalistic and imperialist streaks in Solzhenitsyn's idea of care for the nation. Following the invasion of Ukraine in 2022, the language of state care was further militarized, expanding the object of state care beyond the sovereign borders of the Russian state and excluding those unwilling to follow its ideological imperative.

Perhaps some of the most troubling and pernicious forms of state care have been allegations of the Russian state kidnapping Ukrainian children and moving them to Russian boarding schools and foster care (Gall et al. 2023; Landay and Lewis 2023; Konstantinova 2023). At the time of writing, Ukraine reports twenty thousand children kidnapped to Russia (*BBC News* 2023; "Diti viini" [Children of war] 2024). While Ukrainian and international authorities speak about the displacements in terms of possible war crimes for which Russia might be prosecuted, the Russian government claims it is a humanitarian effort to save and protect children whom the Ukrainian state has failed (Yapparova 2024). The children, Russian commissioner for children's rights Maria L'vova-Belova claimed, were evacuated from war zones and saved by the Russian state (Nazarova 2023). L'vova-Belova herself personified the state's malevolent benevolence by adopting a Ukrainian child from Mariupol. She openly acknowledged that children brought to Russia from Ukraine and in the process of receiving Russian citizenship go through a process of reeducation to transform their initially negative attitudes toward Russia into love for the country (*Meduza* 2022a; Yapparova 2024).[9]

Caring for the Population, Caring for the People?

To begin unpacking the political influence of demographic expertise on post-Soviet state care and cultural narratives about the demographic crisis, a discussion of concepts central both to demography and state care programs is required. In Russian state discourse on the demographic crisis, people (*narod*), nation (*natsiia*), and population (*naselenie* or *narodonaselenie*) have been interchangeably used to name the entity in need of urgent state intervention for population growth. The Russian term for the problem of population (*problema narodonaseleniia*) stresses population as the object of immediate state intervention, although unlike its English equivalent, the word *narodonaselenie* merges *people* (*narod*) with *population* (*naselenie*) and emphasizes the shared territory a group of people might populate.[10] State programs aimed at improving demographics switch focus from *population* to *people* or *nation* as the political entity the state is committed to preserving and protecting. They have been interchangeably called state programs for taking care of or preserving the people (*programmy narodosberezheniia*) and programs for taking care of or preserving the nation (*programmy sberezheniia natsii*).

The late Soviet and post-Soviet comedian and keen observer of everyday life and politics Mikhail Zhvanetsky once reflected on this conceptual muddle and the contradictions between the two terms—*people* and *population*—in the language of state officials. Not long before his death, he published a short sketch called "Population and People" (*naselenie i narod*) in which he satirized the formulaic nature of bureaucratic language—a long-standing punch line of Soviet and post-Soviet comedians. Poking fun at bureaucratic red tape, the sketch describes an imaginary dialogue between two state officials, seemingly of the same rank. At one point, one official says to the other: "Oh, people . . . The people are incomparable with the population. You feel the difference too, right?" The officials then lament that "the people" interfere with efforts to make the lives of "the population" better. When one asks a question about a certain public service "for the people" (*dlia naroda*), the other replies: "The population (*naselenie*) shouldn't be worried." Then, one of them inquires: "Could our population count on a small meeting with the people? . . . The letters from the population [*naseleniia*] keep asking if there's a way for them to catch sight of the people [*narod*] somehow." "Unfortunately, I'm not authorized to make that call," the other replies (Zhvanetsky 2018). The juxtaposition of "the people" and "the population," both ostensibly under the purview of the officials, creates a satirical gap in the highly formulaic and standardized bureaucratic language. In the dialogue, the people's desires and wishes are depicted as a burden, interfering with the officials' work for the population. In contrast to the people, in the bureaucratic parlance of the officials, the population is a faceless and desireless object of state intervention.

Zhvanetsky's insightful observation is relevant to the ways in which the object of state care has been delineated in discourse on the demographic crisis. Although often used interchangeably to identify the problem of population in Russia, the concepts of population and people have different political and historical underpinnings. People (*narod*) and nation (*natsiia*) are grounded in the ideology of the modern nation-state. Population (*naselenie*), on the other hand, is a statistical artifact; although also historically related to the birth of the modern nation-state, it is grounded in a logic of scientific measurement.

Throughout modern history, population measurements such as censuses and surveys have been part and parcel of administrative technologies and governing tools of nation-states, empires, liberal democracies, and socialist/communist federations (Blum 2001; Curtis 2001; Kertzer and Arel 2002).[11] As scholars of modern politics and science have repeatedly demonstrated, the statistical artifact of population, born and nurtured in the modern political era, effectively turned the ideological construct of the people or nation into an object of state power and control. The work of statistical categories and techniques made an amorphous composite of people into *population*—a coherent entity uniformly recognizable by the authorities—making society legible to the state (Alonso and Starr 1987; Curtis 2001; Desrosières 1998; Greenhalgh and Winckler 2005; Porter 1995; Schweber 2006; Scott 1998).

As the book dives deeper into the production and circulation of discourse on the demographic crisis, it demonstrates the role of the post-Soviet science of demography in providing the government with knowledge about population and imbuing the statistical construct of population with a variety of ideological imperatives. Sustained tension between population and people and between the descriptive and prescriptive aspects of demographic knowledge, as the examples in this book show, shapes the object, understood by a variety of social actors as deserving care and protection.

The Political Arithmetic of Numerical Decline

The shape of Russia's population structure warrants special attention as the country's population dynamics are both similar to and different from those of other industrialized societies. Russia's birthrates have been declining steadily since the late 1960s, on par with birthrates in other Eastern and Western European countries (Zakharov 2008). Total fertility rates (TFR)—the average number of children born per woman—began to fall below the replacement level of 2.1 children per woman in the late Soviet period.[12] In 1991, following the dissolution of the Soviet Union, fertility rates fell to 1.75

per woman; in 1997, they fell to their lowest recorded level, 1.2 per woman (World Bank Indicators 2022b). When I began my research in 2009, birthrates were between 1.2 and 1.4 children per woman, which, along with a rapidly aging population, resembled population trends in other industrialized countries, many of which are anxious about low fertility (Frejka et al. 2008).

Unlike other industrialized societies, however, Russia also has high mortality rates and an unbalanced life expectancy at birth for men and women. Russia's excess mortality following the fall of the Soviet Union was unprecedented for a country neither at war nor experiencing an acute health crisis (Parsons 2014; Leon, Shkolnikov, and McKee 2009). Mortality rates were particularly staggering for men of working age. In 2000, the difference in life expectancy between Russia and other industrialized countries was fifteen years for men and eight years for women (Ivanov, Vishnevsky, and Zakharov 2006). In 1995, life expectancy for men was as low as 58.1 years. In 2009, the estimated life expectancy was 62.8 years for men and 74.7 for women (Rosstat 2011a).[13] The immediate upshot of these population trends was that by 2010, Russia's population had declined to 142.9 million from 148 million in 1990, a loss of 5.1 million people over a twenty-year period (Rosstat 2011b).[14]

Over the next decade, as the economic situation gradually improved, birthrates began to rise and life expectancy at birth for men began increasing; it reached 68 years in 2019, although life expectancy in Russia remains one of the lowest of the entire Eurasian region (World Bank Indicators 2022c).[15] The annexation of Crimea in 2014, generating a little under 2.3 million new Russian citizens, temporarily compensated for the natural population decline (the difference between birth and death rates), and from 2009 until 2018, Russia's population was indeed growing in its absolute numbers (Rosstat 2022a).

In 2018, Russia's population began to decline once again (Rosstat 2020, 75). Between approximately 2015 and 2018, a new and much smaller cohort of women, born in the late 1990s and early 2000s—the worst years of the population decline—entered their reproductive phase, considerably reducing the absolute number of women of reproductive age. The lower fertility rates of this cohort were accompanied by an increase in the age of mothers at first birth (twenty-six years old in 2017 compared to twenty-one in 1999), slowing natural population growth as the population continued to contract (Berishvili 2018). In 2020, TFR—the main focus of Russia's population concerns—dropped to 1.5 children per woman (World Bank

Indicators 2022b). With the number of women of reproductive age down 30 percent over the last ten years, in 2022, birthrates were as low as in 2001, and it seems unrealistic to expect a rise any time soon (Guskova 2022; *Moscow Times* 2023). As a reminder, birthrates of 2.1 children per woman are needed for the population to reproduce itself.[16]

Outmigration since the beginning of the war in Ukraine, adding to the decline, has been visible but hard to quantify (Starostina 2022; *Re: Russia* 2023b). Although exact numbers are difficult to ascertain, media reports indicate that an estimated six to eight hundred thousand men and their family members have crossed the borders of neighboring states in opposition to the war or to flee the draft (Light 2022; *Novaya Gazeta* 2024; Otte 2022; *Re: Russia* 2023a; *Reuters* 2022b; Sauer 2022a). The Russian authorities themselves do not deny that since the beginning of the war, more people have left the country than have arrived in it (Rosstat 2022b, 200–203; Zlobin 2022).[17]

When looking at demographic rates since 1991, save for a few years (2013–2015), the trend of more deaths than births per thousand people is continuous (Rosstat 2022a). While these numbers validate the state's preoccupation with population, they also showcase its chronic failure to improve the demographic situation and reproduce Russia's population.

The Origins of the Demographic Crisis:
Spiritual Deficit or Social Change

The dangers of depopulation (*opasnost' depopuliatsii*), as it is often called in Russia, have long been at the center of debates about the unique character of the Russian political system (Rosenholm and Savkina 2008). As I searched for the media's portrayal of the population problem, I collected a variety of bold titles about demography and the viability of the Russian nation. Building on the tendency to anthropomorphize the nation-state through somatic metaphors (Oushakine 2010; Rivkin-Fish 2006), titles forwarded dire claims such as "Russia is not healthy and it is losing its viability" (Pechenkin 2010), or "We are about to lose [the patient] our country" (Meshkov 2008). A newspaper article began with the dramatic statement, "Russia is sick with 'demography'" (Nevinnaya 2007).[18]

Important public figures and leading businessmen joined the discussion (Yakunin, Bagdasaryan, and Sulakshin 2007; Yuriev 2007). Vladimir Yakunin, former CEO of Russian Railways, published a series of essays on the demographic crisis, all saturated with somatic metaphors of the suffering, unwell Russian nation in acute need of speedy recovery. Promoting a sense of urgency, Yakunin and his coauthors employed bold metaphors such as "the demographic Chernobyl" and "the demographic genocide of the nation" to describe the gravity of the problem (Yakunin, Bagdasaryan, and Sulakshin 2007).

In addition to the centrality of somatic metaphors, spirituality (*dukhovnost'*) has figured prominently in cultural narratives about the demographic crisis in Russia. Even though the concept of spirituality has roots in a variety of theological and philosophical traditions, its use here originated in Soviet attempts to secularize spirituality, offering post–World War II Soviet citizens a new way to imagine sociality (Luehrmann 2011, 165–92; Smolkin 2019).[19] In discourse on the demographic crisis, spirituality is portrayed as a fundamental, traditional national value that guides appropriate and virtuous ways to relate to oneself and others as well as an important prescriptive element in the country's demographic recovery (*Demoscope Weekly* 2003; Sulashkin 2008).

Similar to its Soviet iteration, *dukhovnost'* is conceived here as an individual code of behavior and a means for fulfilling ideals the state promotes. Quite literally, enhanced spirituality is depicted as a pronatalist factor encouraging birth and stimulating fertility among women. Mixing religious and secular meanings of spirituality, one prolific commentator offered a convoluted quantitative model for the revitalization of Russia's demography based on the nation's "vitality coefficient," in which the ideological-spiritual condition (*ideino-dukhovnoe sostoianie*) of Russian society was the main variable (Sulashkin 2008). In this iteration of the discourse, adopting a moral code of behavior helps reestablish the appropriate, seemingly authentic spiritual condition of the nation, eventually reversing the decline in population numbers.

The framing of the problem of population as a consequence of a spiritual deficit (*defitsit dukhovnykh tsennostei*) has been ubiquitous, employed by population experts, laypersons, and political contenders alike. The perceived antinatalist values of the Soviet regime and emerging consumerist society have been presented as skewing people's moral compasses and thus as causing low fertility rates (Antonov 2009). Underpopulation as a sign of moral-spiritual degradation has been prominent in nationalist discourses that explain depopulation as the goal pursued by foreign forces working systematically to impede the organic development of the Russian nation and to exterminate the Russian people (Oushakine 2009b, 2010). In 2012, a famous post-Soviet author with nationalist inclinations and a huge reader-ship published an open letter accusing cosmopolitan liberals (read, Jews) of devising a deliberate plan to eradicate the Russian nation by means of depopulation (Prilepin 2012).[20]

The Soviet regime, under which the idea of secular spiritual develop-ment was invented, has been blamed for the spiritual deficit, the moral confusion, and ruptures with imagined traditional lifestyles. Proponents of this view argue that reintroducing "the normative need for children" into women's reproductive strategies and rewarding women for fulfilling their moral and social duties will strengthen the importance of family as a valuable social institution and change population dynamics regardless of people's material conditions (Rivkin-Fish 2003, 2010).

Since the full-scale invasion of Ukraine in February 2022, discussions about the threat of population implosion have intensified, and the language of demography has been further militarized. Prompting anxiety over dwin-dling population numbers and fear of foreign others attempting to over-power the country, population implosion-cum-explosion became a major rhetorical device employed by both supporters of the war and those who openly opposed it. As the war ravaged neighboring Ukraine, the projected demographic hell also became an important rhetorical tool in the revan-chist politics of the current regime.

Tapping into anti-Western sentiment and the sense of foreign threat, political contenders invoked demography as a weapon with which anti-Russian forces were endeavoring to destroy Russian sovereignty. To fight this destructive influence, Putin's propagandists and political contenders urged the government to implement a more proactive approach to encour-aging families to have more children (*TASS* 2024a). Conservative values were presented as a positive force capable of protecting Russia's population, political sovereignty, and national unity (President of Russia 2022a, 2022d; *TASS* 2022b). Strengthening nearly extinct traditional values was narrated as fundamental to the state's efforts to remedy its population problem and guard the nation's imagined moral integrity. Large families (i.e., families with more than three children) were championed as the foundation of such traditional values. Once they become a social norm, it was argued, these families will be effective weapons in the battle against demographic chal-lenges (*Izvestiia* 2022).

Discussions of the demographic crisis in Russia are rich with apoca-lyptic metaphors meant to convey the urgency of the problem and its grave implications for the health and wealth of the nation. Apocalyptic framings of the population problem laid the groundwork and provided language for conservative ideologies based on imagined traditional values as well as for anti–human rights legislation and political decisions. Purportedly designed to guard the moral integrity of the nation, these legislations and policies are often justified by a profound social necessity to solve the demographic problem. Thus, one of the main reasons for urgently protecting traditional values from the mores of the LGBTQ community has been its purported "destructive ideological influence on Russia's citizens that threatens the demographic situation in the country" (President of Russia 2022d, 4).

Moralized arguments about the dangers of depopulation compete with lived experiences of impoverished childcare and health systems that make it difficult for families to plan a reproductive future (Arkhangelsky et al. 2015). During the initial period of economic liberalization in the early 1990s, newly privatized factories and other industrial enterprises, possessing social infrastructure inherited from their Soviet predecessors, responded to an economistic disaggregated analysis by eliminating facilities that were not profitable, including many childcare facilities. In the decade between 1990 and 2000, a drastic drop in TFR—from 1.8 in the early 1990s to 1.2 in 2000—meant that remaining childcare facilities, salvaged by local governments, were working at half capacity, prompting municipal decisions to rent the buildings out for other purposes (Ivanov, Vishnevsky, and Zakharov 2006). Because some of these facilities had been spacious buildings made to accommodate children of different ages under the same roof, during my fieldwork, it was not uncommon to see a former day care or kindergarten, haphazardly renovated, operating as a bank or a gym—or, at one point, as a local branch of a federal university.

Once the birthrate began rising again around 2008–2009, the shortage of kindergartens and other social facilities became a real obstacle for working parents and their children. Private preschools were slow to develop because of bureaucratic difficulties—preschool education is a highly regulated field of governance, and new legislation could not keep up with the growing shortage of kindergartens—and a more general distrust of private childcare institutions. To compensate for the shortage of childcare facilities, parents had to rely on themselves or their extended families for several years before they could enroll their children in day care (Arkhangelsky et al. 2015, 56–57). Consequently, because child-rearing responsibilities fall disproportionally on women, young mothers were often in danger of losing their employment. Many of my interviewees cited such impoverished social infrastructure as the main reason for their reluctance to have more children and for the population decline more generally.[21]

However divergent and politically contingent views on the sources of the demographic crisis and crisis of infrastructures of care, fear of underpopulation—and by extension, of state collapse—has been palpable in Russia. My encounters during fieldwork captured the emotional poignancy at the heart of this preoccupation with demography and adjacent pronatalist state interventions. With matters of population high on the public agenda, the language of demography has impacted debates about other important social issues, offering Russian citizens means for articulating their relationships with the state and perceptions of changing social reality.

Tracing Socio-demographic Knowledge

The book traces socio-demographic knowledge from sites of production through policy and popular discourse to the subjective experiences of people targeted by these policies. From social scientists who produce and use statistical representations to translate ethical concerns about demographic behavior into seemingly objective facts to nonstate actors who circulate ideas about appropriate targets of state care to citizens who respond and reconfigure official expectations, informed as they are by demographic data—the book provides a detailed portrait of the social organization of the Russian demographic crisis and the meanings of care it generates.

I conducted a little over twenty-four months of ethnographic research in Yekaterinburg (formerly Sverdlovsk). My research consisted of two three-month visits, one in 2007 and another in 2008; a year of fieldwork in 2009–2010; summer visits in 2011, 2013, 2016, and 2018; and continuous conversations with my interlocutors through email, social media, and phone calls. During my yearlong stay in Yekaterinburg, I spent most of my days in a large social scientific research institute, where I joined a group of scientists involved in the production and dissemination of demographic knowledge. I specifically focused on scholars' intellectual and professional practices and research interests, as well as their descriptive and prescriptive research designs, and generally followed their work routines. I participated in weekly meetings, assisted in research by crunching data collected in surveys, and prepared research proposals. I also helped organize and attended a variety of conferences, workshops, and roundtables dedicated to the problem of underpopulation in Russia. At these conferences, I made contacts with and became increasingly aware of the expanded range of experts pertinent to the production and enactment of discourse on the demographic crisis.

I paid close attention to interactions among social scientists conducting population-related research and local and regional state bureaucrats, seeking to ascertain the means by which knowledge about the population problem is produced and disseminated. Following the trajectory of socio-demographic knowledge, I also observed a variety of demographers' pedagogical activities and participated in professional development trainings they facilitated. Studying population experts' disciplinary culture and dispositions as well as their engagements with state power shed light on the social processes of vernacularization of socio-demographic knowledge for statecraft. In turn, this vernacularization illuminated the processes by which certain scientific ideas were determined to be true and authoritative.

I began my participant observation in the institute in 2009; although I arrived from the US, I was given easy and inclusive access to the institute and research team.[22] My status in the institute oscillated between that of an apprentice helping with questionnaires and number crunching and a colleague from an American university researching the organization of demographic research in Russia. My main interlocutor, Prof. Alexandrov, would often introduce me to colleagues from other departments in the institute as a student who had come all the way from the US to study with him. To regional government officials, he would introduce me as a colleague from a foreign university who was nevertheless fluent in Russian. I was satisfied with both roles as they gave me access to different aspects of Alexandrov's and his colleagues' professional and personal trajectories.[23]

Social scientific knowledge in general and socio-demographic knowledge in particular have of course played an important role in shaping state reasoning in a variety of historical and political contexts (Camic, Gross, and Lamont 2011; Curtis 2001; Kreager 2004). The post-Soviet context is no exception. The fame of post-Soviet demographers has been less predictable, however. The first decade of the twenty-first century was a heyday for the professional community of demographers in Russia, and their celebrity status was undeniable. In our conversations, state officials, public figures, and representatives of NGOs would often reference specific scholarly arguments or professional disagreements between schools of thought in Russian demography to justify political statements about the problem of underpopulation.

The demographers' presence in media, publications, and intellectual quarrels could only be compared to the popularity of population debates in the mid-twentieth century prompted by Paul Ehrlich's (1968) bestseller *Population Bomb*. Like Ehrlich, who popularized Malthusian perspectives on the threat of global overpopulation using fatalistic and dramatic language, Russian demographers did not shy away from applying an apocalyptic style to warn about consequences of a national population implosion. They portrayed Russia's future as an impending demographic hell and emphasized the prescriptive dimensions of their knowledge to morally legitimize their expertise. These dynamics, the book demonstrates, have made Russian population experts into important social actors who shape how socio-demographic reality has been displayed to and perceived by the public.

Grounded in the "public trust in numbers" (Porter 1995), with their perceived impartiality and objectivity, the science of population has been used in different social and historical contexts to promote a sense of political and social crisis and to solicit a response of care (Bashford 2007; Connelly 2008; Douglass 2005; Greenhalgh 2008; Kravel-Tovi 2018, 2020; Ipsen 2002). These public discourses about population have been framed by the genre Andreu Domingo (2008) refers to as "demodystopia"—"dystopias that are brought about by demographic change or that make population matters a salient concern" (Domingo 2008, 725). Although Domingo is writing about literary works of science fiction, popular discourse about the problem of population follows a similar logic (see also Shriver 2003). In France, the late nineteenth-century organization National Alliance produced scientific brochures passionately alerting politicians and the general public to the dangers of depopulation (Quine 1996). In the 1930s in Western Europe, indicators of Soviet population growth were presented as an immediate and undeniable threat to Europe (Blum 2005, 54). Paul Ehrlich encouraged literary authors to write books and plays emphasizing the apocalyptic impact of overpopulation on humankind and the nature of social existence (Domingo 2008, 729). The alarming language of scientific demographic discourse in contemporary Italy has provoked fears of immigration and moral panic over the shrinking Italian population (Krause 2005). In contemporary Asian countries, discourses about low fertility and aging populations often follow the rules of the demodystopian genre (Whittaker 2022). After the fall of the Berlin Wall, in newly established Eastern European countries, demography was used as moral currency; the goal of rising fertility rates was seen as a major mission in national recuperation (Gal and

Kligman 2000). In post-Soviet Russia, a variety of social actors—health professionals, religious activists, and political contenders—have mobilized the demodystopian genre to advance political and social agendas (Leykin and Rivkin-Fish 2022; Luehrmann 2016; Rivkin-Fish 2005, 2006).

Framed, in Laura Nader's oft-repeated phrase, as "studying up," scrutinizing social scientific expertise and its implications is a particularly apt means to gain insight into key sites of power (Boyer 2008; Carr 2010; Gusterson 1996; Holmes and Marcus 2005). Rather than studying up, however, my research is better described as what anthropologists of policy and international aid call "studying through," which links knowledge production, discourses, policy prescriptions, and targets across levels and processes (Ellison 2018; Shore and Wright 1997, 14; Wedel 1998, 2005). Tracing links between seemingly unrelated processes occurring in the social sciences, politics, and the everyday lives of Russian citizens provided an opportunity to focus on how professional practices and knowledge produced by population experts have provided policymakers and policy implementers with a means for describing social reality as a grave existential crisis necessitating immediate state intervention. It also allowed me to examine the impact and the burden of the state's performances of care on Russian citizens.

The Fraught Relations of Care

With the aim of following science and policy in more intimate domains of social life, I complemented participant observation in the institute with research on other social actors disseminating knowledge about population and the role of the state in solving the crisis. I followed a local NGO's programs educating university students about family matters and intergenerational relations. Attending training sessions allowed me to follow the role of nonprofit organizations loyal to the state in promoting dominant cultural narratives about family as a core object of state intervention and governance. Working with a nonprofit designated by the state as socially oriented (*sotsial'no orientirovannaia*) also helped crystallize social and political processes through which, along with increasingly neoliberal social policies and the outsourcing of their provision, the Russian state has preserved its image as singular and chief distributor of care and social support.

Young women, some of whom participated in the NGO's programs and others whom I found through my growing networks of acquaintances, became my interlocutors, offering insights into the range of popular reactions to the state's pronatalist agendas and efforts to care for its population. For the better part of the year, I participated in the daily routines of twenty women between the ages of twenty-three and fifty-five, and I continued to visit them in the following years. Spending time in their midst and learning about everyday strategies of caring for their families laid bare reciprocal dynamics between models of state care and mundane familial care practices. It transpired in my ethnographic explorations of kinship care practices that the new pronatalist regime, while clearly failing in its explicit goal to transform people's reproductive decisions, has been influential in affecting the redistribution of kinship care in post-Soviet Russia. Using strategies of kinship care inherited from Soviet political and economic policies—grandmother care and the distribution of living spaces among relatives—my interlocutors negotiated two conflicting forces: state pronatalism and its burden.

My ethnographic account of post-Soviet attempts to care for population builds on anthropological meditations on biopolitical and relational forms of care. General debates about care in anthropology range from understanding it as a moral practice that sustains social relations through lateral forms of solidarity to seeing it as a practice that generates hierarchical relations and inequality (Buch 2015; Martin, Myers, and Viseu 2015; Shohet 2021; Yarris 2020). Relations of care are necessarily shaped by social structures of inequality (Han 2012). They can be experienced as a matter of course, an obligation, or a burden, shaped by socially and historically situated expectations and practices (Alber and Drotbohm 2015; Cook and Trundle 2020; Han 2012; Read and Thelen 2007). Care is essentially a responsive and reactive practice, relational in nature and foundational to making and breaking social relations (Noddings 2013; Gelsthorpe, Mody, and Sloan 2020a).[24] As Lisa Stevenson (2014) poignantly demonstrates in her ethnography of care in the Canadian Arctic, although we tend to attribute a positive meaning to the word *care*, it is never only benevolent and can be perceived by those receiving it as malicious and uncaring. In other words, care is fraught with contradictory motivations, practices, and interpretations, blurring binary distinctions between benevolent and uncaring, inclusion and exclusion (see also Cook and Trundle 2020; Garcia 2010; Han 2012; Gelsthorpe, Mody, and Sloan 2020b). As the book will demonstrate, the Russian case exemplifies these contradictions: The state's efforts to care for the reproduction of its population are often perceived by those asked to reproduce as a burden and a strain on their lives.

There is a general consensus that care is also a political practice foundational to biopolitics (Ticktin 2011). Biopolitical care, as a mode of governance in modern societies, implies caring for individuals as members of a specific population. Solidified in the late eighteenth century, caring for population is a form of *regulatory* power. Unlike *disciplinary* power (e.g., schooling, policing, welfare), it is not executed by institutions on individual bodies. Rather, through a diverse set of institutional practices and legal regimes, biopolitical care operates at the level of general rates that determine population structures—birthrates, mortality rates, ratio of birth to death, migration rates, and so on. It creates a manageable and countable social terrain with standardized characteristics, making the social environment legible to the state (Scott 1998). This form of biopolitical care guides state ideologies and policies. However, it is also an ethical practice that governs how individuals engage with each other and with the state more broadly, although these different dimensions of care do not always commensurate (Foucault 2003, 239–63; Garcia 2010; Han 2012; Matza 2018; Stevenson 2014; Thelen and Coe 2019). Tomas Matza, in his compelling ethnography of the development of psychotherapy in post-Soviet Russia, demonstrates how models of self-care brought about by the psychotherapeutic turn following the fall of the Soviet Union do not necessarily align with, and often contradict, the biopolitical norms of care of the new post-Soviet state. This situation places post-Soviet subjects at the crossroad of different and contradictory demands for and meanings of care (Matza 2018).[25]

There is no and cannot be a stable notion of care; this multiplicity and ambiguity of meaning are reflected in the demographic crisis discourse I want to bring into focus. In Russia, state ambitions to care for population are fraught with contradictory prescriptions of what care should entail. The spiritual revival of the nation, promoted by nationalist discourses and translated into quantifiable concepts of population growth, coexists with the market model of pronatalism (e.g., Maternity Capital), aimed at changing demographic behavior through monetary means (see also Rivkin-Fish 2010). How self, family, normativity, and engagement with the state are conceived through models of care also shapes relations of care in the everyday lives of Russian citizens endeavoring to raise families in an economically and socially uncertain context. As much as this book is an ethnographic exploration of the Russian state's ambitions to care for and regulate its population, it is also a meditation on everyday forms of care that rely on social resources and cultural ideas of support and responsibility.

Revisiting the story that opened this introduction, it is clear that Nikolai identified emotionally with the state's demographic anxiety, pervasive in public discourse. His story also reveals that in Russia the demographic crisis is as much about the fear of not having enough people as it is about the burden of having them. It is the plight that Nikolai shares with other Russian citizens, whom the state asks to care for the reproduction of population without providing sufficient resources. Nikolai's final thoughts on the problem of population—"What's to be done?"—encapsulate this plight. The fiasco of the state's care has failed Nikolai and his family, compelling them to rely on the informal distribution of support necessary to care for their daughter and grandson. Throughout the book, I consider these demographic anxieties, zoom in on political, social, and cultural processes that constitute the state's efforts to reproduce its dying population, and highlight tensions and contradictions between these efforts and their burden on the lives of ordinary Russian citizens.

A Note on the Field Site and the Cultural Idea of Remoteness

I conducted my research in Yekaterinburg, the fourth largest city in Russia (after Moscow, Saint Petersburg, and Novosibirsk). Between 1924 and 1991, Yekaterinburg, then called by a different name—Sverdlovsk—was a city at the center of one of the main industrial regions of the Soviet Union, tightly sealed off from foreigners. Over 1500 kilometers east of Moscow, Yekaterinburg is located in the middle of the Eurasian continent and is the capital of the Sverdlovsk district (*oblast'*)[26] and the Urals federal province. The city was erected at an imaginary border between Europe and Asia, and tourists can be spotted visiting the obelisks that mark the boundary.[27]

In the national historical imagination, the region surrounding Yekaterinburg is associated with the incursion of the Russian empire into eastern lands, an expansion that began in the sixteenth century and eventually built grounds for the colonization of Siberia (Lincoln 2007).[28] The city is surrounded by small industrial towns with a concentration of defense research and development facilities, a number of which are still closed to outside visitors. The region has large deposits of metals and minerals, and a significant percentage of Russia's steel and iron industry is located there.[29] By the 1980s, the Sverdlovsk oblast was one of the largest industrial centers in the Soviet Union. The social scientific research institute where I conducted my research, as well as other institutes in the city, maintain close ties with the industrial sector.[30]

For my interlocutors in Yekaterinburg, the cultural concept of remoteness, not as a reflection of absolute geographical distance or an essential attribute of a particular place but rather as a resource that can be mobilized in different situations and contexts, played an important part (for more on remoteness, see Edwards 2000; Gohain 2019; Saxer and Andersson 2019). They often invoked the region's remoteness in relation to the European parts of Russia.[31] Calling the Urals a traditional backbone of Russia (*khrebet Rossii, opornyi krai Rossii*)—a cultural cliché popularized by renowned author and self-identified patriot of the Urals Alexei Ivanov—they would stress the importance of the region and city to the development of Russia.[32] However, in other social situations, when emphasizing the decay brought by the dissolution of the Soviet Union and the neoliberalization of Russia's economy, the metaphor of backbone could easily slide into a metaphor of backyard (*zakholust'e, podvorotnia*), forgotten and not cared for by the state.[33]

In many ways, Yekaterinburg and its surrounding area resemble other post-Soviet regions. As Stephen Kotkin (2007) writes: "The Soviet phenomenon created a deeply unified material culture. . . . Consider the children's playgrounds in those places, erected over the same cracked concrete panel surfaces and with the same twisted metal piping—all made at the same factories, to uniform codes. This was also true of apartment buildings (outside and inside), schools, indeed entire cities, even villages" (520). This unified material reality continues to manifest in the post-Soviet context, with industrial collapse rendering standardized spaces all the more visible (Collier 2011). Indeed, the neighborhood and apartment in which I lived during my year of fieldwork, the building housing the research institute where I spent most of my mornings and afternoons, as well as the homes and neighborhoods of my interlocutors were all, in a sense, manifestations of this "gigantic *tipovoi proekt*—a standardized, prefab civilization" (Kotkin 2007, 520).

However, thirty years after the fall of the Soviet Union, this material resemblance is misleading as vibrant social and political transformations have begun to crumble the standardized image of post-Soviet spaces. Economic, political, and cultural disparities between the better known and studied Russian urban centers of Moscow and Saint Petersburg and the rest of the country continue to grow, and these changes inscribe existing oppositions between center and periphery with new meanings and associations (Clowes 2011).

The Book's Structure

The book begins with an exploration of the role of population experts and their professional practices in constructing categories that constitute discourse on the demographic crisis in Russia. The first chapter carries much of the contextual burden as it elaborates on the historical background of the national preoccupation with demography and shows how Soviet ideas and disciplinary structures of science have contributed to the post-Soviet state's approach to population.

The following two chapters introduce the everyday world of population experts and government bureaucrats involved in the production and circulation of demographic knowledge related to underpopulation in contemporary Russia. These chapters focus on demography as the vernacular that shapes the practical language of state care. The second chapter documents routine practices and strategies population scholars use to enact expertise and claim authority over matters of population. The third chapter follows pedagogical engagements through which they disseminate expertise and teach state bureaucrats to read the social reality they are in charge of governing.

Together, the first three chapters show how population experts responsible for the production and dissemination of demographic knowledge provide ideological and moral orientations that shape normative understandings of the population problem and contribute to policy ideas about care. In spite of putatively divergent conceptualizations of the problem, Russian population experts orient their work around individual behavioral change, which they claim to be the foundation of the crisis. Some claim behavioral changes to be irreversible, and some propose policy solutions and other means to alter them. Despite these differences, for Russian demographers, individual behavioral patterns have become the central problem that must be addressed in research and in policy prescriptions for population care.

Chapter 4 traces the role of so-called socially oriented (*sotsial'no orientirovannye*) NGOs in shaping normative ideas about behavioral change as the core of the population problem. Strengthening traditional values has been a particularly salient motive in discourse on the demographic crisis. Using an ethnographic example of a large NGO focused on youth education, the chapter follows the organization's communicative practices aimed at popularizing the idea of family, particularly the idealized image of the normal/fit family (*blagopoluchnaia sem'ia*) in its heteronormative incarnation, as the core object of state care and an effective cure for the population problem. It demonstrates how weaving neoliberal ideologies of the family as a self-sufficient unit into conservative ideas about family and normativity determines which targets are deemed deserving of state care.

Chapter 5 examines how ordinary Russian citizens' responses to state pronatalist demands reflect ethical practices of care not necessarily captured in state discourses and programs. It focuses on practices of intergenerational kinship care in the context of state pronatalist ideologies and traces social institutions of familial care—grandmother care and housing—through which families, but most of all women, navigate the pronatalist terrain. The chapter shows how these forms of kinship care interact with the rapid marketization of social policies and emerging ideals of self-reliance. When exploring actual manifestations of the privatization of care embedded in state marketized pronatalism—regulating demographic behavior through monetary and market means—it becomes clear that connotations of care and understandings of self embedded in this logic do not neatly align with lived relations and practices of care.

The concluding chapter discusses Russia's continuous concern with the problem of population, now in the context of the Russian invasion of Ukraine. It describes depoliticization of citizenship as foundational to relations of care between the Russian state and its citizens. The chapter also examines the regime's overt imperial aspirations, expressed, at least since the annexation of Crimea, through the idiom of extending Russia's sovereignty beyond its territorial borders. It argues that this scaling has infused the language of demography with a new imperial imagination and political poignancy. However, it has also challenged practical applications of sociodemographic knowledge, grounded in the conceptualization of population as a territorially bounded object of state intervention. This conceptual inconsistency, the chapter demonstrates, denies state institutions the practical ability to turn the population living in occupied territories in Ukraine into a full-fledged object of state power, restraining the Russian state's imperial ambitions of care.

Notes

1. Recently, echoing Shevchenko's insight about the ubiquity of the crisis in Russia, Nikolai Travkin, a former politician, jokingly reinterpreted Genesis: "However, on the seventh day, instead of resting God decided to continue working. He created temporary difficulties for his chosen people [Russians] and then . . . he made them permanent" (Travkin 2024).

2. Throughout the book, I generally use pseudonyms. There are a few occasions in which I use real names for publicly recognizable figures whose statements are easily identifiable in the public discourse.

3. The idea of caring for the nation appears in several interviews Solzhenitsyn gave not long before his death. Solzhenitsyn himself attributed the idea to Ivan Shuvalov, an eighteenth-century public figure and a favorite of Empress Elisabeth. In his interviews, Solzhenitsyn stressed the Russian state's main task as "the preservation of a dying people" (Neef and Schepp 2007); by "the people," he was referring to "25 million compatriots cut off from Russia by the insane Belovezhsky conspiracy [treaty signed by the heads of the Soviet Republics dissolving the Soviet Union]" (Tretyakov 2006).

4. Putin's regime consolidated power by invoking the national strength of the new "vertical of power" as an antidote to the social disarray experienced by Russian citizens following the dissolution of the Soviet Union (Sharafutdinova 2020).

5. For a highly perceptive analysis of the direct line as a political technology aimed at consolidating Putin's power and forging the image of a new, strong, coherent national identity, see Gorham 2014.

6. Near abroad (*blizhnee zarubezhie*) is a concept that emerged following the dissolution of the Soviet Union; it usually indicates former Soviet republics turned into independent states.

7. In the following years, regional governments added monetary incentives for the birth of a third child. The federal government began to provide certain reductions in mortgage payments and monthly allowances for the first child in low-income families (Chepovskya 2017; Ivushkina 2017; *Izvestiia* 2017). For more detailed information on the Maternity Capital program, see Gosudarstvennaia Duma 2023.

8. Russian demographer Igor Efremov has argued that this change had a counterproductive effect, disincentivizing parents to have subsequent children as it turned Maternity Capital into a welfare policy, helping people make ends meet in a time of crisis (Starostina 2022).

9. Another political figure, Sergei Mironov, the leader of the Just Russia party and Putin's close ally, has allegedly adopted a child seized from Kherson, Ukraine, after Russian forces occupied the city (Andersson 2023).

10. The Russian name for the discipline of demography, inherited from pre-Soviet and Soviet periods, further highlights the complex affinity between *people* and *population*. Its official name—*nauka o narodonaselenii* (the science of people populating a specific territory)—is

a combination of both, emphasizing the political and historical origins of the discipline. On the global history of ideas of space, density, and territory in population thinking, see Bashford 2007.

11. Despite a divergent history of Soviet demography, to which chapter 1 is devoted, knowledge produced by Soviet statisticians and population specialists played a crucial role in the project of establishing a modern administrative state and central planning, in which population scholars were obligated to maintain accessibility of population knowledge to the government (Blum 2001; Blum and Mespoulet 2006; Holquist 2003; Hirsch 2000; Slezkine 1994).

12. Replacement level fertility indicates an average number of children born per woman needed for the population to reproduce itself from one generation to the next. It is usually estimated at 2.1, as two children per woman would replace both parents (Smallwood and Chamberlain 2005).

13. One implication of high mortality rates for men is that approximately 45 percent of males who reached their fifteenth birthday in 2009 will not survive to celebrate their sixtieth birthday (World Bank Indicators 2022d).

14. In 2009, as population trends began to improve, negative population growth was only 1.8 per thousand people, compared to 6.6 per thousand in 2000 (Rosstat 2011d). In 2010, the number of deaths still exceeded the number of births (12.5 births per thousand vs. 14.2 deaths per thousand) (Rosstat 2011c), but in the following two years, natural population balance showed signs of positive growth.

15. The global COVID-19 pandemic and full-scale invasion of Ukraine contributed to a renewed increase in mortality rates, reversing previous positive trends in life expectancy at birth and decline in mortality rates (Dik 2023; World Bank Indicators 2022a, 2022d). Scholars estimated that in Russia, due to the pandemic, there were 351,158 excess deaths in 2020 and 678,022 in 2021 (Scherbov et al. 2022). The pandemic further affected life expectancy; according to the authors of the same study, an average person who died of COVID in 2020 would have lived for fourteen more years, and in some Russian regions as many as eighteen more years (Scherbov et al. 2022). As of late 2022, there were not enough data to project the effects of the invasion of Ukraine on mortality rates in Russia, although independent demographer Aleksei Raksha pointed out that alcohol consumption has been on the rise since the invasion, which might reverse the positive trends of declining mortality rates over the last twenty years (Dik 2023).

16. In fact, the most realistic prediction made by the Russian federal statistical agency prior to both the pandemic and the war estimated that by 2035, birthrates will decline from 1.5 to 1.3 (Rosstat 2019). Natural population decline (the difference between birth and death rates) in 2021 was one of the worst in post-Soviet history—7.1 per thousand (Rosstat 2022b, 199). In 2000, the beginning of Putin's first term, the rate of negative population growth (number of deaths vs. number of births) was 6.6 per thousand (Rosstat 2011c).

17. Between January and August 2022, there was a decline of 475.5 thousand people (0.32 percent) in the population of the country (Rosstat 2022b, 199).

18. Over the last twenty years, somatic metaphors have become an important part of political discourse, and the health of the nation has been referenced both literally and metaphorically. For example, in closing statements during the highly publicized show trial of feminist punk group Pussy Riot, both prosecutors and accused used somatic metaphors in which the assault on the political system or the political system itself were represented as destructive to the nation's health (Pirogov 2012).

19. In the secular discourse on spirituality, attending to the spiritual needs (*dukhovnye potrebnosti*) of Soviet citizens and transforming their spiritual values (*dukhovnye tsennosti*) were paths to the important spiritual development (*dukhovnoe razvitie*) of economically productive and well-educated members of society—a development leading to a new and improved communist society (Luehrmann 2011). The revival of religious life during Perestroika and after the fall of the Soviet Union augmented the secular discourse of spirituality with Orthodox Christian meanings and practices, making religious ideas of spiritual development part of hegemonic narratives about the Russian nation's future (Smolkin 2019).

20. Antimigration sentiments characteristic of the nationalist discourse fuel apocalyptic scenarios of the consequences of population decline on the vast territories of Russia. These openly xenophobic discourses, however, have been countered by less popular liberal proposals to enhance migration waves into Russia in order to secure territorial dominance and augment the workforce (Gritsuk 2010; Vyzhutovich 2017). Since 2000, Russia's migration policies have oscillated between actively soliciting migration into the Russian Federation as a means of strengthening population growth and economic development and restrictive antimigration measures (Leykin and Gorodzeisky 2024; Schenk 2018). In the years 2001–2005, the Russian government liberalized its immigration policies for migrants from the CIS—an interregional organization of nine, initially ten, former Soviet republics established following the dissolution of the Soviet Union (Molodikova 2007). In 2012, the government launched the Compatriots program for the return migration of expatriates, mostly from former Soviet republics, aimed at facilitating permanent resettlement in Russia to increase population (Myhre 2017).

21. In 2009, a little over 50 percent of children of preschool age (under six years old) and only 16 percent of children under three years had been placed in childcare. As a comparison, in France, approximately 90 percent of children under six and 48 percent of those under three were placed in childcare (Arkhangelsky et al. 2015).

22. The last time I visited the institute freely was in 2019; I was stopped short of visiting again when Russian forces invaded Ukraine.

23. As much as my ambivalent status reflected population specialists' agendas, it also reflected dilemmas and unique aspects of anthropological research of expert culture and experts. Far from being classical ethnographic subjects, experts—or rather, knowledge specialists—have gained center stage in anthropology (Carr 2010). Through participant observation, knowledge specialists become more than just a sum of rational professional practices or an embodiment of specific social roles as fieldwork allows following them inside and outside their professional lives and workplace (Boyer 2008; Gusterson 1996; Matza 2018).

24. John Borneman (2001) argues that caring is an ontological process that precedes any practice and form of kinship and should thus be prioritized in anthropological studies of social relations and their reproduction.

25. Analyzing the politico-ethical modalities of new models of psychotherapeutic care, Matza shows that "care is an ethical practice with a politics through which people wrestle with social concerns, seek lines of flight, and, of course, sometimes marginalize others. Care is politico-ethical" (Matza 2018, 13).

26. Since 1991, the name of the oblast has not corresponded to the name of its capital city. From 1924 to 1991, the city was called Sverdlovsk after a revolutionary hero, Yakov Sverdlov. In 1991, the city regained its prerevolutionary name of Yekaterinburg. Sverdlovsk oblast with its current administrative borders was founded in 1938, long after Yekaterinburg became

Sverdlovsk. The charter of the Sverdlovsk region stipulates that the name of the oblast must remain the same regardless of the name of its capital city (Kalutzkova, Goryachko, and Speransky 2004).

27. There are several obelisks signifying the border: an old, pre-Soviet obelisk, a post-Soviet column, and spontaneously erected posts celebrating a recently invented tradition of couples visiting the site before their wedding ceremony. In close proximity to the historical site, a gigantic IKEA store also inadvertently marked the overland border between Europe and Asia before it closed following the Russian invasion of Ukraine.

28. During the reign of Peter the Great, deposits of iron, copper, and other metals and minerals were discovered in the Urals, and the region became the site of strategic industrial development for the Russian state. In the mid-eighteenth century, Yekaterinburg emerged as the center of the mining industry, with factories that supplied both Russian and European markets with the military and civil products of smelting works. Since gold was discovered in close proximity to Yekaterinburg in 1745, the region is also known for having had one of the earliest episodes of a gold rush in world history (Ivanov 2010).

29. During the Soviet era of industrialization, gigantic factories, such as "Uralmash," "Khimmash," and other heavy industry enterprises, were erected in Yekaterinburg, then Sverdlovsk. The industrial power of the region was sustained by the developed system of professional and academic education. During the Soviet period, the State Polytechnic Institute (later the Ural State Technical University), Boris Yeltsin's alma mater, for example, had close ties with local industry and was oriented toward educating engineering specialists needed by the local industry. In the late 1980s, prior to the dissolution of the Soviet Union, the region had a vibrant political life, with Boris Yeltsin being only one (very important) example of the vanguard of democratic changes in the Soviet Union the city produced. Other political leaders who joined Yeltsin in the first post-Soviet government began their careers in Sverdlovsk (Barazgova 2007).

30. During the late Soviet period, one of the most important sociological projects conducted in the institute where I did my fieldwork was a longitudinal study of the lives of the working class that constituted a significant percentage of the region's population (Pavlov 1989).

31. During the volatile early 1990s, many regional political movements mobilized remoteness in order to invoke authenticity of their campaigns and sharpen distinctions between themselves and center-based parties and movements (Denezhkina and Campbell 2009).

32. Alexei Ivanov popularized the metaphor of the Urals as the backbone marking the eastern-most boundary of Europe in a book and a long TV exposé, both titled *The Backbone of Russia* (*Khrebet Rossii*), devoted to the four hundred years of the history of the Urals (Ivanov 2010).

33. Discussing widespread corruption in Russia, a journalist reflected on the moral decay of political elites using his trip to a remote village in the Urals as an example. Romanticizing that way of life, he concluded that there is power and pride in remoteness—the farther away from power you are, the better. Elites, spoiled by perpetual power grabbing, lose their dignity, while the people he met in the Urals showed pride and solidarity (Loshak 2010).

1

THE AFTERLIFE OF SOVIET DEMOGRAPHY IN THE DISCOURSE ON THE DEMOGRAPHIC CRISIS

THE FIRST DECADE OF THE TWENTY-FIRST CENTURY WAS a heyday for Russian demographic experts. In an era of heightened preoccupation with demography, their knowledge was in high demand—it added scientific authority to the alarmist discourse of impending demographic doomsday. A demographer from Moscow State University I interviewed in 2009 put it eloquently: "Politicians desperately need us. Those who want to win a Duma seat or just advance their career need to be able to speak demography. That's where we come in."

In gaining their fame and operationalizing the problem of population as an object of state care, post-Soviet demographers drew on the Soviet history of their discipline. This chapter traces the effects of the checkered history of demography in the Soviet Union on the language of its post-Soviet practitioners. This history structured the authorized language they used to speak about the origins of the demographic crisis and about the role of the state in managing it. In this authorized language, demographers' epistemological and political positions on the possibility of individual behavioral change dictated the angle from which they represented demographic problems and offered prescriptions for the state's interventions.

Malthus and Anti-Malthus: Early Conceptions of the Soviet Science of Population

The science of population (*nauka o narodonaselenii*)—an institutionalized name for the discipline of demography in the Soviet Union and contemporary Russia—occupies a controversial position in Soviet political history. On the one hand, as with other modern states, the science of population had been an important instrument of Soviet biopolitics, producing knowledge to serve its main form of governance: central economic planning (Blum 2001, 2005; Blum and Mespoulet 2006; Herrera 2010). On the other hand, the Soviet science of population lacked a cohesive theory on which demographers could design research and prescriptions for government. When the early Soviet science of population disputed the Malthusian formula—the theory of population dominant since the nineteenth century—it failed to provide a comprehensive theoretical alternative that would serve its scientific needs. These contradictory forces—the modernist aspiration to make population legible to the state accompanied by the lack of a comprehensive alternative to Malthusianism—shaped an uneven development of Soviet demography and the Soviet state's approach to population dynamics.

Like any other modern polity, the new Bolshevik state relied heavily on numbers and political arithmetic (Holquist 2003; Blum and Mespoulet 2006).[1] The new state initiated massive amounts of data collection and statistical surveys, culminating in a grandiose census in 1926 (Hirsch 2005; Blum 2005, 29–41; Herrera 2010, 111–13). This early period in the history of the Soviet Union has been described as one of "statistical enthusiasm" akin to the period following the French Revolution, with its wealth of statistical studies (Blum 2005, 31). The fervor was fueled by statisticians trained in the prerevolutionary imperial tradition of regional statistical administration (*zemstvo*), who brought expertise and knowledge to the newly established Central Statistical Bureau (TsSU) and to demographic institutes in the country. Much like their Western contemporaries, these specialists saw statistical sciences of population as crucial in the apparatus of a scientific government—a concept born out of the modernizing projects of the nineteenth century (Porter 1986).[2]

However, despite the prominence of counting in Soviet biopolitics, the new Soviet state had a problem with Malthus's theory of population. Malthus saw population as a natural phenomenon guided by a set of universal rules. His calculations showed that the geometric rate of population growth exceeds the arithmetic rate of food production growth, leading to the doubling of population size every twenty-five years (Malthus 1798). The logical conclusion to be drawn from Malthus's theory is that the universal laws of population inevitably cause poverty (Malthus 1798; Dean 2015). Paired with life-table construction techniques developed in the seventeenth and eighteenth centuries, the assumptions of Malthus's theory became fundamental to the discipline of demography and to the administrative apparatus of the modern state (Bashford and Chaplin 2016; Briggs 2004; Dean 2015; Desrosières 1998; Unger and Hartmann 2014; Villadsen and Wahlberg 2015).

The new Soviet state developed its conceptualizations of population out of the Marxist-Leninist rejection of Malthus's epistemological assumption that population is guided by the universal laws of nature. Marx famously turned the Malthusian law of population on its head, arguing that overpopulation and by extension poverty—Malthus's grim prediction—are not a universal law but rather a form of surplus labor necessary for capitalist expansion. For Marx, what Malthus called overpopulation was in actuality the latent workforce enabling the dominating class to continue to extract limited resources and accumulate wealth (DiMaio 1981; Perrot 1983; Vilquin 2005).[3]

Although Marx rejected the general principle of population devised by Malthus, neither he nor Lenin was able to provide a comprehensive alternative to guide their new socialist regime.[4] Instead, in the Soviet Union, generalized modes of production became the ultimate determinants of population structure. Official Soviet ideology posited that in the more adequate socioeconomic system of socialism (or communism), with the help of a planned economy, unemployment—overpopulation in Malthusian terms—would eventually disappear. The new socioeconomic order would regulate and calibrate population fluctuations according to the Bolshevik state's central economic plans. In 1935, to assure the public of the validity of the new population theory, the head of the statistics division of the central economic planning committee (Gosplan) misleadingly claimed that fertility rates in the Soviet Union were growing due to improved economic conditions and that the country's high birthrates compared to other countries in Europe were in accordance with socialist central planning (Blum 2005, 52–55; see also Hoffmann 2011, 133).

The institutional development of the early Soviet science of population, similar to that of other scientific disciplines, was punctuated by the political purges of the 1930s. Soviet demographers, many of whom had contributed to the new Bolshevik state's "statistical enthusiasm," did not escape Stalin's terror and suffered a series of massive purges (Blum 2001; Blum and Mespoulet 2006; Vishnevsky 1996).[5] During the Great Terror, all demographic institutes were shut down, as was the TsSU's academic journal, *Vestnik Statistiki* (Blum 2001). The 1937 census marks the most tragic moment in the history of the profession. The census data clearly contradicted previous statements made by party leadership and Stalin himself, who in 1934 had announced that the population had grown to 168 million, about eight million more than reported in the 1937 census. The results were therefore suppressed, and Stalin arrested and purged most of the statisticians involved in the census efforts (Blum 2001, 2005; Tolts 1989, 2004, 2008; Volkov 1997, 2014).[6]

Stalin's political repressions did not, however, mean that counting was no longer important to the Soviet state. Counting and studying population was critical to central planning and as such remained an enduring characteristic of Soviet biopolitics. Despite Stalin's insistence on the primacy of party truth over science, party officials and scientific experts employed by the state continued to share a strong belief in the modernizing political project and the importance of statistics for rational management of the population. Employing the most rigid methodological standards, Soviet statisticians continued to scrupulously count the population and conduct statistical surveys even throughout collectivization and the period of the Great Terror (Blum 2005).[7]

The conceptual lacunae left by the Marxist-Leninist rejection of Malthus was evident in state approaches to the problem of population. Time after time, central economic plans failed to stabilize rising mortality rates caused by a wide range of social calamities and political transformations (e.g., famine, the Great Terror, World War II, and more). Gender imbalance as a result of large-scale loss of life during World War II contributed to falling fertility rates, and—along with apparent stagnation in life expectancy, especially for men—led to major warning signs that the Soviet labor market and the state's military power were threatened.

To overcome these troubling trends, despite its anti-Malthusian and anti-interventionist population ideology and without explicitly stating its intentions, the Soviet state began to introduce pronatalist policies aimed to change behavior and to mitigate the shrinking labor force. The ban on abortion introduced by Josef Stalin in 1936 was a punitive pronatalist measure meant to increase birthrates. The 1944 family policy, proposed by Nikita S. Khrushchev, then head of the Ukrainian Communist Party, levied a tax on childless citizens and made the practice of common-law marriages illegal, leaving institutionalized and registered marriages the only legitimate marital union (Ironside 2017; Nakachi 2021).[8] All of these measures were taken with the explicit goal of preventing further population decline (Nakachi 2021). None of them improved demographic trends. But they were highly successful in rendering the reproductive behavior of Soviet citizens, especially women, an object of government intervention (Nakachi 2021; Rivkin-Fish 2024).

This early Soviet history of the discipline became foundational to the professional identities of post-Soviet demographers. The history of the 1937 census, in particular, was formative in shaping the professional identity of demographic experts I came to know during my fieldwork. In 1987, following the policy of Glasnost, population data became publicly available and population handbooks began to be regularly published by the TsSU, spurring an avalanche of publications about the results of the 1937 census and the politics of early Soviet demography (Heleniak and Motivans 1991). The released data were used to reconstruct the demographic reality of that period, but some of the most iconic publications, frequently referenced by my informants, were memoirs published by demographers who witnessed the census and the suppression of its results (Lifshitz 1990; Tolts 1989; Volkov 1990, 1993, 1997).

Professional Identity and Post–World War II Institutional Developments in Soviet Demography

Two main political demands shaped the reemergence of the science of population in the postwar period. First, there was a clear need to assess the demographic consequences of the war on the national level (Blum 2001; Nakachi 2016, 2021). Second, in the context of the Cold War, a stance had to be taken in the international debate surrounding interventionist population politics in developing countries. In this regard, the Soviet science of population was used to express opposition to the United States' policies regarding population control in the developing world, prompting state institutions, in particular the Central Committee of the Communist Party, to support the resurgence of the discipline (Blum 2001, 286; 2005).[9]

The first postwar census of 1959 marked the institutional revival of the discipline of demography (Blum 2005, 39; Pokshishevsky 1966, 201).[10] Andrey G. Volkov, head of a new research center for demography and labor resources founded in 1963 under the auspices of the TsSU, retrospectively described this period in almost military terms. He situated his research center at the forefront of "the battle for demography" (*bitva za demografiiu*) and, despite recurring resistance from TsSU officials, continued to cultivate authority over population matters (mostly against political economists) (Volkov 2001, 2003). The Institute of Applied Social Research, founded in

1968, provided additional institutional grounds for revitalizing the discipline. Its first director, Aleksei M. Rumyantsev, an economist by training, sought to employ sociologists alongside demographers, economists, and political scientists, all of whom would conduct social research in their respective fields. Although Rumyantsev's plan was never fully realized, the institute—from its founding until the dissolution of the Soviet Union in 1991—hosted scholars who contributed to the resurgence of demography and ignited debates that would later define the field and its further development (Batygin 1999).[11]

The Department of Economics at Moscow State University and the Center for the Study of Population Problems, under the long-standing leadership of founder Dmitri Valentei, not only produced demographic research on a large scale but also offered the first professional training program for demographers, including those from the developing world (Rotova and Denisenko 2006).[12] Murray Feshbach's brief but highly informative report on Soviet demography, prepared for the United States Air Force in 1986, showcased Valentei's prominent role (Feshbach 1986, 12–40). According to one of Valentei's colleagues, when Feshbach's policy report was translated into Russian and presented at a faculty meeting shortly after its publication, Valentei's achievements and international fame greatly impressed his party patrons, perhaps contributing to his personal acclaim and the discipline's credibility among the party leadership (Ivanov 2006).[13]

The demographic seminar series at the Moscow Central House of Scientists (TsDU), founded by Boris Ts. Urlanis in 1964, played an important role in consolidating Soviet demographers' professional identity (Borisov and Vishnevsky 2011). Urlanis, the "bad boy" of Soviet demography and a revered figure among Russian demographers of all intellectual stripes, taught statistics at the Moscow Economic Statistical Institute and was known for his irreverence and scientific rigor. He was hugely popular among younger scholars, and his seminar became an important stepping-stone in any aspiring demographer's professional socialization.[14] The seminars encouraged informal discussions and facilitated social ties among participants, creating a tight-knit professional community. One demographer I interviewed recalled that for him, a young, aspiring researcher at the time, the seminar was an informal gathering of like-minded people. In his recollection, attending the seminar felt like getting away from the more ideologically rigid atmosphere of his home institution. The discussions, chaired by Urlanis himself, were lively and loud. Participants would drill down into a specific issue, turning it upside down and sometimes arguing ferociously about one small methodological point for hours on end. The seminar's informal atmosphere and some memorable intellectual (at times bordering on physical) fights between both senior and junior scholars helped shape Soviet demographers' professional identities and their research agendas.

Other institutional forces were at play in resuscitating demography after World War II. Academic publishing houses specializing in demographic research, most notably *Statistika* and *Progress*, further shaped the scope and boundaries of the discipline (Batygin 1999, 118, 608). Several demographers mediated population-related issues for larger audiences, publishing opinion pieces in the print media. In communicating the problems to the general public, demographers highlighted the implications of falling birthrates and the consequences of aging and much lower life expectancy for men than for women for Soviet economic development (Perevedentzev 1966, 1968; Urlanis 1968; Bestuzhev-Lada 1976).

Crucially, in all these popularizing efforts and interactions with party leadership, Soviet demographers stressed the utility of their discipline for central economic planning. When Urlanis advocated for the introduction of demography as a universally taught discipline at the university level, he stressed its importance to Soviet state efforts to revive the post–World War II economy against the backdrop of the country's labor shortages (Borisov and Vishnevsky 2011). In the post-Stalin period, Soviet demographers attributed the failure of Stalin-era policies to lack of empirical and scientific foundations, presenting the science of population as grounds for a new phase of socialist development capable of remedying previous shortcomings (Boyarsky 1975a). Aron Ya. Boyarsky, one of the few surviving prewar demographers who led the TsSU research institute after the war, justified the primacy of demography over other administrative sciences. When demographers approach the main object of their study—population—Boyarsky reasoned, they consider a wide range of factors that shape population processes, including economic as well as cultural, ethnic, biological, and psychological dynamics. This synoptic view gives demography an edge over other social sciences in devising scientifically and empirically based policy prescriptions (Boyarsky 1959, 1975a; Valentei and Sudoplatov 1982).

In the wake of World War II and Stalin's terror, setting the scope and defining the boundaries of the discipline became crucial to demographers consolidating a shared professional identity and articulating their contribution to state governing techniques and mechanisms. Post-Soviet demographers, whose ideals, know-how, and disciplinary structures were formed during this period, have been carrying this legacy, presenting themselves as invaluable partners in the state's work of care. Demography as a more encompassing discipline and as capable of designing scientifically and empirically sound foundations for policymaking was reiterated to me by the majority of my interlocutors socialized during the Soviet period.

The Cold War and New Conceptual Developments in the Soviet Science of Population

In the early 1960s, the revitalized discipline of Soviet demography was still relatively isolated from the international community of demographers, but new channels of communication were opening up. Foreign publications became accessible through exchanges between Soviet and Western libraries, but many were placed in *spetskhrany*—special collections of books, journals, and other publications with highly restricted access (Richmond 2004, 136–52). To increase accessibility, the Institute for Scientific Information on Social Sciences helped translate some of the publications in the social sciences and make them available to scholars (Pugacheva 1994; Kurakin 2017, 402). Publications also made their way to the Soviet Union through Eastern European colleagues who had opportunities to interact with their Western counterparts (Vishnevsky 1996; Arab-Ogly 1999). In the 1970s, new concepts and fields of study penetrated Soviet demography thanks to translation efforts of Russian scholars proficient in foreign languages and thanks to encounters at rare international conferences (Vishnevsky and Kon 1979; Volkov and Darsky 1975, 1979; Pokshishevsky 1966).

Although the official anti-Malthusian stance was not about to disappear, during this period Soviet scholars began to openly question the economic determinism dominant in the Soviet science of population. In 1966, Vadim Pokshishevsky, a demographic geographer, summarized his visit at the 1965 World Population Conference in Belgrade in the pages of a popular literary journal: "For a long time, demographic research in our country was undervalued. . . . The leading doctrine was that the centrally planned socialist economy could automatically rebalance demographic proportions. Estimates that showed inconsistencies between the country's population growth and its capacity to effectively use its labor force were denounced as malignant Malthusianism [*zlostnoe maltuzianstvo*]. . . . Today, we do not discard population research originating in capitalist countries as it provides us with a lot of useful information, ideas and methodological strategies" (Pokshishevsky 1966, 201–2).

The shift of tone from the previous World Population Conference was palpable. Soviet representatives at the 1954 World Population Conference in Rome had firmly rejected Malthusianism and the notion of population control as an overt justification for capitalist expansion (Desfosses 1981). In contrast, Pokshishevsky reported that during the 1965 World Population Conference in Belgrade, Soviet delegates officially rejected the validity of population control policies in the developing world but were nevertheless attuned to the framing and discussion of population issues in capitalist societies. Thus, addressing questions of overpopulation in India discussed at the conference, Pokshishevsky wrote that "brushing off emerging problems based on the assumption that acknowledging them would be considered accession to Neo-Malthusianism does a disservice to the international cooperation between the countries" (Pokshishevsky 1966, 202).

In November 1965, following the World Population Conference in Belgrade, revered Soviet demographer Boris Ts. Urlanis published an op-ed in *Literaturnaia Gazeta*, the official journal of the USSR Writers' Union. In it, he questioned the official Soviet position on family planning policies in the developing world taken at the 1965 conference—a position that fundamentally rejected the importance of population policies in developing countries. From November 1965 to June 1966, *Literaturnaia Gazeta* became a battlefield where prominent demographers and economists attempted to reexamine the Marxist-Leninist population doctrine, arguing for or against its rejection of Malthus (DiMaio 1981, 169–74). Writing in language framed by the rules of the Soviet ideological genre, they nevertheless questioned the official line taken by the head of the census department of the TsSU, Piotr Pod'yachikh, who at the Belgrade conference had resolutely rejected any interventionist population policy offered by other delegates. The economic determinism of the official population doctrine, Urlanis and others claimed, prevented the discussion of future and long-standing effects of current demographic trends, limiting it to thin descriptive statements (DiMaio 1981; Feshbach 1986; Volkov 2001).

In 1968 Boris Urlanis published another op-ed, also in *Literaturnaia Gazeta*. With the emotionally charged title "Protect the Men!," this short text was reprinted over one hundred times in newspapers and magazines across the country (Syrokomsky 2001). Pointing to the growing gap between men's and women's mortality rates and life expectancy, the op-ed was an urgent call for action because "demographically speaking, there is every reason to suggest that men and not women are 'the weaker sex'" (Urlanis 1968). Urlanis's plea was the first instance in which Soviet men's health and its effect on the country's demographics were discussed publicly. Without protecting men's health, Urlanis suggested, the demographic situation would worsen. Still relevant to Russia today, the op-ed had a surprising conclusion, suggesting that because the majority of the country's physicians—"four fifths"—were women, women should protect and take care of men's health: "Women, please take care of men! . . . Let's make sure that we have not only grandmothers, but grandfathers too, who are currently a great rarity" (Urlanis 1968).

While preserving the Cold War framework of ideological conflict and diligently critiquing his Western colleagues for employing erroneous bourgeois assumptions about population, Soviet demographers absolved Malthusianism of its status as a malignant or hostile theory. The fact that their overt disagreement with the official position was published in several highly reputable Soviet outlets means that moving away from a rigid anti-Malthusian stance was approved by party officials and deemed suitable for publication.

During the decade between the World Population Conferences of 1965 and 1974, theories previously rejected as malignant Malthusianism entered the conceptual vocabulary of Soviet demography. Thus, the theory of demographic transition or revolution popular in Western demography began to take hold (see, for example, Fedorov 1975; Zabelin 1977). This theory was formulated by French demographer Adolphe Landry in the interwar period and revised by Frank W. Notestein and Kingsley Davis after World War II. In very broad terms, the theory of demographic transition postulates that all societies are on a path from premodern regimes of high mortality and fertility to modern regimes of low fertility and mortality. This theory provided a unifying theoretical framework for Western demography, much as modernization theory provided such a framework for sociology (Notestein 1945; Davis 1945; Sharpless 1997).

Demographic transition theory was rejected by early Soviet demography because it suggested that population processes have a semiautonomous nature and are not entirely determined by specific politico-economic regimes—a formulation too reminiscent of the Malthusian definition of population and thus inacceptable in Soviet population doctrine, dominated by economic determinism. In the 1970s, Soviet demographers began borrowing from the conceptual apparatus of the demographic transition theory and applying it to their analysis of time-dependent changes in demographic trends, fertility in particular (Kvasha 1971; Vishnevsky 1979; Borisov 1976). Masterfully weaving the Malthusian model of population with Marxian dogmas, Soviet scholars posited that demographic trends in pre-Soviet and Soviet Russia might have followed a general European trajectory independent of the specific economic and political structures of these societies (Vishnevsky 1979).

Another conceptual development that made its way into the mainstream of Soviet demography was critical engagement with the optimum theory of population, which seeks to determine an absolute size of population that would yield maximum return on its economic activities. Reminiscent of Malthusianism, this macroeconomic theory claims that the optimum population size is determined in relation to the scarcity of natural resources and capital stock. Aron Ya. Boyarsky, a highly respected figure in the history of Soviet demography, criticized the theory for its Malthusian assumptions, but rather than dismissing it outright, he proposed a revised model based on a dynamic understanding of the optimum in relation to production. This revised version, Boyarsky argued, could be applied to a socialist economy without falling (in his view) into the ideology of Malthusianism or "populationalism" (pronatalism) (Boyarsky 1968).

To smooth over ideological inconsistencies, Boyarsky translated the theory's basic assumptions into abstract mathematical formulas and emphasized the theory's—and, by extension, the discipline's—practical utility for central planning: "The question of the optimal, i.e., the most desirable population size in relation to specific economic goals and in the context of specific relations of production is a rightful one. . . . Because the population size and structure, as well as the dynamics of its growth, although never primary, but still are highly important determinants of social development, there is no reason for the state not to shape them in a favorable direction. Marxists have never rejected that kind of 'intervention,' which we now call demographic politics" (Boyarsky 1975b, 76).

Despite palpable resistance from political economists, population optimum, or rather "the theory of economic-demographic optimum," founded on a solid mathematical basis, progressively became a legitimate field of Soviet demographic research that sought to provide the state with an instrument for effective central planning. Interestingly, while Boyarsky still referred to it as the "bourgeois theory" of population optimum in the 1960s, the following decade saw the theory stripped of its bourgeois reference (Elizarov 2014; Kvasha 1973). Boyarsky's domestication of the optimum theory of population illustrates how institutional and intellectual developments within the discipline shaped the privileged role of demography for central planning and expanded the scope of what was considered ideologically tolerable in the Soviet approach to population.

During this period, the Soviet state adjusted its population doctrine and softened its hardline stance on Neo-Malthusian family planning programs in the developing world. Thus, at the 1966 World Health Organization (WHO) meeting, the Soviet delegation, still asserting its position regarding population growth as a function of the mode of production, nevertheless backed the WHO resolution to provide support for the development of global family planning activities (World Health Organization 1966). Less than a decade later, at the 1974 World Population Conference in Bucharest, the Soviet delegation already fully supported the US initiative to establish a global strategy focusing on family planning (although disagreeing on numerical targets). In fact, when the Chinese delegation vehemently opposed the plan and accused the USSR of submitting to the US-backed imperial appetites expressed in its population control campaigns, the Soviet delegates turned to their American counterparts, who were leading the initiative, and shook their hands (Connelly 2008, 313).

When the demographic experts I worked with would speak of their professional history, they would index the decade following the World Population Conference in Belgrade as a defining period that shaped both the scope of their disciplinary practices and their identities as experts in population matters. Regardless of the differences in scientific approach and the antagonistic relationships between representatives of different schools of thought in contemporary Russian demography, all of them identified this period as formative to their professional identity.

The Emergence of Demographic (Reproductive) Behavior

Perhaps the most important development during the decade following the 1965 World Population Conference in Belgrade was the emergence of demographic research with the central focus on social norms and cultural values as determinants of population structure (Belova and Darsky 1972; Belova 1975; Belova, Bondarskya, and Darsky 1983; Volkov 1981, 1971; Bondarskya 1977; Sifman 1974). The primacy of norms and values in social research might seem like an obvious development aligned with global social scientific trends of the time. However, within the Soviet science of population, itself grounded in the primacy of economic structures, this development was quite revolutionary and had major consequences for the discipline and its contribution to the state's work of caring for its population.[15]

One concept added to the analytic vocabulary of the Soviet demographic discipline during this period was that of demographic behavior (*demograficheskoe povedenie*). In a demographic encyclopedia published in 1985, an entry on demographic behavior notes that the concept's integration into research began a decade earlier with the scholarly realization that social norms and attitudes regarding childbearing, child rearing, marriage, and health determine behavior (Matskovsky 1985). There are different types of demographic behavior, the entry suggests—matrimonial behavior (norms and values that determine marriage and family formation patterns), reproductive behavior (norms of childbearing and child rearing), and vital behavior (health and hygiene habits). Social norms and attitudes determine these forms of behavior, which in turn affect population trends and structures (Matskovsky 1985; see also Elizarov 1980; Volkov 1986). Not only in scientific publications but also in the popular press, transformations in behavior began to be presented as driving overall population structure (Valentei 1980; Valentei and Sudoplatov 1982; Elizarov 1980; Bestuzhev-Lada 1976; Perevedentzev 1983).

Although Soviet demographers used the general qualifier *demographic* to describe their research on the effects of behavior on population structures, in most cases, it came to indicate research on the effects of social norms and values on fertility. The combination of falling birthrates, visible in the country since the 1960s, and the importance of demography for central state planning rendered demographic research on reproduction of particular interest to the state. This interest was evidenced in the growth of commissioned demographic research on fertility, family, and reproductive behavior.

In a collective volume, the director of the TsSU research institute, Andrey G. Volkov, explained that demographic trends in different parts of the Soviet Union could only be understood in light of the effects of long-standing cultural values on the demographic behavior of families (Volkov 1971). Put differently, Volkov suggested that fertility rates in Soviet republics with different ethnic compositions depended on social and cultural norms that might have been indifferent to the effects of Soviet economic structures. Exploiting research conducted in Soviet republics with low and high fertility rates, the volume accounted for regional differences in fertility by pointing to reproductive behavior characteristic of various ethnic groups as determinants of fertility rates (Bondarskya 1971; Bondarskya and Kozlov 1971; Bondarskya 1976). Works based on this research underscored the lingering effect social and cultural norms have on families and reproduction, implying that population structure has its own regulatory rules and should thus be studied independently of economic structure (Volkov 1976).[16] Although it might seem like a reiteration of conventional demographic research to a reader unfamiliar with the Soviet reality, it was quite an innovative pivot in demographic studies within the Marxist-Leninist scientific dogmas dominant at that time.

The Communist Party and the Science of Population

During this decade, conceptual developments in studying reproduction and family were accompanied by efforts to strengthen the disciplinary power of demography as an effective administrative tool for state intervention (Kvasha 1973; Valentei 1980; Valentei and Sudoplatov 1982; Urlanis 1974). Volkov, for example, argued that the most effective way to move demographic trends in a favorable direction is to actively facilitate the formation and internalization of social norms that affect reproduction (Volkov 1976). He proposed that the state execute an essentially moral pedagogical project to influence the behavior of the coming-of-age generation by encouraging new cognitive and behavioral patterns among individuals: "self-control, the recognition of the inherent value of family life and the cultivation of a personal interest in the well-being of other family members" (Volkov 1986, 248). In 1973, Valentei recommended instilling in youth the idea that "large families are happy families" and that the social utility of women hinges on a combination of work and motherhood (cited in Desfosses 1981, 115). The primacy of party goals over individual needs in these recommendations was indisputable, but in order to change demographic trends, the state could and should not only intervene in economics but also use other means to motivate Soviet citizens to procreate. In a communist society, demographers argued, the endgame of an effective demographic policy is to modify motivations, values, and needs such that people eventually learn to regulate their own demographic behavior in accordance with socialist goals (Zvereva 1980).

Demographic behavior as the cornerstone of late Soviet demographic know-how indeed played an important part in larger discussions within party leadership about the country's population decline. Soviet demographers contributed heavily to these discussions, and Dmitri Valentei in particular promoted the notion that demography and policymaking are natural bedfellows. Reportedly a master networker and skilled politician, Valentei advanced the discipline's interactions with state leadership, which culminated in the implementation of the 1981 comprehensive demographic policy following the XXVI Party Congress (Sudoplatov 2006).

In 1981, the party adopted a generous pronatalist policy, implementing for the first time yearlong maternity leave, job protection policies, and a child allowance that constituted 30 to 60 percent of an average monthly wage (Avdeyeva 2011, 368–69; Avdeev and Monnier 1995; Zakharov 2008). The policy had an immediate effect on fertility timing, increasing birthrates to 2.2 children per woman in 1987. However, reproductive patterns seemed untouched. Parity between children declined; by 1987, people had exhausted their reproductive needs, and all the children they wanted had already been born (Avdeyeva 2011). Notwithstanding differences between intended and actual consequences, historically, the 1981 policy was the most comprehensive Soviet population policy aimed at reproductive behavioral change, and it continued to affect both policy experts and people targeted by the state long after it was introduced.

During the late 1970s and early 1980s, demographers and party leaders discussed the regionalization of population policies, an idea spawned by conceptualizations of reproductive behavior as determined by cultural and social norms. In policy briefs and proposals, Soviet demographers stressed the national (ethnic) and cultural nature of reproductive behavior and attitudes, a notion previously rejected by Marxist-Leninist demography (Bondarskya and Kozlov 1971; Sifman 1974). Some suggested that policies concerned with stimulating fertility should differentiate between Soviet republics with high and low birthrates, urging pronatalist measures and welfare support only for those with low birthrates (Litvinova 1981; Lovett 2023; Urlanis 1975). In fact, the 1981 policy was first introduced in the European republics of the Soviet Union and only later spread to the rest of the Soviet Union (Litvinova 1989). Following the XXVII Party Congress in 1986, the party pledged to continue developing and implementing "demographic policies that would more fully address particular characteristics of different national regions" (KPSS 1986, 273).

These ideas of differentiated pronatalist measures reverberate in current post-Soviet articulations of the impending demographic catastrophe. One of my interlocutors, a demographic economist, was very upset with the universal nature of the 2007 Maternity Capital policy, which offered a lump-sum payment to all women giving birth to their second child regardless of regional or ethnic affiliation. In conversation, he told me: "it's as if the Russian state is more socialist than its Soviet predecessor. Even Boris Urlanis was talking about differentiated demographic policies in the 1980s, so why can't we do the same now? Why should women in the depressed regions of Siberia get the same as women in South Caucasus where fertility is already high?" Concepts of demographic behavior as affected by social and cultural norms (and, by proxy, the differentiated approach to population policymaking) continue to mold the post-Soviet scientific demographic landscape and contribute to ways in which the post-Soviet state articulates its problem of population and designs interventions.

To Intervene or Not to Intervene: The Post-Soviet Science of Population

Demographic behavior as a key object of state intervention and self-regulation lies at the heart of the demographic scientific landscape in post-Soviet Russia. It is particularly pronounced in the long-standing intellectual rivalry between two prominent post-Soviet demographic experts: Anatoly Vishnevsky and Anatoly Antonov. Their rivalry, which can be traced back to the 1970s, captured the imagination of the professional community of Soviet demographers. It became even more prominent after the dissolution of the Soviet Union, when the problem of low fertility transformed into an apocalyptic discourse about the nation's looming demographic catastrophe. The unprecedented population decline in the wake of the Soviet Union became a source of profound moral panic among politicians, public figures, and state officials, carving out a special place for Russian demographers such as Vishnevsky and Antonov. For them, the demographic crisis became both a discursive resource with which to communicate ideas about how Russian society should imagine its present and future as well as symbolic capital to popularize demographic expertise as a foundation for new post-Soviet statecraft (Rivkin-Fish 2003). As previously mentioned, their fame could be compared to that of Paul Ehrlich, whose publication *Population Bomb* in 1968 in the West granted him the celebrity status of a potent social critic.

Both Vishnevsky and Antonov agreed that behavioral and attitudinal changes are the crux of the matter when it comes to transformations in population structures. However, their ideas diverged on the question of *regulating* behavior. Anatoly Vishnevsky, a proponent of demographic transition theory, spoke of an inherent inertia and relative independence of population processes that make demographic behavior virtually impenetrable to direct state interventions. Anatoly Antonov, on the other hand, saw the state as capable of altering individual behaviors and changing demographic trends.

Vishnevsky, a highly respected and internationally recognized scholar, was head of the Institute of Demography at the Higher School of Economics until his death in 2021. He began his career in 1971 at the center for demography at the TsSU's research institute, where for thirteen years he worked with some of the most important demographers and statisticians of that time—Boris Urlanis and Aron Boyarsky, among others. In the mid-1980s, Vishnevsky moved to the Institute of Sociological Research at the Academy of Sciences. Working under another important demographer, Leonid Rybakovsky, Vishnevsky began collaborating internationally, particularly with French demographers, but soon left the institute because of ideological and scientific conflicts with Rybakovsky (Blum 2021).

In 1976, Vishnevsky published a monograph titled "Demographic Revolution"; in it, he set out the idea of the demographic transition of fertility and mortality from high to low as applied to pre-Soviet and Soviet demographic fluctuations. Analytically moving away from Marxist dogmas, he argued that current demographic trends reflect a modern conflict between individual and social interests related to procreation. This conflict produces new social norms, values, and expectations, affecting patterns of reproductive behavior and leading to low fertility. However, these changes do not necessarily lead to the population's disappearance. In this highly functionalist conceptualization of population, reproduction is the main function of any demographic system, necessary for its survival. Therefore, the demographic system always finds a way to recalibrate itself to reach equilibrium and fulfill its main function—reproduction (Vishnevsky 2005).

Vishnevsky's work combined two major developments in Soviet demography. First, he introduced the Malthusian model of population into Soviet demography by promoting the idea of an autonomous set of rules and regulations that guide population processes. Second, he saw changes in demographic behavior as determining population trends (Vishnevsky

1977, 1979). His diagnosis for modern society was that a changing social value of children affects reproductive behavior and alters population structures worldwide (Vishnevsky 2014). His conceptualization of demographic change was harshly critiqued by his colleagues at the Institute of Sociological Research, particularly his boss, Rybakovsky. The conflict around Vishnevsky's Malthusian assumptions led to them accusing each other of holding antiscientific and ideologically biased views (Blum 2021).

The post-Soviet incarnation of these ideas also made apparent Vishnevsky's political assessment of behavioral changes. A great believer in the power of modernization, he viewed individual autonomy positively, understanding the role of the modern state as ensuring individual freedom (Rivkin-Fish 2003). He critically assessed the post-Soviet state's attempts to intervene in the reproductive choices of citizens as an infringement on individual freedom and described these attempts as scientifically unsubstantiated (Rivkin-Fish 2003; Vishnevsky 2007). His theoretical and political positions led him to stress the futility of state policies in increasing fertility and underline reproductive behavior as an object of self-regulation of autonomous individuals (Rivkin-Fish 2003, 2024).

Taking his arguments from the late Soviet period into post-Soviet debates on the country's demographic future, Vishnevsky rejected the idea of demographic exceptionalism, opposing claims that Russia's declining fertility is somehow unique and should be understood as a severe and urgent crisis. Vishnevsky insisted that Russia, in fact, was joining other European countries in the universal and socially inevitable transition to low fertility rates and an ever-growing aging population, a transformation characteristic of all developed nations. He saw state attempts to increase birthrates through direct monetary policies, such as the Maternity Capital policy introduced in 2007, as doomed to fail because, in his view, such efforts contradict the universal law of population, which states that there is an internal mechanism through which the demographic system regulates itself (Vishnevsky 1979, 30; Vishnevsky 2007; Zakharov 2008). Instead, he considered large-scale migration a promising avenue of recovery from Russia's population decline—a highly unpopular and controversial stance in contemporary Russia, where labor migrants from former Soviet Asian republics are often politically conceived as a threat to the nation's sovereignty and security (Gritsuk 2010; Vishnevsky 2007).

The other side of this debate finds its origins in the value-based theory of reproductive behavior that gained ground in the mid-1970s.[17] The theory was voiced by Anatoly Antonov, a professor of sociology at Moscow State University and Vishnevsky's personal rival. For him too, changing behavior caused by new norms and values was at the center of demographic fluctuations. However, Antonov located the essence of the population problem not in the inertia of demographic processes but in changing morality underlying individual behavior. For him, the demographic crisis was really a crisis of morality and ethics, and plunging fertility rates were directly related to a diminishing value of childbearing and declining normative need for children (*potrebnost' v detiakh*) in contemporary society (Antonov 1980). This theory, as well as Antonov's public and very vocal polemic with Vishnevsky, gained further popularity in the post-Soviet period, influencing popular discourse on the demographic crisis (Rivkin-Fish 2003).

Although Antonov's assertions largely aligned with Vishnevsky's historical diagnosis in regard to the diminishing value of children and family, Antonov saw the problem as waiting to be remedied by direct state intervention. Contrary to Vishnevsky's skepticism of the state's ability to alter established social norms, Antonov and his colleagues claimed that by strengthening the family's moral and economic values, the state can stimulate fertility and reverse worrisome population trends. In his Soviet and post-Soviet publications, Antonov called for pronatalist interventions to reinstall the value of family life as both an economic value and a moral and normative ideal, positioning the state as key to reversing demographic trends (Antonov 1980, 2005, 2006; Antonov, Medkov, and Arkhangelsky 2002).

If, for Vishnevsky, the state should safeguard individual autonomy in relation to reproduction, for Antonov, the task of regulating and changing demographic behavior properly belonged to the state. Contrary to Vishnevsky's suggestion of a predetermined trajectory of demographic dynamics not amenable to state engineering, Antonov stood staunchly by the capacity of social and political forces to alter individual attitudes toward birth, marriage, and family. Soviet paternalist state policies and the integration of women into the workforce had stripped the family of its significance as the basic unit of production and caused declining demand for children (*potrebnost' v detiakh*). Therefore, it is the obligation of the post-Soviet state and its agencies, he argued, to provide structural (but not necessarily monetary) incentives for childbearing to change citizens' normative behavior (Antonov 2005).

Regulating demographic behavior, according to Antonov, is a two-tiered process. First, families that decide to have multiple children should be able to do so without fearing for their material well-being, "because in our country, giving birth to a second child usually throws a family under the poverty line," he told me in an interview. "Only after that," Antonov continued, "should we restore the prestige of family and marriage and introduce policy that will ensure that people want to get married and have more than just one child, as is the case today."[18] Although conservative in his views, in my interview with him, Antonov argued against dogmatic Russian Orthodox Church interventions and attempts to frame abortion as murder, noting that then "one would have to call millions of Soviet women murderers." In writings, he nevertheless stressed relations between falling birthrates and moral decadence leading women to abandon reproductive roles (Rivkin-Fish 2003).

In an interview, I asked Antonov how he knows which state policies might restore people's desire for children. By way of an answer, he scribbled a series of rectangles and triangles with corresponding arrows to show the complex relations between the state and its scientific experts. Using a set of arrows, Antonov outlined the relationship between the state and demography based on a feedback loop that, in his view, devises and implements pronatalist policies that ultimately yield the best possible demographic outcomes. Under the supervision of its scientific advisers, the state ought to reallocate resources, crafting a comprehensive regulatory policy aimed at fostering new norms of reproductive and demographic behavior. In this scheme, demographers stand as the main theorists of state interventions.

Antonov and Vishnevsky's large personalities and sharp-tongued debates had a dramatic effect, elevating their expert status and popularizing the discourse of impending demographic catastrophe. Notwithstanding their conflicting views on the nature of population processes and the role of the state in regulating them, both construed change of conduct as the primary object of analysis and administration. Both also made moral and political arguments about behavioral change and its effects on the population structure.[19] Their debates were fierce, and advocates of their theoretical approaches tended to discredit opponents as no less than responsible for the demographic crisis in its current form. One of my interlocutors, a former student of Antonov, reflected on Vishnevsky and his theoretical approach: "He made others believe in the equilibrium of the demographic systems [that in the long-term, the demographic system will independently strive to reproduce itself] and that we should do nothing. Look where it got us." Vishnevsky and his colleagues often accused Antonov of an antiliberal approach encroaching on individual freedom of choice and for being scientifically illiterate (Rivkin-Fish 2003).

The post-Soviet demographic community inherited a Soviet conceptual toolkit that views population structure as a function of behavioral change, population growth as essential to economic modeling, and state intervention as central to addressing population change. While for advocates of Antonov's theory, individual behavior and reproductive values can be transformed through targeted demographic policy, proponents of the demographic transition theory like Vishnevsky contend that demographic behavior will change in response to the basic need of society to reproduce itself, irrespective of governmental intervention. Thus, while they differ in their understanding of the role of behavior in population structure and blame each other's approaches for either causing the crisis or being morally corrupt, both approaches take behavior as the basic unit of analysis for scrutinizing, predicting, and changing demographic trends. Their engagement with policymakers—another Soviet legacy—has rendered behavior the target of governmental population interventions, either through direct intervention or through the cultivation of mechanisms for self-regulation (Leykin 2019). Through this late Soviet legacy, demographic expertise contributes ideas about what kinds of behavior ought to be valued by society and shapes the categories of the post-Soviet discourse on the demographic crisis.

* * *

Liberalization of the social sciences during the Khrushchev thaw brought about a fresh attempt to interpret Malthusian and Marxist population doctrines. The disciplinary move to a more behaviorist approach to population affected the ways party leadership and executives conceived of the population problem, leading to new policy problematizations.

These developments were induced by ongoing tension between the Marxist population doctrine, which claimed the primacy of economic structures, and population forecasts, which showed perpetual threats to Soviet labor resources. While postulating that population problems could be solved through the economy's social organization, experts were also producing analyses that showed that without state intervention, fertility rates would continue to decline, leading to dwindling population numbers. Against the backdrop of this tension, the primacy of economic determinism gave way to new scientific concepts, highlighting behavior as an object of either self-regulation or state management. From these developments emerged the epistemological and methodological assumptions of the Soviet science of population, which one demographer described as an "odd scientific mixture" in which Marxian dogmas coexisted with haphazardly transmitted Western demographic concepts (Vishnevsky 1996).

This late Soviet transformation in population doctrine has had long-lasting effects on post-Soviet demographic expertise and its role in policymaking. Knowledge produced by Soviet demographers in the decades following the 1965 World Population Conference has become a means for generating contemporary political ideas about normative and desirable reproductive behavior, evident in the post-Soviet state's work of care. In this formative period, divergent scholarly traditions and professional trajectories within Soviet demography led to its intellectual bifurcation and the creation of two competing schools of thought. Even though both schools of thought shared a view that stresses change of conduct as the core of population regulatory processes, their main point of contention was the power (or lack thereof) of the state to regulate such behavioral change.

Arguments about behavioral change as determining population structures, originating in Soviet demography, contributed to contemporary discussions about reproductive behavior as a legitimate target of state interventions as well as a key object of self-regulation. While a small but vocal group of Russian demographic experts has always been skeptical of the state's ability to regulate reproduction, other experts advocate active state intervention. The skeptics' argument is based on the idea that patterns of reproductive behavior are guided by their own regulatory rules and not easily altered by state policies, however generous those may be (Vishnevsky 2007). Advocates for state intervention reject such demographic determinism and highlight the explicit role of the state in regulating reproductive behavior through structural incentives. They see behavior as more modifiable, believing that changes can be achieved by strengthening the value—both economic and social—of family and reproduction (Antonov 2006).

In administrative terms, the rivalry between these two schools of demographic thought in Russia can be boiled down to the question of whether or not introducing pronatalist policies, and specifically the Maternal Capital policy, alters normative perceptions of family and practices of procreation. In the process of formulating demographic policies, new post-Soviet state agencies turned to experts in demography, whose knowledge practices and conceptual models grew out of Soviet intellectual and institutional

trajectories. Their ideas about demographic behavior as affecting population structures were reproblematized by post-Soviet policymakers into
political solutions framed by individualized behavioral logic. According
to this logic, demographic policies, and in particular the monetary incentives of the Maternity Capital policy, should assist individuals, especially
women, in changing reproductive behavior and attitudes toward family and
childbearing. The individualizing logic embedded in this policy designated
women as responsible for regulating their own reproductive behavior in
accordance with the state's demographic needs. When the policy failed to
produce the desired result, this logic made it easy to present those who had
failed to change their behavior as responsible for the failure of the policy.

This chapter has focused on knowledge and normative orientations produced by the Soviet science of population. The next two chapters focus on the
professional practices of post-Soviet demographic experts as they continue to
provide authoritative knowledge affecting governing practices and popular
discourses about population. They demonstrate how, through interactions
with local and national administrations, demographers exploit the specific
characteristics and historical development of their discipline to authenticate
their role as valid partners in the post-Soviet state's work of care.

Notes

1. The etymology of "state-istics" reveals its original meaning of *political arithmetic*,
offering modern governments practical knowledge to solve specific problems (e.g., annual
numbers of birth and life expectancy to estimate population size) (Desrosières 1998, 9, 25).

2. *Zemstvo* statisticians shared a strong modernist and technocratic ethos with the
party leadership that influenced both Russian imperial and Soviet policies. They envisioned
demography to be independent of politics and yet saw it as the best instrument by which to
govern their new, modern society (Blum and Mespoulet 2006; Herrera 2004; Holquist 2010;
Stanziani 2017).

3. Hostility toward Malthus was not only the Bolsheviks' prerogative. Malthus was
translated into Russian in 1868, some seventy years after the original publication of "An
Essay on the Principle of Population" in England. The essay sparked an immensely negative
reaction among Russian intellectuals from the Left, Center, and Right. This hostility was refracted through a variety of ideological premises, but it was largely shaped by the discrepancy
between Malthus's gloomy predictions of overpopulation and the existing circumstances
related to population and agriculture in nineteenth-century Russia. It seems as though applying what Malthus was describing in terms of the relation between population growth and
scarcity of resources onto the Russian reality required too large a cognitive jump for Russian
intellectuals to consider his theory viable (Todes 1989).

4. In the 1970s, a growing number of Marxist demographers in the West placed proletarianization at the center of their analyses, perceiving it as a protracted and uneven demographic revolution that began in the eighteenth century—two hundred years prior to the formation of the proletariat—with the rise of a mass of rural landless laborers (see, for example, Seccombe 1983, 25–28). This development was not, however, at the forefront of Soviet demographic research.

5. In 1930, the TsSU, originally an equal member in the Council of People's Commissars (Sovnarkom), was subordinated to the Soviet agency responsible for central economic planning (Gosplan) under its new name, the Department of Economic Accounting (TsUNKhU). Deprived of its somewhat independent status as a member of Sovnarkom, the bureau's official mandate was reduced to recording population dynamics for Gosplan (Herrera 2010; Blum 2005). In 1948, the TsUNKhU was given independent status under the Council of Ministers of the USSR and renamed TsSU. The move did not necessarily change the department's methods or the level of political control. In 1987, at the height of Perestroika, it was given the new name GosKomStat. The new political atmosphere transformed its independent status and role in governance significantly (Herrera 2010).

6. The official reason given for censoring the census results was that the Trotskyist counterrevolutionary group within the statistical administration had sabotaged the data collection procedures and final results of the census (Vishnevsky 1993, 593).

7. Although accusations of doctoring data are abundant, research demonstrates that raw data used by Soviet statisticians and demographers were not fabricated; it was only the final and very general numbers made available for use by party leadership that were altered (Blum 2001, 2005; see also Rosefielde 1986, 302–3). Evgeny Andreev, a prominent demographer who began his career in 1970 in the demographic research institute of the TsSU, remembers that he and his colleagues were asked to calculate life expectancy for the years 1969–1970. The result they got was 69.34—slightly lower than life expectancy trends previously published by the TsSU (70). Rather than manipulating the data by adding several decimal points to the result and publishing it, which, according to Andreev, they could have easily done, Aron Boyarsky, head of the research institute, instructed them to recalculate life expectancy for four years instead of two, adding the slightly more favorable trend of the two previous years (Andreev 2011). This recollection demonstrates that even though Boyarsky could have easily published concocted data, he was committed enough to the discipline to manipulate the data in a way that would not impinge on the perceived scientific principle of objectivity.

8. Khrushchev's policy also made divorce proceedings more difficult and costly (Nakachi 2021).

9. Similar processes were occurring in other social sciences, Soviet sociology among them. In 1958, after decades of virtual nonexistence, the Soviet Sociological Association was established because of a growing demand to represent the Soviet Union at international sociological conferences (Kurakin 2017).

10. Demographers and statisticians who survived the purges of Stalin's terror continued to conduct research, although many found themselves torn between disciplinary approaches and demands of the party and its Marxist-Leninist ideology (for other examples of this dilemma, see Pollock 2006). One of them was Mikhail V. Ptukha, founder and director of the Kiev Institute of Demography, which was shut down by Stalin in 1938. Despite multiple arrests during the 1930s, he continued his research and participated in preparing the first

postwar census (Steshenko 2001). Aron Ya. Boyarsky also survived the purges to become the director of an important research institute in the postwar period. He and Ptukha were a living bridge connecting pre-Stalin demography with post–World War II debates about the revival of demography as an independent scientific discipline.

11. The Institute of Applied Social Research at the Soviet Academy of Sciences—Institut konkretnykh sotsial'nykh issledovanii (IKSI)—was renamed the Institute of Sociological Research (ISI) in 1972 and the Institute of Sociology in 1988. Other institutes of the Soviet Academy of Sciences, most notably the Institute of Economics and its regional branches, also hosted demographers and scholars interested in demography from related disciplines such as geography (Osipov 2004; Batygin 1999).

12. It was first established as the Laboratory for Population Research in 1965 (Problemnaia laboratoriia po voprosam izucheniia narodonaseleniia na ekonomicheskom fakul'tete MGU). In 1968, the Center for the Study of Population Problems was established in the same department (Tsentr po izucheniiu problem narodonaseleniia). From the late 1970s until after the fall of the Soviet Union, the center hosted professional training courses in demography sponsored by the UN for specialists from African, Asian, and Latin American countries (Rotova and Denisenko 2006).

13. It is possible that Murray Feshbach had a direct impact on late Soviet demography, although I could not find any tangible evidence to prove this point.

14. It has been suggested that Urlanis's intrepid behavior can be traced to his "freedom" from any official position in the Soviet academic and political establishment. A Jew, Urlanis was fired from his position at Moscow State University in 1949 as part of Stalin's campaign against cosmopolitanism. He never held a position at the TsSU or any other politically sensitive department or laboratory (Vishnevsky 1996; Borisov and Vishnevsky 2011).

15. During the Khrushchev thaw, behavioral change became an important framework of reference in other social scientific disciplines, too. Thus, Viktoria Smolkin (2019) writes that the Institute for Scientific Atheism, established in 1965, was charged with finding alternatives to religious practices. Its research showed that adherence to Soviet ideology did not necessarily guide changes in behavior and that believing in communism did not prevent Soviet citizens from observing religious rituals. To change behavior, the research concluded, Soviet institutions needed to create new and emotionally viable secular rituals (142–64).

16. It is notable that despite their explicit focus on women's role in the reproduction of families, these studies were based on a shared ideological and welfare model of women as active participants in the labor market.

17. It is very likely that the emergence of this theory was influenced by concepts associated with American sociologist Talcott Parsons. However, in reading Antonov's and his colleagues' writings from that period, I could not find direct evidence of connections between the two.

18. His proposals for structural incentives included a variety of tax policies and state investment in the development of family businesses (Antonov 2005).

19. Both understood Russia's population decline as a geopolitical and economic burden that works against Russia's position within the "global demographic hierarchy," preventing Russia from competing with the rapid pace of population growth in developing countries (Antonov and Borisov 2006, 5; Vishnevsky 2007, 44–45).

2

HOW TO DO THINGS WITH DEMOGRAPHY

IN DETAILING THEIR PROFESSIONAL TRAJECTORY, the demographic experts I spent time with during my research would typically follow a particular narrative arc. They would commence in the 1960s or the 1970s, a formative period in the history of the post–World War II Soviet science of population. The story goes that during this period, concerned with declining birthrates visible in population projections, demographers began to ring the warning bell, urging the Soviet state to take proactive steps toward preventing further population decline. They were heard, it transpires in these narratives, and in 1981 the Soviet state enacted its comprehensive pronatalist policy aimed at changing the troubling trend.

The narrative form of this success story includes an element of heroic endurance; demographers are portrayed as having to overcome political censoring in order to preserve professional integrity. Recollecting their Soviet professional past in the first decade of the twenty-first century, they would stress that their intimate knowledge of population—an important object of Soviet biopolitics—had always been a double-edged sword. On the one hand, as for any modern political entity, their expertise was a useful resource, contributing significantly to the Soviet state's capacity to govern rationally and effectively. Thus, stories about demographers' interactions with party leadership regarding the emerging fertility decline were abundant, and they emphasized the high esteem in which the leadership held the demographers' expertise. On the other hand, population knowledge could pose personal and professional danger as it might reveal that experts knew too much about the state's faults and weaknesses. The story goes that when presenting research and projection results to party executives, my interlocutors had to pick the right words to avoid, as one of them put it, "accidentally calling out loud that the king has no clothes."

These narratives were shaped by early Soviet history of the discipline, particularly the history of the 1937 census. A defining feature of Soviet demographers' oral and written memoirs was that statisticians and demographers were punished by Josef Stalin for knowing the ramifications of collectivization and famine on population numbers and for refusing to falsify results to align with his predictions (Tolts 1987, 1989, 1991; Vishnevsky 1993; Volkov 1997, 2014). Their narratives stressed that those counting population possessed knowledge about social reality kept concealed from the public eye. Even if they wholeheartedly believed in party goals of building communism, as many did, professional ethics prevented them from falsifying results of the 1937 census to smooth over consequences of collectivization and industrialization.[1]

The trope of the double-edged nature of population knowledge was also based on my interlocutors' professional experiences during the late Soviet period. Access to population statistics in the Soviet Union was highly restricted, which significantly obstructed the professional activities of Soviet statisticians and demographers (Lovett 2024). They were routinely denied access to the fruits of their own research, designated by the state as "top secret" or "classified information" (Tolts 2004; Rindzevičiūtė 2015, 15–17; Denisenko and Elizarov 2014, 40).[2] Then, during Perestroika and inspired by the policy of Glasnost, public discussion of the data previously concealed from the public (e.g., the effects of collectivization and industrialization on population growth, suicide rates, infant mortality rates) provided demographers with credibility and even some fame (*Demoscope Weekly* 2017; Heleniak and Motivans 1991). My interlocutors often described Perestroika as "the golden age" of Soviet demography; it allowed them to shed light on a past they had always known about but had been unable to share with the public. When the post-Soviet Russian state once again began prioritizing demography, the historical credibility of population experts socialized during the late Soviet period received a wave of political support, reinforcing their efforts to authenticate themselves as irreplaceable partners in the new state's work of caring for its population.

This chapter follows a group of population scholars at the social science research institute in Yekaterinburg as they navigated transformations in institutional conditions and shifts in political contexts while endeavoring to produce and circulate policy-relevant knowledge about population. Focusing on the minutiae of these specialists' professional practices, the chapter reconstructs and elucidates the strategies scholars employed to enact expertise and claim epistemic authority over care for the population. Its organizing argument is that in order to substantiate their expert status, population scholars capitalized on the inherently porous boundaries of the science of population, which were shaped by both the modern political origins of the discipline and its specific historical trajectory in the Soviet Union.

Despite being attached to the state by the umbilical cord of Soviet political history, the population specialists I followed worked hard to instantiate their autonomy from the state and avoid having their work perceived as marred by interests interfering with pure scientific goals. To protect their domain of jurisdiction and navigate changing conditions in the production of social knowledge, experts exploited the porousness of the science of population as both an essential tool for modern government and an autonomous scientific discipline. In other words, population scientists appealed to the flexibility of the boundaries demarcating their discipline to preserve their authority as experts in matters of population.

Becoming Population Experts

I met most of my interlocuters at the social scientific institute in Yekaterinburg, where I joined an interdisciplinary research team involved in producing knowledge pertaining to the population problem. The team, consisting of fifteen scholars and several graduate students, studied regional fertility patterns, migration trends, labor markets, and economic development in conjunction with demography and public health, providing population forecasts to regional and municipal governments in the Urals and writing policy briefs for state officials. I participated in the team's research projects, helping prepare survey questionnaires and collecting data on the results of demographic policies launched in 2007. I was also involved in composing policy papers based on the team's population projections and in a series of conferences where demographic experts and their allies in the government would meet and create alliances and partnerships.

The institute where I conducted my fieldwork is heir to a Soviet research institute, founded in 1971 in the Ural regional capital, Sverdlovsk. It is the largest research center dedicated to the study of social and industrial life in the Urals. Every weekday, I would ride a tram to the intersection of two broad avenues where the institute occupies a monumental, Stalinist Empire-style building with visible signs of disrepair. During my fieldwork, in order to increase revenue, the administration rented out large parts of the building to a private medical clinic, a tourism firm, a restaurant, and an insurance company, banners for which were slightly more colorful and visible than the sign marking the institute itself.[3]

Despite the changes the Russian scientific field underwent following the dissolution of the Soviet Union, there is a sense of continuity between the old and new structures of the institute and the organization of science more generally. As a direct descendant of the Soviet system, which kept universities separate from specialized research centers, the institute is almost entirely devoted to research, with no undergraduate students and only a small number of graduate students. Developed shortly after the revolution in 1917, specialized research institutes for training the country's scientific vanguard were often directly related to the development of Soviet industrial complexes (Vucinich 1984; Graham 1993; Graham and Dezhina 2008).[4] Emphasis on applied research and close ties to industry played a significant role in the history of these institutes. Even today, although largely a formality, graduate students defending a dissertation are required to provide proof that their study has practical significance for a particular industry or policy and that practitioners in that field have validated the applicability of the research.

Also inherited from Soviet times is the institute's official mission to promote interdisciplinary research on the social and economic aspects of life in the Urals and in Russia more generally. Whereas interdisciplinarity has been critiqued as a mode of investigation arising from the neoliberal knowledge economy produced by Western academia (Brenneis 2009; Hoffman 2011; Shore 2008; Strathern 2003), scholars at the institute often lamented what they saw as an undesirable move toward a larger conservation of hierarchical divisions of labor between disciplines. In this new hierarchy of knowledge, economists and strictly macroeconomic research dominate all four major research departments and dictate research agendas. When I joined an interdisciplinary research department at the commencement of my fieldwork, the head of the department, an economist himself, reflected on this growing division of labor: "We're segmenting. Disciplines are segmenting. Just within economics we have over twenty sub-disciplines and they rarely overlap and never interact with each other. The result is that instead of studying social reality, it's all about abstract theoretical and methodological issues. That's what is valued today [*eto to chto prokhodit*]." His department, he assured me, intended to counter this tendency; he stressed the multidisciplinary nature of the department's research, reflected in the department's name—the Department for the Study of Regional Socioeconomic Systems (*otdel issledovaniia regional'nykh sotsial'no-ekonomicheskikh sistem*).

My interlocutors' scientific routines and structural positions within the social scientific field also bore the legacy of the Soviet science of population. As discussed previously, although counting population was an important feature of the Soviet regime, numbers produced by statisticians and social reality construed by demographic research were largely censored, and the number of people with access to data was extremely limited (Blum 2001; 2005; Tolts 2008).[5] As an important part of their professional narratives, my interlocutors shared stories about working in an institute that was as closed as the city itself—research and access to classified data even more so—during the late Soviet period.[6] To work with confidential and classified data, they had to have a special permit from the KGB department in charge of the institute's political surveillance, known as the First Department (*pervyi otdel*). They worked under strict surveillance while researching in state archives or copying data into notebooks and were not allowed to take materials or notes outside the archives or libraries. Only when provided an official request from the institute could these places send data to researchers' workplaces via special courier.

Once, over a glass of wine, Dr. Raisova, an elder in the research department I joined, told me a story about what it meant for her to do demographic research in the Soviet Union. In the late 1970s, Raisova was on a research trip in Moscow. She was in the archive, meticulously copying numbers into her notebook to compute in the evening, when a librarian, the only person on duty that day, approached her. They were friendly. The librarian had been greeting Raisova every morning for a few weeks by then, and Raisova had occasionally, as a token of appreciation, brought the librarian snacks. That morning, the librarian told Raisova that she needed to go out and leave Raisova alone in the library. She explained, "I have to run to the GUM [a large department store in Moscow]. There's a sale there. They have boots in stock today [*segodnia sapogi daiut*], and I really need a pair." Her reference to a sale is somewhat different from what people living in a capitalist society might associate with the word. Here, the notion of "they have boots in stock today" indexes a practice of mass consumption in which Soviet citizens kept a finger on the pulse of the distribution of goods and services to know when goods were not "on sale" but rather "for sale."

The economy of storage and shortage both Raisova and the librarian were living in required a degree of social skills and connections to acquire and accumulate goods—an important material condition for shaping and displaying social identities (Cherkaev 2018; Ledeneva 1998; Oushakine 2014). It was clear to both of them that the librarian could not and should not miss this opportunity. Raisova recalled that the librarian promised it would not take long. Reflecting on the moment, she noted that this promise did not mean much; they both knew it was impossible to predict the length of the queue or the amount of time it might take.

Because Raisova was working with classified documents, the librarian would have to lock her inside the research room to ensure she could not take any materials out. Raisova agreed, but after four hours, she was in dire need of a restroom. When the need became unbearable, she had to be creative, using the only thing she could find to substitute for a toilet: a potted plant. The librarian finally returned six hours later, explaining that the line had been very long. "I pretended nothing happened. I didn't want to embarrass her [*I pritvorilas', chto nichego ne proizoshlo, choby ee ne smushchat'*]," Raisova told me. To avoid an uncomfortable situation, she snuck the potted plant out when she left.

Raisova's story encompasses the multilayered social fabric of the Soviet Union. It is a story about the effects of Soviet economic and security regimes on people's everyday lives. The Soviet culture of mass consumption forced the librarian, though ostensibly at work, to wait six hours in line to buy a pair of shoes, literally interfering with Raisova's most basic human needs. It is also a story about shared understanding and compassion between two women living in the same context—instead of being angry for being locked inside a room for six hours, Raisova not only accepted the librarian's plight but also, out of concern she might embarrass her, made sure the librarian would not find out that Raisova had urinated in a planter (on the idea of mutual aid in late socialism, see Cherkaev 2018). Finally, it is about state mismanagement, which, alongside strict security protocols, left Raisova with unrestrained access to the library for six hours.

At first glance, demography does not play a special role in the overdetermined reality of Raisova's story; she could have been studying anything. The irony, however, is that it was state concern with demographic statistics and restricted access to data that fueled the story's unfolding. Access to statistical data concealed from the public made Soviet demographers' expertise an important yet threatening resource in the eyes of the state. Raisova and other members of the team inherited this structural position. In the emerging context of heightened concern with the problem of population, they employed the tension as a valuable asset in their relationship with the state, particularly to attract funding and political support for their research.

Performing Relevance

I arrived at the institute at what appeared to be a very busy time. While introducing myself to other researchers and getting used to my brand-new desk in the office I shared with Prof. Alexandrov, a leading demographer at the institute, I quickly recognized the familiar agony of approaching grant application deadlines, which dominated conversations and cut introductions short. Although government investment into science has increased since the early 2000s (Graham and Dezhina 2008), the financial crisis of 2008 wounded state and regional budgets. At the first general meeting I attended, the head of the institute announced a 20 percent cut to the institute's budget. Although the move toward external, nonstate funding had already begun as part of larger, market-oriented reorganizations of scientific research in Russia, the director took the announcement of the budget cut as an opportunity to encourage researchers to solicit funding from nongovernmental granting agencies.[7] The administration was struggling to redistribute the significantly reduced budget to secure salaries and claimed that renting out parts of the building to commercial enterprises would fund ongoing research projects and equipment purchases. Scholars, skeptical of the administration's concern for their well-being, busily applied for competitive grants from federal and regional funding agencies.

Demography seemed to be an unusually popular topic in the grant applications I saw, even those written by scholars outside the team I joined. Proposed titles ranged from "The Demographic Security of Russia and the Ural Region" to "The Demographic Modernization of Russia," from "The Role of Business in Improving Russia's Population Growth" to "The Study of the Social Effects of the New Demographic Policies in the Sverdlovsk Region." The abundance of demographic titles reflected a preoccupation with population, a concern I quickly came to recognize. However, it did not correlate with the number of researchers at the institute either trained in demography or self-identified as population specialists.

Prof. Alexandrov reflected on the pragmatic nature of these titles: "Of course. Even if there are no demographers around, people put 'demographic' in their titles to show they're doing relevant and important research." Alexandrov half-jokingly used his Soviet academic upbringing as a point of reference: "It's like when we were writing our dissertations [*kandidatskie*] back then. The date for which your defense was scheduled was an important part of it: were you to defend before or after the upcoming Party Congress? It was always better to do it after the congress, because then if there was a new decree issued or a new program announced, you'd still have time to adjust your work to reflect the change before the defense. If you did it before the congress and the party suddenly changes its program, then there's a danger your work becomes irrelevant."

Alexandrov's professional trajectory as a demographer in the Soviet Union and in post-Soviet Russia illustrates how public performance of the political relevance of his expertise is grounded in inherent tension between administrative (applied) and pure scientific (theoretical) aspects in the epistemological apparatus of the science of population. Performing the relevance of his expertise, a skill mastered in the Soviet political culture, became an important instrument in Alexandrov's scientific toolkit during the post-Soviet period. Focusing on the problem of dwindling population—a clear object of state concern—was an opportunity to showcase relevance and attract resources to support his expertise.

Ivan Borisovich Alexandrov was born, as he once told me, in "the cold summer of 1953," referring to the 1987 film of the same name, which depicts the havoc the death of Stalin wreaked on the country. He grew up in the family of a college teacher and a high-ranking civil servant and came of age in the late socialist period. After graduating from high school, he enrolled in the Department of Marxist-Leninist Philosophy, a trajectory that should have trained him to become a member of the party nomenclature, the main ruling strata of the Soviet Union. Alexandrov told me that in his junior year, he and his classmates grew tired of the Soviet ideological axioms: "In our third year at the university we no longer liked the idea of developed socialism [*k tret'emu kursu my uzhe ne liubili razvitoi sotsializm*]." Their disappointment with the system did not, however, mean he or his classmates became dissidents. To the contrary, after graduating, Alexandrov went to work as a research assistant in the Department of Marxist-Leninist Philosophy at one of the universities, where he was also leader of the Youth Communist Organization (Komsomol).

In many ways, Alexandrov belongs to what Yurchak (2005) calls the last Soviet generation—people who came of age during the 1970s and 1980s and whose shared identity was shaped by the highly normalized political discourse of the Brezhnev period. Reduced to performative and ritualistic dimensions, hypernormalized political discourse enabled Alexandrov's generation to relate to the Soviet system by producing meanings, identities, and forms of sociality not limited to official rhetoric without rejecting authoritative discourse (Yurchak 2005). The Ural State University and his Komsomol career were influential in Alexandrov's life trajectory, as they provided social and political skills he used in his post-Soviet political and scientific career. Through his studies, he became friends with some of the people (most notably Gennady Burbulis) who eventually constituted the first post-Soviet Russian government under Boris Yeltsin, himself a native of Yekaterinburg.

In the late 1970s, Alexandrov began his graduate training (*aspirantura*) in Marxist-Leninist economics. His adviser was a former high-ranking bureaucrat in the regional health department (*oblastnoi otdel zdravookhraneniia*) of one of the autonomous Soviet Socialist Republics. According to Alexandrov, his adviser had been "expelled" from his ministerial position and given a post in the institute as consolation: "He was doing medical statistics. He worked with vital statistics a lot, but he wasn't a demographer." Explaining his own encounter with demography, Alexandrov continued, "I didn't learn demography from my adviser. We didn't study demography. I don't think anyone did. Maybe a few people in Moscow did. For us, in Sverdlovsk, it was out of the question." He concluded with a refrain I often heard from him and his colleagues: "Plus, as you know, the Soviet state wasn't interested in teaching demography. It was too threatening [*slishkom opasno*]."

Before defending his dissertation about the economic history of family in the Ural region, he wrote to several Moscow-based demographers whose work he had studied independently. He wanted to share his work with them and solicit their advice. Meetings were set, and Alexandrov boarded a train, dedicating the twenty-four-hour-long journey to preparing to meet demographers working in the Soviet Academy of Sciences and at Moscow State University. The meetings did not go as well as he expected. In fact, he was devastated. He sat on a bench next to the academy after receiving what in his recollection was a very harsh critique from one of the scholars: "I remember holding the draft of my dissertation with all these margin notes written in red ink. There were hundreds of them. I just wanted to toss it away. I realized that whatever I thought I was doing was not demography, it was mere population counting [*uchet naseleniia*]. All the people I was working with previously were bookkeepers [*schetovody*], not demographers." The realization that knowing the technique did not mean he had mastered the science propelled him to postpone his defense for three years; during those years, he trained himself in demography primarily through contact with students of Prof. D. I. Valentei, one of the most prominent demographers to have emerged in the post–World War II period.

Alexandrov defended his dissertation in the mid-1980s, when Mikhail Gorbachev came to power and the era of Perestroika and Glasnost began. Like many others socialized in the Komsomol organizations during late socialism, Alexandrov tried to convert his skills to fit a new reality and briefly considered a political career. He joined the vibrant political scene of Yekaterinburg, then still Sverdlovsk. Such transitions into politics were not unusual for the Komsomol nomenclature; in the early 1990s, he joined the newly established liberal political party and even ran for local parliament, an episode he would avoid talking about every time I would push him on it. Trying their hand at politics was characteristic of the last Soviet generation, and many brought ideological versatility, shaped by the hypernormalized political discourse of the late Soviet Union, into their post-Soviet realties (Yurchak 2005; for a particularly illuminating example, see Derluguian 2005).

I repeatedly asked Alexandrov about his political career, but I sensed that he felt uncomfortable talking about that period in his life. He recalled it as an era of political naïveté (*politicheskii naivniak*) and democratic schizophrenia (*demshiza*). This stigmatizing and pathologizing reference to demands for democratic reforms in the late Soviet and early post-Soviet periods is widely used by both people who previously identified with the movement and those who blame the reforms for ensuing social and economic problems (Boym 2002).[8] "It was when we had no idea what we were doing and we didn't know how to go about what we wanted to do," he once lamented. In the mid-1990s, Alexandrov became disillusioned with politics, which prompted his return to academia. He defended his doctoral dissertation (*doktorskaia*) on the ethno-demographic development of the Urals in the nineteenth and twentieth centuries and soon after secured a research position in the institute where he works today. He also has close ties with the Ural Academy of Public Administration, teaching demography to civil servants and public administrators in professional development courses.[9]

Navigating changes in Soviet and post-Soviet politics and academia honed Alexandrov's ability to not only perform but also recognize performances of the political relevance of scientific expertise. His overt cynicism over such performances was hard to miss. One day, I was in Alexandrov's office sipping tea and reading a grant application when, without knocking, another researcher entered. It was Dr. Donov, a macroeconomist and head of another research team in the institute. A fast talker, Dr. Donov paused briefly to exchange pleasantries and quickly moved on to talk about a large federal grant his research team was hoping to win. Their proposed research, he explained, focused on "the demographic security" of Russia and the Ural region.

His team, I learned, consisted of several very talented economists and mathematicians who had created solid models with which to study demographic trends. "But we need a demographer to apply for this grant," Donov said, turning to face Alexandrov: "Do you want to be part of the team? Can I put your name in? You'll get the title of lead demographer on the team and I'll pay you 15,000 RUB [$500 USD]." Alexandrov frowned, which Donov seemed not to notice. Donov continued, "I'm not a sociologist or a demographer and frankly I'm very skeptical about what these disciplines do, but for this grant, we need a more holistic team, we need a demographer." Alexandrov looked uncomfortable, a disconcerted expression on his face. Averting his gaze, he rejected Donov's proposal: "I have my own grants to apply for. I have two applications that are due soon and I don't even have time to think about anything else."

The practice of soliciting a scholar from a different field to be part of a research grant application did not seem strange to me. Indeed, globalized institutional practices of assessment and evaluation of scholarly work often encourage a particular mode of interdisciplinarity: several independent disciplinary experts turn a specific chunk of research into digestible information to distribute, usually to inform policy (Strathern 2003; Hoffman 2011; Brenneis 2009; Shore 2008). I was, however, struck by the direct, businesslike nature of the conversation between Donov and Alexandrov. There were no pleasantries exchanged about the importance of Alexandrov's expertise in population studies. It was pure pragmatics, and in fact, Donov was very honest about the utilitarian nature of his request. To improve his chances of winning the grant, he had to appear relevant. To appear relevant, his proposal had to include an expert with appropriate credentials, preferably one with *Professor* attached to his name.

Pacing back and forth after Donov's exit, Alexandrov appeared more frustrated than angry: "He's an economist but he puts demography in the title because this is what brings him money. He pretends to be a demographer [*eto pritvorstvo*]. Because it's popular, I guess. But if you ask him, he can't tell you the difference between fertility and mortality." Clearly, Alexandrov was unconcerned with Donov's blunt approach to asking favors; at stake here was Donov's graceless incursion into Alexandrov's domain of expertise, a common experience for Alexandrov, who has been working with economists since defending his dissertation in 1984. For him, economics is an interpretive framework he sees and analyzes social reality not through but against: "They [economists] don't see demographic trends as an object of study; they just want to identify very basic causal relationships between demographic and economic variables. This is very different from how I think about social reality." He once told me that within the institute, he feels "at home among strangers and a stranger at home" (*svoi sredi chuzhikh, chuzhoi sredi svoikh*): "I understand them, they understand me, but we're strangers."

For both Alexandrov and Donov, the rhetoric of the demographic crisis provided a foundation for receiving funding, and both were quite open about it.[10] What bothered Alexandrov and seemed to him a deceit (*pritvorstvo*) was that Donov had attempted to instrumentalize Alexandrov's expertise to perform the public relevance of his own research. At one point, complaining again about Donov's attempt to use his expertise, Alexandrov exclaimed, "He doesn't understand what he's talking about!" Relatively frequent exchanges between them helped Alexandrov crystallize the distinction between his credentials as a population expert and those of pseudoexperts who use demographic variables without doing demographic research. I was a perfect audience—a student but also a fellow social scientist interested in demography—to whom to showcase the distinction and highlight the deception.

This practice of drawing symbolic boundaries around population expertise often came up at dissertation defenses I observed and participated in at the institute. In one, as part of a larger corpus of works bearing demographic titles but conducted by economists, Donov's graduate student defended her dissertation devoted to "the demographic security" of a particular region within the Urals. After a long presentation, comments, and student responses to twelve examiners, time was allotted for open discussion. One of the researchers on Alexandrov's team, Dr. Baranova, was the first to raise a hand. Rather than speaking to the student, she turned to the student's adviser, Donov: "Professor, you call this demographic research, but mathematics is your evil genius. You put too much trust in mathematical calculations. You think your macroeconomic models can substitute for demographic research?" Only then did she address the student: "Here," she pointed to the dissertation abstract we had received at the beginning of the defense, "income is not a demographic variable, it's an economic one." Tongue in cheek and clearly addressing the adviser, Baranova asked the student what she thought made her research demographic. The director of the institute, an economist himself, was chairing the defense, and he responded to Baranova's remark: "Prof. Alexandrov and his colleagues are demographers, and they like to find any chance to remind us about it. But let's not forget, this is an economic study that should be evaluated as such."

Interactions between population experts and macroeconomists in the institute were interesting variations on the theme of boundary work in science, an inherently social process always affected by cultural practices, science's social institutions, and beliefs independent of scientific data (Collins and Evans 2002, 2007; Evans 2005; Fuller 1991; Gieryn 1983, 1999). As the exchange during the defense illustrates, both demographers and economists carried out the interpretive work of drawing boundaries around expertise and presenting claims about social (in this case, demographic) reality as scientifically credible. For economists, the dominant status of their discipline and the institutional development of the Soviet and post-Soviet science of population as subordinate to economics instantiated their expertise. By drawing boundaries around demography as the domain of her expertise, Baranova (in orchestration with Alexandrov) challenged economists' privilege as credible authorities on the population problem. Pointing out that the student, as well as her adviser, lacked the necessary scientific instruments to interpret reality was a means for Baranova to draw a boundary of legitimacy and demonstrate who has a monopoly over her domain of expertise and who can perform the public relevance of demographic research (Gieryn 1999).

Conflict over the performance of public relevance is framed here by the allure of demographic research and the applicability of population expertise in the current political context. In this particular genre of boundary work, it is not simply that the value of demography is downplayed or ignored and thus requires additional effort to showcase. Rather, its value is both acknowledged and deployed by too many. The popularity of demography both makes Alexandrov's expertise relevant and threatens his autonomy as a population expert (Carr 2010; Collins and Evans 2002, 2007). To preserve authority over the domain of population expertise, Alexandrov and Baranova stressed their close engagement with the object of the study and called out Donov's ignorance (via his student) of the distinctions between basic population-level indicators and economic variables. Understanding neither the object nor the language of the discipline rhetorically excluded Donov from the community of population experts and highlighted Alexandrov's and his fellow demographers' own authority.

State efforts to address the problem of population rendered demographic research a priority for federal and regional funding agencies. In turn, interpretive work was invested in creating distinctions between population experts and pseudoexperts (for whom, from the standpoint of population specialists, demography serves mere utilitarian goals). Within the institute, this boundary work was particularly prominent between Alexandrov's interdisciplinary team of demographers, geographers, economists, and sociologists and Donov's team of macroeconomists. Alexandrov and his colleagues addressed the purity of their craft vis-à-vis research conducted by economists who claim the same epistemic domain. The stakes were high, as both parties competed for a limited range of grants and were forced to package their science legibly for funding agencies and the state. In these contexts, Alexandrov and his team worked hard to perform the public relevance of their research and present themselves as experts with an epistemic monopoly over demography—experts who possess superior skills in reading the country's fragile demographic reality.

Keeping Them Flexible: Pure and Applied Aspects of Population Research

Boundary work was not exclusive to population specialists' interactions with other social scientific disciplines. If in interactions with economists, population specialists sought to draw sharp boundaries between respective fields of expertise when relationships with the state were at stake, another form of boundary work came into play. Here, the tension between pure and applied aspects of the science of population itself became a powerful resource for authenticating expert status and performing the public relevance of expertise.

Although, as the previous section demonstrates, the importance of nonstate funding agencies has been growing, the state and its agents have remained important sources of support. In fact, during my fieldwork, state funding, along with contracts with local industrial enterprises and state ministries, still constituted a substantial part of the institute's budget, and department heads were always on the lookout for an interested party for which to provide a scientific analysis or forecast.[11] In their interactions with different state institutions, Alexandrov and his team invested a significant amount of social energy in maintaining the flexibility and ambiguity of the boundaries between different dimensions of their research. They emphasized or downplayed one or another aspect of their work to accommodate their team's professional needs and interests.

Population specialists on Alexandrov's team targeted different state institutions as potential collaborators and sponsors. In one of the research team's recurring meetings, Dr. Shuvalov, a senior researcher, presented a proposal for the study of relationships between economic development and demographic trends in Russian rust-belt company towns—former Soviet industrial towns built around one industrial enterprise. Ten to fifteen municipal centers in the Urals with similar social and economic characteristics were suggested for the study (a number later reduced to four), all categorized as monotowns or depressed territories (*depressivnye territorii*). Privatization of major industrial sites following the dissolution of the Soviet Union effectively shut down existing material infrastructure in these cities, leading to economic and social decline (Collier 2011; Morris 2016).

The idea behind the research proposal, Shuvalov said, was to identify major social problems caused by population decline in these towns and provide population forecasts for use in managing resources in the region. At one point, he suggested the project as a form of giving back to society, something socially beneficial they could do as a team (*obshchestvenno-poleznyi trud*): "We can do this, or we can volunteer in an orphanage." It seemed as though this volunteer work had the added value of potentially attracting funding from the regional government. "Demography is our trump card [*nash kozyr'*]," Shuvalov added. "We can offer to do simple diagnostics of these places—population fluctuations, labor market trends, migration patterns, social issues, etcetera. We know the situation is getting worse. How bad is it and what investments do they need to improve it? We help them understand the problem, build a few models and they can help fund us."

After introductory remarks about the rationale of the project, a junior researcher raised concerns about the way some of the research questions had been constructed and presented. Exploring relationships between economic development and demographic trends is an extremely sophisticated theoretical question, which might impede the progress of the research. In fact, Alexandrov himself and other senior scholars would raise this concern when debating with macroeconomists in the institute. Here, however, Shuvalov's response was swift: "I hope you all know you didn't come here [to the institute] to do basic scientific research. Our goal here is to do applied science [*prikladnaia nauka*]. We've been doing it well for many years now and we don't need to reinvent the wheel." The conversation about basic versus applied research ensued. "The main goal of this research proposal is to lure bureaucrats [*zamanit' chinovnikov*]," Akhmetov, another team member, suggested: "We want them to become interested in this kind of research, so we need to phrase it in a way that shows that applied [*prikladnye*] aspects of this research are more important. I mean, you know, why would they want to deal with the population problem at all? They might even benefit from depopulation as such—fewer people means fewer people to feed, plus you don't need to take care of the elderly."

A few people in the room seemed taken aback by Akhmetov's overt cynicism about state officials' motives. Also, focusing explicitly on bureaucratic interests to steer the research agenda seemed to spoil the atmosphere. Perhaps Akhmetov had pushed the boundaries too far, so Shuvalov, who was leading the meeting, tried to adjust course: "Thinking about what state bureaucrats can get out of this doesn't mean we would massage data for them. Never. We never hide our scientific results. In our experience, sometimes officials don't want us to publicly share our research results because they don't want people to know the real dimensions of the problem. Sometimes they know that if people knew what the real situation was, they'd run away and never come back. But we would never censor what we find. If they don't want to see what we find, it's fine [*ne khotiat ne nado*]." Raisova, who was sitting next to me, whispered in my ear: "Thank you very much, we concealed plenty in the Soviet Union. Everything was sealed and concealed. What good did it do? [*i chto khoroshego*]." Shuvalov, ever the seasoned manager, seemed determined to persuade the young researcher who had raised the concern that the applied nature of the proposed research would not affect its scientific rigor. "You're thinking like a scientist [*uchenyi*]," he told him, "but we need to think how to attract state bureaucrats [*chinovniki*] and how to make them interested in this project. What do they [government officials] need? They lose people in these towns at a great speed, and they somehow need to attract them back because they need people to keep going to work."

I heard Alexandrov laughing: "That's not true. They [bureaucrats] don't care about people. That's laughable. But they can always use 'demography' as an investment trump card [*investitsionnyi kozyr*'] to attract federal funding. So, we can help them with that." Dr. Akhmetov, Alexandrov's frequent collaborator, chimed in eagerly: "A few years ago we tried something similar in town X. We did a few population forecasts for them and showed how population fluctuations affect their old power plant. And we got paid!" Turning to Alexandrov, he said, "Remember how the municipal bureaucrats were bragging about our projections?" Akhmetov turned back to his team members: "You see, they used our diagnostics and our forecasts as a resource. With our projections, their development plans were now scientifically grounded, so they could use it to attract regional or federal funds." Alexandrov cynically confirmed: "Yes, it was good public relations for them, and those *chinushi* [derogative for *chinovniki*, bureaucrats] would do anything for a little bit of public relations."

In Russia as elsewhere, population forecasts have indeed been a popular techno-scientific tool for soliciting action. Politicians often use population forecasts as a "scare tactic" (for interwar Europe, see Quine 1996; for postsocialist Eastern Europe, see Gal and Kligman 2000). President Putin, for example, has used population forecasts to fortify his anti-Western rhetoric. Addressing domestic audiences, he once pointed to deviations in the UN population forecasts that, in his words, "projected a slow but steady extinction of the Russian nation." State interventions in population trends over the last decade, he assured the audience, "had proved certain domestic and international population experts wrong by a huge margin of at least ten million people" (President of Russia 2013). For Russian population specialists I worked with, quantitative methods of predicting the demographic future have emerged as valid ways to represent and intervene in Russia's crisis. They relied on the forecasts' ability to structure the public's and policymakers' understanding of the population problem in the face of uncertainty.

However, there is an inherent paradox in demographers' efforts to predict the future. Efforts intensify when uncertainty about the future increases, yet this same uncertainty makes the future less predictable and the task of forecasting more difficult. Forecasters have to assume that the future is going to be different from the past—they try to predict it for this very reason. At the same time, because of the inertia and interdependent character of long-term demographic processes (i.e., fertility rates in 1981 necessarily affect fertility rates in 2003), demographers must assume that future changes will resemble past demographic fluctuations in significant ways (Keyfitz 1981).[12] To overcome the inherent uncertainty of forecasting models, demographers need to incorporate certain assumptions about what is perceived as desirable in future transformations. However, the task of forecasting, as I observed in the team's work and as it appears in Russian scientific literature, has been complicated by the fact that specialists, aside from stating that the future should be different, usually lack a clear idea of what an alternative future might entail (see, for example, Arkhangelsky and Elizarov 2016).

Models in general and forecasting models in particular function not only as a means of intervention but also, and first of all, as a means of representation (Krause 2021; Morgan and Morrison 1999). When it comes to the projections of Russian population specialists, demographic change is often presented in terms of impending dystopian disaster. Predictive models of demographic development frame Russia's demographic reality as a collective crisis heralding the death of the nation. Their projections are motivated by the narrative of an imagined, looming catastrophe: if something very radical is not done, Russia's population shrinks until the country ceases to exist. In this sense, demographic projections solicit a sense of crisis to shape political action. In the models, population as a functional unit of government is shown to be in danger of disappearing, as is the state's capacity to govern. The visual nature of models, presented in graphs and charts, is intended to trigger an emotional response to scenarios of population disappearance (Kravel-Tovi 2020). These representations urge the state officials Alexandrov and his team interact with to see numbers as more than just numbers—as an encroaching disaster that calls for immediate action.

The models Alexandrov and Akhmetov built for town X are a good example of how a sense of doom and political goals were incorporated into the forecast to shape emotional response and action in the present. The experts created a series of future demographic scenarios drawing from a politically informed notion that the town in particular, and Russia in general, is in dire need of rapid population growth to survive economically as well as geopolitically. The quantified results were later circulated among state agencies and in the media.

In their population growth forecast for town X, Alexandrov and Akhmetov showed how desired and undesired migration movements might sustain or suspend positive population growth. A scenario in which internal rather than international migration flows into the town are enhanced was shown as the ultimate response to the population problem. In their final quantified form, projections informed both political and popular representations of the population in the region and shaped the ways in which regional and federal bureaucrats understood the problem. More importantly, these projections dictated what is appropriate and what is not in terms of possible policy solutions. However simple or sophisticated these models and their methodological tools might have been, the practice of forecasting demonstrates how population specialists mobilize narratives about a looming catastrophic demographic future, narratives present in both public discourse and the epistemological apparatus of the discipline.

I was intrigued by the openly cynical atmosphere of the meeting where these projections were discussed. To me, it resembled the tone of Donov's exchange with Alexandrov about grant applications. I shared my thoughts with Alexandrov on our way back to the office. In his usual, somewhat world-weary tone, as if spelling out an obvious fact to a child, he replied, "As of now, the state is ready to invest in the economic revival of monotowns, so we need to get creative with this feeder [*kormushka*]." When we were back in the office, Alexandrov silently pulled out a letter he had crafted addressed to the regional branch of Putin's political party, United Russia (Edinaia Rossiia). The letter stated that the objective of the research proposal on monotowns, designated as "depressed territories," was "to create an innovative project of improving the quality of life for people in monotowns." It requested that the local branch of the party sponsor "the social and cultural healing of the depressed territories." The letter was signed by the director of the institute, whose status as an academician, Alexandrov told me, lent the signature more weight than his own. In another letter addressed to the governor of Sverdlovsk region, Eduard Rossel, Alexandrov wrote: "The scope of depopulation processes is such that it requires the work of well-trained population scientists who could diagnose and offer solutions to the population problems in the region." Alexandrov offered the resources of his research team as the foundation for such work. Although his large-scale monitoring project never materialized, the institute's population projections were used in plans for the development of Yekaterinburg and several smaller municipalities (*URBC.RU* 2015).

Capitalizing on the popularity of population as an object of state care, Alexandrov and his colleagues highlight some and downplay other aspects of their scientific work. Instances in which researchers interpret their intellectual activities in varying and often contradictory terms function to justify scientists' claims to authority, autonomy, or state resources. Depending on the goal they are pursuing in their research, their scientific work is "purified" or "impurified" (Gieryn 1999; Latour 1987, 145–76). Thus, when speaking about his and his colleagues' cultural authority as scientists, Alexandrov emphasized the purity of his scientific work vis-à-vis its consumers, namely bureaucrats and government officials. On the other hand, when faced with political conditions that required new ways to secure research funding, Alexandrov and his colleagues purposely blurred boundaries between the pure and applied aspects of their research, focusing on its practical benefits.

The applicability of the science of population as the science of government threatens the sense that demographers' work is autonomous from the state. Thus, to preserve objectivity as the main attribute of their expertise and to maintain flexibility, demographers' labor must be temporally organized in such a way that the state enters only *after* the real scientific work has been done. The research team can only maintain the purity of the scientific process by suggesting that "we do the research and then tell them what to do with it." In other words, to appear credible, their engagements with the objects of their expertise have to precede their engagement with audiences. Objectivity and autonomy must go hand in hand. More importantly, experts need to demonstrate that this fragile relationship between objectivity and autonomy would be marred were alien interests allowed any purchase, hence Alexandrov's immediate insistence that he would never doctor data. The research teammates I worked with pursue both objectives. They strive to remain autonomous to preserve their cultural authority and credibility as a vanguard in matters of population care. But to secure the support of the state, they highlight possible applications of their research at the risk of appearing nonobjective and nonscientific. As a result, the boundaries between these two aspects of their work remain flexible and purposefully vague.

* * *

The strategies population specialists pursue in order to sustain credibility as experts are the outcomes of two important political and social processes. First, they are an outcome of the historical development of the Soviet science of population, which throughout its history cast population specialists as both ally and threat to state interests. Second, these strategies are products of contemporary political transformations in which government-dictated priorities of population growth have ascended in significance, enhancing the value of population expertise and experts. The historical conjuncture where knowledge about population becomes valuable and the historical trajectory of the science of population as both ally of the state and troublemaker is reconsidered can shed light on how experts maintain their status and make strategies recognizable in the eyes and ears of their audiences.

These scholars' interpretive work, grounded in their professional socialization during the Soviet Union, and the different styles of boundary work they engage in simultaneously protect their authority over population expertise and offer opportunities to seek the support of the state and its agents. Thus, by effectively posting "keep out" signs to other epistemic authorities, such as economists, around their domain of expertise, population specialists represent epistemic rivals as pseudoexperts who engage with the object of study without the skills and language necessary to enact expertise in population matters.

Resisting their subordination to the discipline of economics, demographers employ one or another form of boundary work to claim authority in scientific matters of population vis-à-vis economists who also claim epistemic expertise in these matters. This boundary work enables population specialists to not only expand their claims for epistemic authority but also demand greater access to material, and often political, resources. As the exchange between Donov and Alexandrov demonstrates, this particular genre of boundary work is often accompanied by funding wars between experts within the same academic institution and the same social scientific field. To emphasize their privileged position as authorities in matters of population, population specialists do the interpretive work of convincing audiences that their representation of social reality is more reliable and socially and publicly relevant than that of others, who only pretend to know demographic reality and are mistaken when they seek to represent it.

To secure the support of the state while protecting their autonomy, scholars purposefully sustain flexible and vague boundaries between two aspects of their scientific work: pure and applied research. Maintaining the flexibility of the boundaries between these forms of social scientific knowledge constitutes these scholars' positions as cultural authorities and expert communicators in matters of population policy and the demographic crisis. To maintain an aura of objectivity crucial to their status as experts, they devise a special temporal regime of representing their expertise in which engagement with research always precedes engagement with the audience that desires it. In other words, they represent their research as not determined by state interests and wishes but rather as a factor that should dictate and direct the state's inclinations and aims.

As demographers continue to both protect and transcend the boundaries of their epistemic authority, they gain access to new material, organizational, and conceptual resources and redefine themselves as experts with ever-greater authority over population as the object of their knowledge—and over political processes to which this knowledge is applied. As the following chapters demonstrate, the cultural authority of demographers to speak about and on behalf of the population is an important element in making demography a new vernacular for the state to think about how to fight the demographic problem.

Notes

1. In his memoirs, recorded by Anatoly Vishnevsky in 1959–1960 and published only after the fall of the Soviet Union, Mikhail Kurman, who worked in the Department of Economic Accounting (TsUNKhU) from 1932 until his arrest and imprisonment in 1937, recalls that he and his colleagues were well aware of dramatic population loss following the famine of 1932–1933. This realization prompted them to classify all population data and publish the last figure on January 1, 1933. No data was published after that, but they kept meticulous records for themselves (Vishnevsky 1993, 600).

2. After the death of Stalin, certain indicators became publicly available, but since 1974, most of the data (age distribution, life expectancy, birth parity, and more) have been reclassified as "for internal use only" (*dlia sluzhebnogo pol'zovaniia*) (Vishnevsky 1996; Tolts 2001; Heleniak and Motivans 1991, 475–76). It is important to note that during the Cold War, certain topics deemed relevant to national security could not be published on both sides of the Iron Curtain. Such was, for example, the case of mathematical economics (Bockman and Bernstein 2008, 591).

3. The practice of renting out institute space to commercial enterprises was born out of the financial crisis Russian academia underwent in the decade after the dissolution of the Soviet Union (Graham and Dezhina 2008, 29). Several months after I left the field, the district attorney ordered a thorough legal examination of the institute's real estate operations and found serious violations of laws regarding use of state property (https://fedpress.ru/66/polit/society/id_207153.html).

4. In terms of both state support and public imagination, research centers and the researchers who worked in them were situated higher on the Soviet social ladder than their university colleagues (Vucinich 1984, 72–91, 144–46). In post-Soviet Russia, however, this hierarchical system came under attack, with higher education reforms aiming at recalibrating the system toward greater unity and standardization (Medvedev 2020). Funding opportunities behind the reform prompted departments within the institute to create collaborative ties with regional universities. The full-scale invasion of Ukraine in February 2022 and the

international sanctions that followed introduced severe restrictions on funding, and political reforms rendered universities and research centers isolated from international partners.

5. See also chapter 1.

6. As noted in the introduction, until 1991, Yekaterinburg (then Sverdlovsk) was a city tightly closed to foreigners because of the high concentration of defense research and development facilities.

7. Many scholars had to get accustomed to this new mode of funding; educated during the Soviet Union, few were familiar with it. In Soviet academic structures, research projects had been centrally funded by the state, complemented by contracts with specific industrial enterprises and ministries interested in research and development (Graham 1993; Graham and Dezhina 2008; Ninetto 2005).

8. The schizophrenia in *demshiza* also alludes to a coerced psychiatric treatment many Soviet dissidents were subjected to for their political activism (*Signal* 2022).

9. The Ural Academy of Public Administration is the current incarnation of the Sverdlovsk High Party School (Vysshaia partiinaia shkola, VPSH), where party members could receive degrees in four years (compared to the regular five). In 1991, VPSH was transformed into the Ural Center for the Government Cadres (Ural'skii kadrovyi tsentr), which trained experts in market economy and offered courses for government and municipal bureaucrats. In 1995, the center was transformed into the Ural Academy of Public Administration and become a branch of the Russian Presidential Academy of National Economy and Public Administration (RANEPA). See also chapter 3.

10. Olga Shevchenko (2009) writes about the dependence of Russian scholars in the humanities and social sciences on international grant-making agencies in the first decade after the fall of the Soviet Union. She notes that there was a general consensus among Russian scholars that agencies favored projects dealing with severe social crises. In effect, affirming the crisis became a necessary condition to solicit funding from agencies (27–29). Although international grant-making agencies are long gone, Russian scholars are very attuned to the specificity of formulations new national granting agencies are interested in.

11. For other forms of monetization of scientific research in Russia, see Golub 2018.

12. This philosophical dilemma has preoccupied a professional community of demographers since at least the 1950s, and population forecasts have long been a defining feature of demographers' professional identity. North American demographers often evoke their failure to predict the post–World War II baby boom when they reflect on the history of their discipline (Keyfitz 1981, 1982; Ahlburg and Lutz 1998; Ahlburg, Lutz, and Vaupel 1998). The last Soviet forecast conducted in 1989–1990 played a similar role for Russian demographers as it failed to predict the dramatic rise in mortality rates following the dissolution of the Soviet Union (Andreev and Kharkova 2002).

3

DEMOGRAPHY—A NEW VERNACULAR
FOR THE STATE

"I'M INVITED TO THE OMBUDSWOMAN'S RESIDENCE NEXT WEEK.[1] You know, the one next to the governor's," Alexandrov told me with a wink when I entered his office one morning. As a researcher at the Russian Academy of Sciences with expertise in demography, he had been asked to join a committee of experts from various scientific institutions and state agencies around the region, including demographers, sociologists, economists, educators, and public health professionals. The committee's mandate was to assess the effectiveness of new federal and regional policies aimed at facilitating population growth. "You see, sometimes they [the government] need evidence [*dokazatel'stva*]. That's when they call us, the scholars [*uchenye*]," he concluded in his familiar cynical tone.

During the meeting at the ombudswoman's office, which I joined, experts spent two hours discussing the long-term plan for population policies approved by the federal government in 2007 and adopted by its regional counterpart later that year.[2] Alexandrov and his senior colleague Raisova lamented the inadequacy of available statistical data to assess the demographic situation in the region two years into implementation of the new policy. Nodding her head approvingly and looking at the reports provided by the regional statistical authority, the ombudswoman replied, "Indeed. I don't know whether it's because you, Ivan Borisovich [Alexandrov], taught me well or because I'm simply clever, but I noticed there is no information on the number of first, second, and third children per woman in this or any other reports we've received." Alexandrov looked very pleased at the remark.

On our stroll back to the institute, both Alexandrov and Raisova returned to the ombudswoman's comment. Some years ago, Alexandrov told me, he had spent a considerable amount of time explaining to her that number of first children does not necessarily indicate sustainable population growth. "The basic demographic wisdom that in order to know if population is really growing, we need to know if there are more women giving birth to second and third children was hard for her to understand. But it seems as though she's finally internalized it [*vpitala*]." Chiming in, Raisova, a former physician and medical demographer who had working relationships with state officials spanning different political eras, emphasized the educational nature of her and Alexandrov's interactions with the ombudswoman: "[When we met her,] she was demographically illiterate [*demograficheski bezgramotna*] and couldn't distinguish the total fertility rate [TFR] from the absolute number of births. Today, she knows that in demography absolute numbers are not good indicators for anything. She knows not to trust newspaper reports that claim that population has been growing in 2010 because we have over 1000 more births than we had last year."

The metaphor of demographic illiteracy Raisova used here, as well as its eradication, was a common refrain every time she or another member of Alexandrov's team recounted pedagogical interactions with state officials, journalists, or representatives of nonprofit organizations. *Likbez*—short for the eradication of illiteracy, *likvidatsiia bezgramotnosti*—indexes a particular moment in Soviet history when, following the Bolshevik revolution, the government launched a widespread and highly successful campaign aimed at the total eradication of illiteracy in the country (Fitzpatrick 2002). It is a powerful metaphor, one that puts Russian demographers in the position of initiating a civilizing project on a scale equal to that of the Soviet eradication of illiteracy. Indeed, the metaphor of eradication of (demographic) illiteracy has been extensively employed by post-Soviet Russian demographers from different schools of thought when describing practices of popularizing demographic knowledge for the general public and state officials (for example, demographia.ru 2014; *Demoscope Weekly* 2016).

In Alexandrov and Raisova's portrayal of their interactions with the ombudswoman, attempts to eradicate demographic illiteracy appeared successful. The ombudswoman seemed Alexandrov and Raisova's ideal bureaucrat rendered student. Although she represented the state, which governed the expert' research, the value of their expertise in understanding a pressing political and social issue tipped the hierarchical scale, compelling her to become their grateful student. Both Alexandrov and Raisova assessed the ombudswoman's performance during their interactions as showing the fruits of their pedagogical labor and *likbez* campaign: the ombudswoman was becoming literate. She had learned the terms of their field, such as *rate* and *parity*, and showed an ability to read the sociodemographic reality she was trying to act on using their conceptual framework. Notably, by inviting them to the committee and acknowledging openly and unequivocally their contribution to her demographic literacy, the ombudswoman had validated their expert status as mediators between demographic reality in the form of statistical reports (i.e., TFR instead of absolute numbers) and scientifically informed state care.

This chapter explores pedagogical engagements in the context of the moral panic over Russia's demographic crisis, engagements marked by experts' didactic efforts to vernacularize sociodemographic knowledge for state bureaucrats. I suggest understanding these practices through two main interpretive frameworks. First, following Olga Shevchenko (2009), is the notion of general and ubiquitous crisis that, following the dissolution of the Soviet Union, became an important feature of public discourse—an interpretive framework structuring perceptions of reality and evaluations of often unrelated events. When speaking about population, Russian demographers have employed the readily available rhetoric of crisis to represent demographic reality with a sense of doom and assert their competences in understanding and preventing the catastrophe.

Second, predictions of demographic doom have been characteristic of the conceptual apparatus of demography more generally, with gloomy predictions shaping public perceptions of the problem. As an administrative science of the state, these predictions are primarily concerned with state capacity to regulate population. Any deviation from what is considered a balanced demographic system, in other words, any sign of overpopulation or underpopulation, is perceived as a threat to the state capacity to govern. It also marks the state as chiefly responsible for returning the system to equilibrium (Domingo 2008; Greenhalgh 2008; Shriver 2003).

In the case of Russia, predictions molded by the demographic discipline resonate with a popular interpretive framework in which crisis serves as a chief category through which to explain reality (Shevchenko 2009). The apocalyptic framing of the problem has contributed to the view of demographic reality as a singular threat to state governing capabilities. These two interpretive frameworks—the public discourse, in which the notion of crisis has been central to how people perceive everyday reality, and the disciplinary apparatus of demography that frames the demographic crisis as a crisis of state care—have shaped Russian demographers' pedagogical engagements and didactic attempts to vernacularize disciplinary knowledge for administrative audiences. The chapter argues that by vernacularizing demography for post-Soviet statecraft, population experts have supplied Russian bureaucrats with a set of moral orientations and ideological assumptions with which to reflect and act on the country's social and demographic reality.

Vernacularization is an interactive practice that involves making strategic decisions regarding how to communicate certain scientific concepts; which arguments to omit; how to express particular ideas as universally accepted; and how to convey the practical implications of expert knowledge to validate the status of demographic experts as active participants in a political process. It is through these vernacularizing practices that ideas about population as a dire crisis of the state's potency became dominant. The consensus about the apocalyptic framework of the crisis, embedded in demographic experts' attempts to vernacularize knowledge and educate state officials, has allowed demographers to present their competences as socially and morally beneficial to restoring the state's ability to govern.[3] In the following pages, I explore how motivations and didactic strategies of demographic experts affect and even determine the forms of knowledge vernacularized and produced in engagements with state bureaucrats.

A Note on Vernacularizers

Vernacularizers of sociodemographic knowledge are a particular type of intermediary (Ballestero 2012; Chua 2009, 332; Merry 2006). From Max Gluckman's (1949) village headman and Victor Turner's (1967) Muchona the Hornet to human rights activists (Levitt and Merry 2009; Merry 2006; Michelutti 2007), anthropologists have long been fascinated with social actors who use familiarity with local cultural practices and idioms to negotiate systems of meaning. However, unlike go-betweens who mediate local adaptations of ideas produced elsewhere, the experts in demography I worked with were both producers and vernacularizers of ideas generated by their discipline. Similar to the vernacularizers of Merry's (2006) international human rights language, population experts endeavored to make knowledge resonate with those they were conveying it to, so they used cultural idioms and practices familiar to the state bureaucrats they were teaching. At the same time, they advocated for their role as knowledge producers who not only translate but also possess exclusive theoretical and methodological skills to mediate social reality and political processes of population management.

A considerable amount of my fieldwork involved following experts as they tried to vernacularize basic demographic knowledge for state bureaucrats attending professional development seminars in public administration. Part of the federal initiative Innovative Russia 2020, these training programs were designed to deploy knowledgeable cadres to implement and disseminate new government policies.[4] Training programs for public administrators have been powerful institutional mechanisms, encouraging particular framings of social problems in a variety of national and international contexts. The EU, IMF, and World Bank, as well as local and international nongovernmental organizations (NGOs), all rely on such efforts to craft common policy language at different levels of government (Babül 2012, 2015, 2017; Ballestero 2012; Broome and Seabrooke 2015; Firat 2014, 2016).[5] Russia's strategic program Innovative Russia 2020 was driven by similar motivations, and in 2007, as new demographic policies became part of the national high-priority package (*natsional'nye prioritety*), basic training in demography and social aspects of population trends were incorporated into the curriculum of professional development programs across the country. For my interlocutors, the state's prioritization of demography gave those seeking to convert their skills into other forms of capital an opportunity to offer their expertise.

Another important feature of vernacularizing practices discussed here is that experts, in their pedagogical engagements, needed to balance showcasing the value of their expertise for state-crafting processes and protecting the scientific neutrality and objectivity of their knowledge (Jasanoff 1990; Porter 1995). The experts I followed during my fieldwork worked hard to prompt state bureaucrats to care for the issue at stake. They worked equally hard to preserve distance between the authority of their expertise and that of state bureaucrats, even while praising them as good students able to internalize the fruits of their expertise. The distance between demographic reality in its quantified form and its operators, namely state bureaucrats, created the need for an authoritative intermediary—experts able to translate academic knowledge into the administrative language of the state. For demographic experts, vernacularization became an important instrument with which to stress the demographic crisis as a crisis of state care and underscore their own vitality to the governing project.

The Cycle of Ignorance

The majority of training programs for state bureaucrats where I observed attempts to vernacularize population knowledge were conducted at different branches of the Russian Academy of Public Administration (RAGS), a postsocialist incarnation of the Higher Communist Party School, which was the home for training and educating Soviet cadres until 1991. During my fieldwork in 2010, RAGS merged with another institution, also known for its Soviet legacy of training state bureacrats—the Academy of National Economy (ANKh). Together, they formed one of the largest universities in Russia: the Russian Presidential Academy of National Economy and Public Administration (RANEPA). Through a series of dramatic shifts, RANEPA emerged in post-Soviet Russia as the entity responsible for training state cadres and business leaders (Huskey 2004). It has many regional branches. In the building the academy occupies in Yekaterinburg, this institutional transformation and transition from one political regime to another are still visible. A visitor standing in the corridor leading from an older part of the building to its newer wing might notice a semitransparent curtain that, on closer inspection, veils a carving of a scene with almost biblical overtones in which Vladimir Lenin converses with Yakov Sverdlov, considered to be a proponent of scientific training for socialist cadres (fig. 3.1).

To conduct training programs for state bureaucrats of different ranks and from different regions, the academy commissions specialists from across the city's scientific institutions. Since professional demographers are somewhat rare in contemporary Russia, Alexandrov or one of the members of his research team would usually be offered the job. A concentrated module in demography would be taught before or after other intensive modules devoted to the basics of micro- and macroeconomics, law, and public administration. Always eager to cultivate networks and find new sources of funding for policy research, Alexandrov and his colleagues actively sought out training programs, offering their expertise as an instrument of management and governance. The trainings were a job requirement for bureaucrats, and some were explicit about their lack of interest in taking part in conversations initiated by teachers. However, others were happy to come to the classroom, as doing so relieved them of work duties for the duration of the program. Many were interested in acquiring an additional certificate after completing seminars, as those offered possibilities for career advancement and a salary increase.

Most of the trainees in the dozen seminars I attended worked at regional branches of the Ministry of Social Security as well as for social services associated with various municipalities. The groups were quite diverse in terms of age and gender distribution; rather than signifying the egalitarianism of postsocialist state administration, this diversity reflected its

Figure 3.1. Carving in the building of the former Higher Communist Party School. 2018. It depicts two canonical figures and proponents of the scientific training of socialist cadres, Vladimir Lenin and Yakov Sverdlov, surrounded by new Soviet cadres. Photo by the author.

gendered character in differences in public administrators' ranks. Thus, seminars for high-ranking administrators had clear male dominance. Seminars consisting of what Michael Lipsky (1980) succinctly calls "street-level bureaucrats" were much more diverse in terms of gender. Working in welfare, middle- and low-ranking administrators make decisions on behalf of the state through direct contact with people in need of government services.

The first training seminar I observed was in a classroom full of high-ranking officials from a remote Siberian region with a particularly scarce population. Alexandrov began his introduction to the predominantly male group in suits and ties by cheerfully announcing, "What I like is that since the government launched the new [demographic] policy, a new demographic bureaucracy, in a good sense [*v khoroshem smysle slova*] has been formed . . . I've already taught some of your colleagues, and I can assure you they learned to understand and appreciate demography." Promising that by the end of the module they would be able to "breathe" demography (*dyshat' demografiei*), he handed out a survey questionnaire on the new policy, part of the research he had been conducting since the policy's introduction in 2007. The basic idea behind the survey was to understand how state bureaucrats conceived of the problem of population and how urgent they think it is. However, when asked about the purpose of the survey, Alexandrov told students, "This questionnaire is simply a teaching tool. Fill it out first, and then we'll see what all the questions and answers mean. Maybe you'll even be able to catch my mistakes. There are mistakes there. Let me know if you see them."

It was a trick Alexandrov employed in all his sessions. He wanted students to gain intimacy with the object of his expertise and, in this case, with a basic methodological tool of the trade—a survey questionnaire. The trick is indeed an important part of learning by apprenticeship, as it allows trainees to assess their skills in relation to others' work (Lave 1991, 2011; Makovicky 2010; Portisch 2010). By sharing his research instruments with students and even inviting them to be critics, Alexandrov constructed his students as capable interlocutors. Yet as soon as the students began to fill out the questionnaire, he provocatively shifted the footing: "It's a well-known fact that bureaucrats don't know demography and statistics. Look at you, for instance. You have a sociological questionnaire in your hand, but it doesn't mean you're sociologists."

Alexandrov's provocation, although bordering on offensive, was an important element of his vernacularizing practice. Protecting his authority while cultivating state bureaucrats as novel experts in all things demography required fostering ignorance to protect his base of competence and maintain the distinction between those more knowledgeable and those less so (Knorr-Cetina 1999). I observed a recurring effort on Alexandrov's part, in this and other classrooms, to transmit knowledge to students while reminding them that without his expertise, their knowledge remained insufficient to make scientifically sound bureaucratic decisions.

Ignorance, thus, played an important role in Alexandrov's vernacularizing efforts. As scholars have argued, ignorance is part of, rather than absent from, the social process of knowledge construction, and it plays an important role in forming power relations (Chua 2009; Dilley 2010, 182–83; Gershon 2000; Gershon and Raj 2000; Mair, Kelly, and High 2012). In Alexandrov's case, students' ignorance guarded his own authority. Hence, by offering the opportunity to reflect on the survey, which students were asked to complete both as subjects of research and as students of demography,

Alexandrov created a distinction in which his bureaucrat-students might be able to enact limited expertise by learning to speak the language of demography. Only he, however, had the authority to interpret the survey to which they, as his objects of knowledge, offered evidence. While providing students with the quantitative skills to accurately read social and demographic reality, he continually reminded them of the distance between their partial skills and his contributory expertise that remained pivotal for interpretation and action (Collins and Evans 2007).[6]

The learning process I observed in these classrooms was built around attempts on both sides to evaluate the other's ignorance. As much as teachers attributed ignorance to students, public administrators tended to be suspicious of teachers' knowledge of political reality, portraying them as ignorant of real political processes. On several occasions, I witnessed students calling out teachers for making factual mistakes in describing laws, reforms, or political decisions or accusing them of being politically naïve.

Both sides regularly invoked ignorance when encountering sensitive political issues. In these cases, ignorance was used to morally evaluate the other's ideas and statements. In one class, a particularly active student declared global population growth as, in his view, "the real crisis." The problem, he said, is "not that there aren't enough people here, but that there are too many, and the earth might explode. Why not encourage migration instead of making women have more children?" As mentioned in previous chapters, migration as a solution to the country's demographic crisis has been a highly unpopular political stance in Russia over the last two decades. The teacher's reaction was quick. He attributed the student's argument to what Alexandrov and his colleagues often called general demographic illiteracy—in other words, ignorance. Referencing existing scientific arguments against Malthus's calculations that had led the student to believe in an inevitable population explosion, Alexandrov construed the student's argument as lack of knowledge rather than a political statement. Ignorance was used to avoid political confrontation by presenting a political position as a matter of scientific ignorance.

As much as "knowledge provides people with materials for reflection and premises for action," ignorance and its strategic employment plays a crucial role in producing these materials and premises (Barth 2002, 1). From the perspective of trainers, students' ignorance played an important role in vernacularizing demography as a policy tool, rendering their contributory expertise free of the political interest associated with state agents. State bureaucrats, on their end, were dependent on scholars' knowledge and evidence-based reports but resisted the shift that transformed them from authority figures into subjects in need of education (Babül 2012, 2017; Firat 2014). These tense pedagogical engagements showed the cyclical nature of vernacularizing efforts in which ignorance played a highly instrumental role.

As much as Russian experts in demography showcased the disciplining power of vernacularization, their strategic employment of ignorance also signals its limits. Similar to other contexts of situated learning, experts and trainees in training seminars appeared dependent on each other to pursue often contradictory goals (Lave 1991, 2011). When Alexandrov's tactics of turning his students into ignorant subjects morphed into cynicism—if not direct contempt or condescension, as often happened in his trainings—the strategy lost its empowering qualities. There was a thin line between constructing students as ignorant to maintain his own social position and exhibiting outright disdain by resorting to popular stereotypes of indifferent and ignorant civil servants. Crossing this line undermined Alexandrov's base of competence and the power of his expertise.

Visual Pedagogy of Numbers

Visualization is another pivotal mechanism Alexandrov and his colleagues employed in their vernacularization efforts, as the visual pedagogy of numbers provided bureaucrats a framework for understanding the issue of population. The teachers in the professional development classes I attended made liberal use of visual aids (graphs, tables, charts) and web-based simulators to depict the "grayness of statistics" (Porter 1995), inscribing numbers with political urgency (Greenhalgh 2008) and soliciting a response of care from students (Kravel-Tovi 2018). Visual aids are called *nagliadnye posobiia*, and their use has a long history in Soviet and post-Soviet pedagogy. As Sonja Luehrmann (2011) demonstrates, the concept of *nagliadnost'*—the use of teaching visual aids—in Soviet pedagogy encompasses both the use of visual materials (e.g., pictures, graphs, statistics) and images that emerge in listeners' heads as they reflect on a lecture (144).[7] In the training seminars I attended, representations of demographic reality through visualization tools—either tables and charts on a whiteboard or computer simulations—imbued numbers with symbolic and political meaning, advancing the catastrophic story of Russia's demographic development.

Lacking Alexandrov's confidence in front of bureaucrats, Andrey Shilov, one of Alexandrov's junior colleagues, often let visual representations do the heavy lifting in communicating the political significance of the crisis. He began classes on demography by projecting a slide showing the cover of the book *The Russian Cross: Factors, Mechanisms, and Plans for Overcoming the Demographic Crisis in Russia* (fig. 3.2). The "Russian Cross" (Russkii krest) is a statistical line chart and technical concept that received visibility following the political concern over the demographic situation (Rimashevskya 1999; Khalturina and Korotaev 2013). Revived in a series of debates about the nature of the demographic crisis in the mid-2000s, it serves as a technical as well as popular representation of the crisis. On the one hand, the cross quite literally depicts the moment in Russia's demographic development when, coinciding with the dissolution of the Soviet Union, around 1991–1992, mortality rates became equal to and then rose above the birthrate—the two trends crossed. On the other hand, the cross is freighted with symbolism of moral loss and national suffering in the wake of the Soviet Union (Rivkin-Fish, 2006, 151–55; Oushakine, 2010).

The Russian Cross is a powerful cultural metaphor. As Sergei Oushakine (2010) writes, when presented as a graph, trends of fertility and mortality form an indelible image that recalls the Christian icon of both suffering and endurance, moving the discussion of social policies "towards the predictable fascination with the nation's suffering" (159). When combined with scientific facts and politically conditioned statements, the metaphor contributes to the dystopic narrative of the demographic situation in Russia. The narrative of imminent catastrophe, conveyed by the visual representation of demographic reality, adds to the political importance of the problem and the credence of demographers explaining the problem.

The exclusive focus on the moment of the Soviet Union's dissolution set the tone for Shilov's representation of the demographic crisis. It obscured historical continuities and the inner inertia of demographic trends and processes. In a different context, Shilov, as well as his mentor, Alexandrov, would likely disagree with the short-term interpretation of the demographic processes popularly represented by the cross. They would explain that social upheavals occurring some sixty years ago affect demographic trends visible in today's Russia. Birthrates have been declining in Russia since at least the 1960s (Zakharov 2008). Male mortality rates skyrocketed after 1987; alcohol abuse was a major cause of death, prompting the introduction of an anti-alcohol campaign by Mikhail Gorbachev in 1985–1987, which led to a rapid decline in mortality rates

Figure 3.2. Book cover for D. A. Khalturina and
A. V. Korotaev, *Russkii krest: Faktory, mekhanizmy i puti
preodoleniia demograficheskogo krizisa v Rossii*. Moscow:
URSS Publishing Group, 2013. Credit: URSS Publishing
Group, Moscow (http://urss.ru/104378).

and a sharp increase in life expectancy, especially for men (Shkolnikov and
Nemtsov 1997; Leon, Shkolnikov, and McKee 2009; Parsons 2014). Yet, oriented
almost entirely toward the restriction of public access to alcohol, the campaign
did not produce substantial changes in underlying drinking patterns or related mortality rates. Instead, it postponed deaths that occurred once the anti-
alcohol campaign was lifted in 1987. Thus, in 1994, the life expectancy for men
reached its lowest point in fifty-seven years (Shkolnikov and Nemtsov 1997).

Using the visual of the cross didactically to vernacularize demography
for state bureaucrats associated the problem of population decline almost
exclusively with the collapse of the Soviet Union. The Russian Cross as an
image played an important role in obscuring the relevance of long-term

historical processes, instead highlighting 1991, the year of the fall of the Soviet Union, as a discrete moment marking sudden changes in the demographic trajectory of the country. There is clear continuity in Russia's demographic history, rooted in political and social processes that affected people's lives prior to the fall of the Soviet Union, but the Russian Cross creates an image of a graspable and bounded reality, a clear-cut boundary between two periods in the country's history—the Soviet and the post-Soviet. Evading the continuity of demographic processes that connect the Soviet with the post-Soviet makes it easier to assign responsibility for the crisis to a particular event or social actor; the inertia of demographic processes and their far-reaching effects make it harder to offer immediate, hands-on solutions. Instead, the binary distinction between what was before and what is now disguises this complexity and creates an image of the population problem as a discrete predicament that can be solved by the state's political will.

While the Russian Cross in its graphic form denotes seemingly objective demographic trends, it also indexes the idea of Russia's demographic exceptionalism and unique national course. While a small group of demographers see Russia as part of a global trend of transition to low fertility rates and an ever-growing aging population (Vishnevsky 2007), the dominant camp in Russia adheres to the idea of demographic exceptionalism (Antonov and Borisov 2006). They see Russia as evolving along a path independent of global demographic trends and qualitatively different from demographic transformations in other countries and regions. Unique material and ideological resources will allow Russia to overturn negative demographic trends and reappear on the geopolitical map as a powerful and abundant nation, the argument usually goes (Vyzhutovich 2007). The emotionally appealing and symbolically loaded metaphor of the Russian Cross illustrates this view and solicits a response of care from state officials.

In the process of vernacularization, which inevitably showcases certain aspects of the demographic trajectory while passing over others, the Russian Cross became the visual framework through which bureaucrats were taught to perceive and reflect on social concerns with population. Its symbolically loaded two-dimensional visualization of complex calculations conveyed the threat of demographic crisis for Russia's sovereignty. In one of Alexandrov's classes, he announced in a dramatic tone, "For the past twenty years, the population of our country has been declining by 800,000 to 900,000 people annually." To emphasize the dwindling numbers, he added, "This means that every hour of the day the population is declining by a hundred people. Experts everywhere are concerned that the country cannot preserve its current borders if this catastrophic demographic trend continues."

Pausing for the expected murmur of surprise and disbelief, Alexandrov amplified the effect of his statement through an example about Russia's eastern neighbor: "By the way, Chinese demographers calculated that the optimal population size in China should not exceed 700–800 million people. Where do you think the rest would go? Our neighbor from the East is concerned with the question of how to accommodate the remaining 600 million people." Without elaborating on the statement or explaining why the Chinese would use Russia as a solution to their own population problem, he nevertheless made the link between Russia's population decline and a possible external threat to the country's sovereignty. Beyond framing the problem of population as a threat to national sovereignty and a collective political crisis, *nagliadnost'*—visualizations of this "scientific truth" via dramatic visual representations of the problem—urged students to care about it.

In another instance, to visualize the connection between Russia's demographic crisis and the country's sovereignty, Alexandrov drew two population pyramids on the board. The first was for Somalia, with a broad base indicating an abundantly populated country. Next to it, he drew a pyramid that looked more like a barrel with a narrow base and top, the right side protruding further than the left. The horizontal coordinate was the indicator of fertility rate, he explained, and the vertical one represented age structure. Pointing to the pyramid on the left, he said, "This is Somalia. Do you see how many children are born there?" He then pointed to the pyramid on the right and explained that the right-hand side of the pyramid represented women and the left-hand side, men: "This is Russia's age and gender distribution pyramid, and there is no balance here." Pointing to the bulging right side of the pyramid, he began to explain the implication of the imbalance: "If something happens to Russia, if there's a military invasion from outside, for instance, we're done [*nam kaput*]. We don't have enough people in general and enough men in particular to fight this invasion." His statement turned out to be prophetic. Although no one invaded Russia, Russia invaded Ukraine in February 2022, so the problem of military conscripts became salient. I address some of these issues in the concluding chapter of the book.

Visual displays of knowledge are a powerful means of presenting scientific research and shaping how outcomes are perceived (Latour 1987, 64–79; Greenhalgh 2008, 110). By mapping the country's population structure on the board and comparing it with a different country, Alexandrov emphasized the spatial dimension of the problem—too much territory with too few people. The fear of disappearance resonated with Alexandrov's students; more than simply a numerical problem, population decline had a clear material presence—closed childcare facilities, shortages of healthcare professionals, and decaying infrastructure, especially in rural areas and border regions. When Alexandrov talked about the territorial aspects of population decline, a student from the mayor's office in a provincial town in the southern Urals lamented that in the past, train tracks connecting central Russia with Siberia had been an important part of the town's identity, making it a regional transportation hub. In recent years, however, significant decline in public demand for transportation had led to serious readjustments of the market, resulting in a very few trains passing through the town.

The student's example illustrated the material manifestation of what Alexandrov explained as "too much territory with too few people." It also illustrates what Dace Dzenovska (2020) calls "postsocialist emptiness"—a physical manifestation of the disappearance of people, capital, and state care from marginalized spaces and their concentration in other spaces, usually global cities incorporated into circuits of capital and power. The material reality of de- and reterritorialization has been familiar to post-Soviet and postsocialist subjects, making the issue of population decline an observable phenomenon grounded in material and social relations (Dzenovska 2020).

The visual pedagogy of numbers helped teachers organize the flow of information for students in seminars and provided an anxiety-inducing framework through which to read Russia's problem of population. Put differently, demography and statistics created a language for articulating the widespread postsocialist fear of disappearing from the map, manifested in students' and teachers' observable reality. Displaying the final outcomes of quantitative manipulation, as teachers did in classes, also modified the scale of the population problem. The somewhat amorphous concept of population decline became a graspable and isolated reality that could be conquered and modified using simple quantitative instruments (Desrosières 1998). Visualizations of a temporally and spatially bounded demographic reality framed it as both large enough to be threatening and small enough to be defeated by their knowledgeable teachers.

Vernacularizing the Pillars of Demography: Fertility, Mortality, and Migration

Vernacularizing demography for state bureaucrats entails not only framing and visualizing sociodemographic knowledge but also deciding what to present and what to set aside. In this sense, certain hegemonic cultural and political ideas shared by bureaucrats and experts, as post-Soviet subjects, shape the process of vernacularization. Thus, in the training seminars I attended, fertility and reproduction were much more widely discussed than, say, mortality or migration. Teachers would often begin sessions on demography with the following statement: "Demography stands on three pillars: fertility, mortality, and migration."[8] Despite this oft-repeated axiom, they never apportioned an equal measure of time to each subject. Two-thirds of the time allotted to demography was devoted to fertility and reproduction, leaving mortality, migration, and other topics to be discussed in the remaining third of the time.[9]

Fertility

Teachers often began their discussions of fertility by introducing the concept of replacement level. Using a historical Soviet Union example, one teacher explained, "Already in the 1970s and especially the early 1980s, Soviet demographers began to be concerned with the shrinking population. Why? Because birthrates began to fall below replacement level." He explained that for population to reproduce itself, TFR should be 2.1 children per woman; in her lifetime, a woman needs to give birth to at least two children. "So, falling below this level indicates that population is growing slower and even declining," he concluded. He paused, and before moving to a new topic, the teacher added emphatically: "Less than that and we are about to disappear." In this teacher's delivery, there was almost no rhetorical distance between the statistical manifestation of declining birthrates and the nation's disappearance. The students were offered to read the statistical indicators he provided as a clear sign of the nation's death. To prevent this death, teachers would explain, the state needs to listen to its experts and use their skills.

Alexandrov, who was particularly creative in using classes to boost his expert status in front of bureaucrats, would demonstrate his continuous commitment to the project of governing population: "In the Soviet Union, we were concerned with falling birthrates and so we began writing letters to the Central Committee of the Party to alert the leadership. As a young scholar, I wrote a lot of letters too. The leadership listened." To prevent the decline, he would continue, the Soviet state introduced a series of what he dubbed "paid motherhood" (*platnoe materinstvo*) policies. By paid motherhood policies, Alexandrov meant a policy introduced in the Twenty-Sixth Congress of the Communist Party of the Soviet Union in 1981, discussed in chapter 1. The policy's explicit goal was to raise birthrates while allowing women to remain in the workforce; the policy included extended maternity leave, certain flexibility in work schedules, and a special set of subsidies for women with more than three children. It was introduced gradually, first in the Far East and Siberia and then in the remaining parts of Russia in 1982 (Avdeyeva 2011; Zakharov 2008, 920–22).

At this point in his narrative, Alexandrov would jump to the immediate post-Soviet period in the demographic development of the country, drawing from his and students' shared experience of the dissolution of the Soviet Union: "And then in 1992 came [Egor] Gaidar.[10] Do you remember him? He's the guy who told you, 'Now go forth and multiply . . . only at your own expense.'" The ages of the students would usually indicate that they had some firsthand experience of that period, and many would nod. "In the Soviet Union, the state took partial responsibility for childbearing. And then Gaidar and his cronies [*ego brat'ia*] came to power," Alexandrov would continue. In one class, a female student interjected, "I don't like to remember this time." Alexandrov replied, "No one does because it reminds us of poverty. It is, I think, when poverty appeared on our radar for the first time." His rendition of this historical narrative resonated with students because of their shared experience of free-market economic reforms following the dissolution of the Soviet Union. In his narrative, the retreat of the state from its social duties—the decade of privatization and liberalization of the economy—was personified in Gaidar as chiefly responsible for the population decline.

Alexandrov's historical example served to illustrate an argument, much debated in demography, that considers the positive relationship between economic inequality and population decline. In a different instance, he reversed this relationship, detaching the problem of population from issues of wealth and inequality. Speaking about the wave of population policies initiated by the Russian state in 2007, Alexandrov switched his focus from economics to behavior, rendering declining fertility rates an outcome of changing social norms and values rather than poor economic conditions. In this iteration of the problem, rather than intervening in the economy to change demographic trends, as the Soviets supposedly had, the state must help the country's citizens change their demographic behavior (i.e., their normative ideas about childbearing).

To elucidate the argument that demographic behavior determines population structure, he returned to the visual examples of the population pyramids on the whiteboard. Pointing to the pyramid of Somalia, he asked: "Why is it that in Africa they have birthrates of 5 children per woman, and in Russia, it's barely 1.3? They're constantly at war, and they're poor there, but they continue to have a lot of children. Why is it that in other countries like Somalia,[11] for instance, where there's poverty and lack of political stability, birthrates are high, and in Russia people refuse to have children?" One of the trainees, a civil servant from the Ministry of Social Services, offered an observation: "True, I've seen them. They barely have a room of fourteen square meters to live in, and they have multiple children, and then I see young, healthy women [in Russia] who give up their babies although they have space in which to live and raise a child." Alexandrov turned to the student and stated emphatically, "It's because there are ruins in our heads [*v golovakh razrukha*]."

V golove razrukha, a popular turn of phrase in post-Soviet discourse, originated in Mikhail Bulgakov's novel *Heart of a Dog* ([1925] 1968). In speaking about the state of Russia following the Bolshevik revolution, one of Bulgakov's protagonists exclaims, "Hence, the rack and ruin are not in the bathrooms, but in the heads" (Bulgakov 1968, 37). This phrase, as many other popular tropes from the novel, pertains to a range of social crises construed as consequences of a problem of consciousness (Rivkin-Fish 2009). In this imaginary, consciousness has palpable material and social effects. Along these lines, in 2009, Alexander Surinov, then head of the Russian Statistical Bureau (Rosstat), stated that "the population will continue to decline if there are no revolutionary changes in our heads" (Surinov 2009). In 2013, Surinov returned to this idea when a journalist asked him if he thought demographic policy was responsible for visible population growth in the country. Surinov responded that the policy's effect on collective consciousness (*massovoe soznanie*) might have led to growing birthrates. "Ruin starts in the heads. It also ends there," he said (Kamakin 2013).

"Ruins in the head," as Alexandrov rendered it, refers to a crisis of consciousness that led to a change in women's reproductive behavior, which in turn led to a decline in social norms pertaining to the desired number of children in a family. From this perspective, the demographic crisis can only be resolved by reestablishing the norm of multi-child families. In the words of one of Alexandrov's colleagues: "The new demographic policy's main goal should be changing people's demographic behavior. This means changing the norms, and not simply providing material benefits to people." "What's wrong with material benefits?" one student asked. The teacher replied, "We can't solve the problem of depopulation if we don't start thinking about values and norms. Why do you think the population grew before the revolution [of 1917]? Because family, generational succession, and values were the most important things for people then."

Most, if not all, demographers teaching these seminars were followers of Anatoly Antonov, the Russian demographer who claims that the norm of multi-child families can be achieved by punishing or rewarding families economically and socially for producing a certain number of children (Antonov and Borisov 2006, 111–15). Despite being assiduously anti-Malthusian, Antonov advances what Malthus was essentially preaching: the need to stimulate, adjust, and incentivize people's patterns of reproductive behavior. His views have been echoed by politicians from the dominant political parties and resisted by more liberally oriented public figures and social scientists (Rivkin-Fish 2003).[12]

As an example of a change in demographic behavior advanced by Antonov, teachers would often present the Maternity Capital policy introduced by the government in 2007 that offers women a one-time payment of approximately $13,000 (adjusted for inflation) to encourage them to have a second child.[13] The announcement of the policy hardly took Russian demographers by surprise: many served on federal and regional expert committees dedicated to the issue of population decline, and rumors about the new policy spread fast in their tight-knit professional community. Yet the monetized form of the pronatalist policy did catch them unawares. "This idea did not come from us," I heard again and again. Expert opinions about policy interventions had been countered, they said, by government officials' demands for a simplified cost-benefit analysis of the demographic situation. A leading demographer from Moscow State University recalled in an interview that a high-ranking official, a macroeconomist by training, from a ministry in charge of demographic policies requested that the committee he was heading produce statistical models based on a simple economic analysis of the problem. The official asked a group of experts: "How many more babies do we need? How much money do we need if we decided to pay women to have them? How much would it cost if we paid them directly?"

Behind the scenes many teachers in professional trainings called the monetized policy demographically illiterate and ineffective in changing childbearing norms. They nevertheless used Maternity Capital as an example in their classes when addressing the role of state policies in changing demographic behavior. Regarding the policy, one told his students: "I never thought it would work, but it did. We see that people are having a second and even a third child. It's a new phenomenon; clearly, the policy has had an effect on how people think."

In offering Maternity Capital as an example, they conveyed the argument advanced by the dominant school of demographic thought: with the correct set of incentives, the state is capable of changing the demographic behavior of individuals, modifying their normative desire for children in accordance with social needs. In one of his classes, Alexandrov noted, "We lost a few million in the 1990s. Some forecasts even projected that the population would reach a low of 80 million by 2015, but state efforts have paid off, and the population has been growing since the new policies were set in motion."[14] A civil servant from the governor's administration remarked, "That's true. I had to wait two years to get my daughter into a municipal day care. There are so many children now and not enough kindergartens." Using this remark as confirmation of his argument about the immediate effect of the new policy, Alexandrov replied, "You see? Only recently, to the question about a third and sometimes a second child, Russian women would have answered, 'We're not fools.' But now, you can see that birthrates are going up."

The cultural idiom of "ruin in the head" was particularly helpful in vernacularizing the concept of demographic behavior in relation to fertility. It assumed that population decline is determined by behavioral attitudes and norms. Already popular in depictions of social crises, the phrase rendered the concept of demographic behavior as malleable to normative changes palatable to students attending training seminars for state cadres. Framing the problem of population as exclusively that of norms and collective consciousness helped divorce the problem from political and economic underpinnings, such as changes in the country's welfare policies. It also oriented the moral aspects of having children away from families and toward the state. In this reading, in order to change behavior, the state and its agents need to establish the proper moral coordinates for citizens to follow.

Mortality

Compared to fertility, mortality was left relatively untouched in the training seminars I attended. Alexandrov's teammates do little research on mortality; this was reflected in their teaching curriculum. Given the high mortality rates for an industrialized country such as Russia, this relative absence is especially telling. At the time of my fieldwork, life expectancy at birth was an estimated 61.8 years for men and 74.2 years for women (Rosstat 2010). As a point of comparison, in the years 2010 to 2015, estimated life expectancy at birth for men and women in eastern Asia was 74.7 and 76.6; 77.8 and 80.1 in northern Europe; and 78.5 and 81.2 in western Europe (United Nations, Department of Economic and Social Affairs, Population Division 2015, 190, 194).

It was not only the team members' disciplinary interests that led them to ignore the issue of mortality. Although the problem of high mortality rates among Russian men has been an object of public health and social research (Parsons 2014), popular and state discourses on the demographic crisis attribute greater significance to promoting increased births than to battling male mortality rates (Rivkin-Fish 2006). This bias is evident in the pronatalist nature of social policies aimed at altering population trends, such as the previously mentioned Maternity Capital policy (Rivkin-Fish 2010).

Mortality has nevertheless occupied the popular imagination of Russians. A Russian comedian on the once-popular late-night comedy show *Paris Hilton's Projector* was asked why Europeans live longer than people in Russia. By way of answer, he offered what sounded like an acute anthropological observation: "Russian lives aren't shorter, people here just live at a higher velocity [*oni zhivut ne men'she, oni zhivut bystree*]." Several years later, when increasing general life expectancy became the focus of a presidential decree, Kirill Kleimanov, a host on the pro-Kremlin first channel, suggested that although Europeans might live longer and have better medical care, their lives are more boring: "Our lives are more fun, but they are shorter. And just so that our lives could be both long and fun, the president issued his next, but most important decree to date" (Boletskaya 2018).

During trainings, culturally specific experiences and discourses of mortality informed the ways in which both students and teachers framed the problem of high mortality rates and unbalanced life expectancy. In her seminars, Raisova, who was a medical demographer and former physician, would draw examples from her expertise in public health. She would lead students through a series of thought exercises to show relationships between mortality rates and life expectancy. In the last hour of one seminar, she asked students to imagine a desirable life expectancy for men in Russia. The parity between real and desired life expectancy in students' responses was quite telling. One student suggested sixty-one, which was in fact the life expectancy for men at the time. Several students suggested sixty-four or sixty-five. Others went for seventy. She then encouraged, "Well, let's go wild, let's let our imagination fly." No one proposed a life expectancy above eighty. In one of the sessions in which Alexandrov distributed his survey on state bureaucrats' familiarity with new demographic policy, to a question about desirable life expectancy, seventeen students replied sixty-five to seventy-five years, seven students said seventy-five to eighty, three replied sixty to sixty-five, and only one student suggested eighty-five to ninety. In a larger survey Alexandrov and his colleagues ran among municipal administrators in the region, only four out of one hundred and two respondents suggested a number greater than eighty-five.

Raisova pointed out the appalling differences in life expectancy for men and women in Russia. She asked students if it might be possible to make people live longer instead of encouraging women to have more children. Both men and women in the classroom attempted to reply. In the cacophony of voices, I heard, "What for?" and "Maybe men. Women already live long enough." At that point, Raisova drew a chart laying out reasons for high mortality rates. As in the case of fertility, behavioral patterns and norms became the focal point of the training while structural forces were edged out of discussion. When she spoke about behavior related to health and hygiene, what Russian demographers call *vital behavior (samosokhranitel'noe povedenie)*, and their effects on mortality rates, one of the male students jokingly protested, "Why do we need to know all this? We'll all die in the end regardless, even if we exercise." To that, a female student replied, "Yeah, but I'd like to live a little longer."

These exercises demonstrated the limits of social imagination shared by Raisova's students. They found it hard to imagine a life expectancy significantly higher than the statistically estimated one. Shaped by popular and scientific discourses on the demographic crisis that privilege fertility, these learning exercises reveal the cultural meaning behind statistical regularities (Johnson-Hanks 2007, 2008). They show how these regularities and the discourses that describe them can shape our imaginaries and aspirations for social action. For Raisova as well as her students, numerical signifiers were not simply an intellectual exercise in quantification but also an everyday experience that guided their social imagination. The widespread material effects of statistical regularities, such as unbalanced and low life expectancy in Russia, shaped teachers' and students' experiences of family and reproduction and hopes for the future.

Migration

If mortality received an abbreviated mention, migration was afforded even less time in the teaching curriculum, but for different reasons. Alexandrov's explanation of this absence tended to be quite circular: "Migration is part of demography, but it's a different topic; it's a separate topic although we cannot talk about demography without talking about migration." The conundrum was caused by the politically sensitive nature of migration as a topic. He clearly felt uncomfortable discussing the controversial issue and often cast it as too complex to dwell on in the framework of a training. Glossing over different types of migration, he would say, "Migration can also be dangerous because it sometimes fosters national conflicts." After a pregnant pause, he would add: "Russia is depopulating but migration is not a solution. A sacred space is never empty [*sviato mesto pusto ne byvaet*]. When in the 1990s we had negative population growth, migration was thought to solve the problem. So we opened these floodgates that attracted migrants. But migration doesn't exist to temporarily block holes. Large migration waves might change the national constitution of the country."

Aside from a few occurrences, one of which I discussed in the beginning of this chapter, the framing of migration as a threat to national sovereignty was accepted without much resistance. The issue particularly resonated during trainings with state officials from either border regions or cities with a large migrant population. Articulating a negative sentiment regarding unregulated migration flows from former Soviet Asian republics and China, teachers would insist that migration cannot and should not replace other remedies for the population problem. The trope of demographic change as a threat to national sovereignty—never fear, there is always going to be somebody to fill the vacancy—is widely utilized by Russian nationalists, but it has broader appeal, too. Media outlets add to the xenophobia by framing unregulated labor migration as contributing to the changing national character of the country (Karpenko 2010; Kuznetsova 2017; Markowitz and Peshkova 2016; Pain, Poloskova, and Zaionchkovskaiia 2004; Pilkington 1998; Rivkin-Fish 2006; Schenk 2018).

Using the popular proverb *sviato mesto pusto ne byvaet* (a sacred space is never empty), demographers first of all addressed a shared social experience of postsocialist emptiness—depopulated towns and villages, abandoned industrial and agricultural sites, and thinning social and material relations (Dzenovska 2020). As to what might happen to that vast depopulated space, they excluded migration as an alternative to the emptiness of postsocialism because in the politically dominant discourse, migration poses a threat to national sovereignty and security.

Two contradictory interests motivated this framing of migration in the seminars. On the one hand, it was shaped by the perceived objective nature of the experts' scientific trade. Teachers felt obliged to address all three pillars of demography, including migration and its possible effects on the population structure. On the other hand, the construction of migration as a threat to sovereignty underpinned their demographic reasoning. It also resonated with a hegemonic political discourse and sensitivities of the bureaucrats whose perceived mandate was to implement, not critique, state policies. Strategic framing of the problem for the bureaucrats, working in the name of a state whose ideology toward migration was less than favorable, affected the experts' teaching curriculum and reinforced dominant political ideologies.

Although the demographic indicators of mortality in Russia, especially mortality for men of working age, are highly unusual for an industrialized country, the population problem in Russia has been framed almost exclusively through the lens of fertility and birthrate. Even when mortality and migration are acknowledged as social problems, both state and popular discourse on the demographic crisis focus on falling birthrates, attributing the decline and recovery of the seemingly dying nation to reproductive behavior. Naming fertility rather than mortality or migration as the core of the population problem plays a crucial role in forming public perception of the demographic reality in both cultural narratives and policy-adjacent discourses.

* * *

Vernacularization is an important mechanism for translating expert knowledge for administrative audiences, and it elucidates interactions and ideological orientations that inform popular and state discourses on social issues. In the context of heightened concern over Russia's demographic crisis, the vernacularization of sociodemographic knowledge during interactions between experts and state bureaucrats played an important role in molding ideas about state care. Training programs in demography for state bureaucrats provided epistemological parameters and ideological premises with which to interpret the country's sociodemographic reality: behavioral change as the target of state care, population policies to protect national sovereignty, and expert knowledge as essential in turning demography into an effective governing tool.

A quintessentially performative practice, vernacularization turned the products of experts' labor into a policy instrument for state population care. Recursive relationships between what experts taught and which pedagogical tools they used shaped configurations of power and effects of vernacularization. Vernacularization revealed the decidedly political underpinnings of Alexandrov's and his colleagues' pedagogical practices. The process of vernacularizing sociodemographic knowledge for state bureaucrats brought to life the dystopic discourses of the demographic crisis and ideas about how the state should prevent the nation's disappearance.

For population experts, these interactions were an important means of asserting expert status and probing the possibility of partnership in a larger governing process. In implementing this strategy, ignorance played a crucial role as a disciplining tool. Evoking ignorance, experts marked an unbridgeable chasm between themselves as contributory experts and their trainees to negotiate their role as unbiased interpreters of social reality. In this learning process, they shifted the bases of competence, transforming state bureaucrats into ignorant subjects and themselves into producers and mediators of knowledge. Far from being the opposite of knowledge, ignorance appeared as a critical practice through which knowledge and power relations were constructed.

In the processes of vernacularizing knowledge analyzed in this chapter, experts used a variety of pedagogical tools to teach state bureaucrats to frame the problem of underpopulation and prove the validity of such a framing. Students and teachers negotiated a set of assumptions with which to interpret demographic reality in a series of imaginative (*nagliadnykh*) exercises through which normative and moral foundations of the crisis were displayed. With the help of visual aids, students were taught to recognize sources and effects of the demographic problem, framing it in a way that privileges behavioral change over structural factors and fertility and reproduction over other demographic variables such as mortality and migration.

As teachers sought to guard their reputation as scientific experts, they engaged the perceived objectivity of population statistics to shape the political meanings of demographic reality as a severe crisis while avoiding the appearance of political motivation. Their pedagogical engagements revealed the demodystopic framings of social reality embedded in the conceptual toolkit of the discipline (Domingo 2008). The notion of omnipresent crisis that frames post-Soviet public discourse contributed to the sense of dystopia, making the political and cultural sensitivities of state bureaucrats resonate with the notion of demographic crisis leading to the nation's disappearance.

Crisis as a fact of life and a fundamental element of the demographic discipline provided population experts with the moral and political legitimacy to appear as authoritative interpreters of a salient social problem and as vital forces in the state's efforts to fix it. The next chapter will examine the role of other social actors offering cures to the crisis and shaping normative ideas about families as the core object of state care.

Notes

1. Created in the 1990s as part of the democratic reforms, the position of ombudsman has a semi-independent status. The ombudsman is elected by the legislative assembly of the region to serve as intermediary between the regional government and the public. As part of her responsibilities, the ombudswoman also mediates advisory committees in charge of social policies. Although the institution of ombudsmen functions nominally as a civil society in Putin's Russia, it nevertheless operates under the auspices of the regional government and serves its interests.

2. The regional demographic policy closely followed the federal plan and offered an additional monetary incentive for a third child: http://msp.midural.ru/docs/386.

3. My argument about the vernacularization of demographic knowledge as an important channel through which political ideas about population come into being follows anthropological scholarship that focuses on "the dynamics of expertise-in-practice" and demonstrates the inherently social and performative character of expert knowledge (Brada 2016; Camic, Gross, and Lamont 2011; Carr 2010, 19; Hodžić 2013; Leykin 2020; Mertz 2007).

4. Innovative Russia 2020 targeted public administrators of different ranks and branches of the government (Surnacheva and Gabuev 2012).

5. Ethnographic accounts of training programs for bureaucrats tend to take the perspective of trainees, examining how they accept or resist what they learn (Babül 2012, 2015; Firat 2014). Complementing this scholarship, I take the trainers—experts in demography—as my focus.

6. The distinction between interactional and contributory expertise, suggested by Collins and Evans (2007), is a useful heuristic in this regard. They define interactional expertise as "expertise in the language of a specialism in the absence of expertise in its practice" (Collins and Evans 2007, 28). A high level of interactional expertise allows one to discuss the object of

expertise (scientific concept or technical skill) but not to perform the action in question. An interactional expertise in a given area is always learned through engagements with those who possess contributory expertise in this area (Collins and Evans 2007).

7. On the history of using visual materials and the concept of *nagliadnost'* (visual teaching aids) in Soviet and post-Soviet pedagogy, see Luehrmann 2011, 143–64.

8. They often used the Russian idiom *demografia stoit na trekh kitakh*—demography stands on three whales.

9. Understandably, the balance of other topics seemed dependent on a particular teacher's research interests.

10. Egor Gaidar served as prime minister of Russia in 1992. He was best known as a passionate advocate of the free-market economy and a major architect of the so-called shock therapy reforms implemented by Yeltsin's government after the dissolution of the Soviet Union.

11. The country would vary from one seminar to another.

12. For more on Antonov's school of thought, see chapter 1.

13. See introduction for detailed information on Maternity Capital.

14. In 2008, Russia's population had declined to 142 million from 148.6 million in 1993 (Rosstat 2011b).

4

TRADITIONAL FAMILY VALUES

From Population as a Quantitative Problem to Population as a Moral Concern

IN 2013, VLADIMIR PUTIN, THEN IN HIS THIRD term in office, introduced a national ideology of *dukhovnye skrepy* in his annual address to the nation. To English-speaking audiences it was translated as *spiritual bonds,* imagined as a set of cohesive social values the Russian state purports to strengthen (Shepelin 2013). In this new, conservative iteration of national ideology, spiritual bonds were presented as traditional values (*traditsionnye tsennosti*) characteristic of the unique composite of people populating the Russian Federation (Kremlin.ru 2012, 2013a, 2013b, 2013c, 2021). An apparent social spiritual deficiency (*dukhovnoe neblagopoluchie*), caused by weak spiritual bonds, was presented as impeding the country's upward development and national unity.

Long before the concept of traditional values became almost exclusively associated with regime efforts to set forth a unified and distinct national ideology, they were at the heart of national concerns with underpopulation. In the first decade of the twenty-first century, at the height of national obsession with demography, any conversation or political statement about population care (*narodosberezhenie*) had to include a discussion of traditional family values and the so-called moral and ethical foundations (*moral'no-nravstvennye osnovy*) that ostensibly shape these values. Shortly after the government launched new demographic policies in 2007, the year 2008 was declared the Year of the Family, and a new holiday appeared on the calendar: July 8, the Day of Family, Love, and Commitment (Den' sem'i, liubvi i vernosti), a name later shortened to Day of Family (Den' sem'i).[1] While the holiday has primarily been used by municipal and regional governments as a platform for channeling ideas about so-called traditional family values, its introduction also marked the emergence of secular and religious foundations and nonprofits with a focus on family. One such foundation, chaired by Svetlana Medvedeva, wife of Dmitry Medvedev, then-president of the Russian Federation, declared that its goal was to bring a prosperous future to Russia by protecting traditional values and improving the "demographic and social climate in Russian families" (Fond sotsial'no-kul'turnykh initsiativ 2008).[2]

Medvedeva's campaign is but one example of how idealized family values have emerged as an important element of state discourse on the demographic crisis. In this socially conservative discourse, family values are conceived as both the cause of the population problem and its remedy. The dormant and nearly extinct status of these values, severely damaged by the previous political regime or the destructive influence of the *collective West* (*kollektivnyi zapad*), has been presented as leading to the crisis of family and, consequently, to population decline. The state, supported by civil society, was presented as playing a leading role in reviving and strengthening family values. If resuscitated, the narrative goes, traditional values can change reproductive behavior, eventually reversing troubling population trends.

Demographers have played an important part in entangling gender, sexuality, and family with postsocialist statecraft, shaping the meanings attributed to family in state efforts to remedy the demographic problem. A particularly popular strand of demographic writing, inspired by Anatoly Antonov and described in the previous chapters, foregrounds conservative ideas about family values and gender in the national imagination of population problems and care (Antonov 2005, 2006; Antonov and Avdeev 1990; Antonov and Medkov 1996; Antonov, Medkov, and Arkhangelsky 2002).

However, demographic experts have not been the only social actors involved in modeling the kind of family values the state should invest in and care for. A variety of social actors such as the church (Luehrmann 2016, 2019), biomedical professionals (Leykin and Rivkin-Fish 2022; Rivkin-Fish 2005, 2024), and nongovernmental organizations, or NGOs (Höjdestrand 2016, 2017), have also deployed the ethos of traditional family values as fundamental to the state's interest in higher fertility. In one way or another, these actors have all flagged lack of traditional family values as central to low fertility—the core of the demographic discourse.

This chapter traces the role played by nonprofit secular and religious organizations in cementing traditional values as the object of state care.

In the first decade of the twenty-first century, the regime's increasingly authoritarian efforts to design and manage civil society led to the recognition of certain nonprofits as socially useful or socially oriented (*sotsial'no orientirovannye*). The state welcomed those organizations it deemed loyal to the regime and ostracized those seen as critical (Bindman 2017). Both secular and religious nonprofit organizations working with and around families, gender, and reproduction and marked by the state as "socially oriented" contributed to sharpening the meaning of the population crisis beyond quantity—beyond family size and number of children. Mediating between day-to-day practices of working with actual people and state discourses about a statistically constructed entity called "population," these NGOs have been effective in communicating conservative ideas about traditional family values. In a culturally resonant and socially meaningful way, they portrayed these values as the necessary social force to protect the moral integrity of the nation and its population.

Ethnographically, the chapter focuses on the activities of the socially oriented Sverdlovsk regional public foundation called 21st Century Family (Sem'ia XXI-vek). The foundation has been involved in a series of campaigns and programs aimed at educating high school and university students about family, intergenerational succession, and reproductive behavior. Along with conducting long-term educational projects in colleges and universities around the region, the foundation has occasionally provided free psychological consultations for young families in and around Yekaterinburg (Fond Sem'ia XXI-vek 2022). Aside from that, the foundation has produced an array of happenings celebrating the institution of the family all around the region, continuing the legacy of Soviet mass public festivals around specific holidays or life-cycle events.

The foundation's educational and entertainment programs depict family life in the Soviet past and post-Soviet present as morally decayed and deficient and offer a renewed, idealized image of family bound by traditional values capable of healing these social ills. If loss of traditional values led to the social and economic chaos experienced in the wake of the Soviet Union, then the restoration of these values might lead to a better and more stable future. Thus, these messages ask participants to invest socially and emotionally in the reinvented image of family bound by traditional values as a path to a morally fulfilling and economically prosperous future. Inasmuch as the state is shown to benefit families molded in the image of these values, the messages offered by socially oriented NGOs and foundations such as

Sem'ia XXI-vek implicitly communicate socially meaningful and culturally resonant ideas about what kind of families should be considered normative and thus deserving of state support.

Socially Oriented NGOs and a New Civil Society

The Russian state's persecution of nonprofits perceived as disloyal to the state became particularly visible during Putin's second and third terms. Amendments to the law on nonprofit organizations curtailed and at times criminalized their work (Bederson and Semenov 2022; Duma 2006; *Izvestiia* 2009; Podrabinek 2010). Following Putin's return to the presidency in 2012, after a four-year hiatus, sanctions against these organizations intensified. The Foreign Agent Law, introduced in 2012, stipulated that NGOs receiving foreign funding and engaging in political activities, however vaguely defined, had to declare themselves foreign agents (Duma 2012). Labeling human rights organizations as foreign agents had a quite explicit Cold War connotation. More importantly, though, the law stonewalled the activities of NGOs by subjecting them to audits and unrealistic legal requirements, causing many to self-liquidate (Bederson 2024b; Bogdanova, Cook, and Kulmala 2018; Elder 2013). Another law, adopted in 2015, further curtailed and endangered the work of human rights NGOs. The Undesirable Organizations Act made it illegal to participate in activities of any organization designated as such (Duma 2015). Several months after the full-scale invasion of Ukraine, the Foreign Agent Law was expanded to include individuals and media outlets, constricting or banning freedom of press and human rights organizations almost entirely (*Moscow Times* 2022).

However, the attempt to limit the influence of human rights NGOs was only one side of the regime's relationship with civil society. While zeroing in on civic organizations deemed critical of the government and thus threatening to the political order, the state also pledged to support socially oriented civic or charity nonprofit organizations working with families, youth, and the elderly; supporting disadvantaged groups; or conducting educational and cultural programs (Bindman 2017). In 2007, the state introduced a special presidential fund to distribute grants to socially useful and politically loyal NGOs. The annexation of Crimea in 2014 and ensuing international sanctions effectively eliminated foreign funding of nonprofits, but the state initiated large-scale investment programs to support civic organizations and expanded presidential grants (Bederson 2024a; Bogdanova, Cook, and Kulmala 2018). The state then legally bound its relations with socially useful NGOs in a series of laws providing support and allowing them to register as state-sponsored providers of social services—under the condition, of course, that the NGO had not been declared a foreign agent (Cook, Iarskaia-Smirnova, and Tarasenko 2021; Duma 2010, 2013, 2016).

The new legal definition of a socially oriented NGO put civic organizations and social activists in an uncertain structural position, forcing them to choose between engaging with broadly defined social and political agendas or focusing on issues designated as socially useful to avoid being stigmatized as acting against the state's social interests (Bederson and Semenov 2020). However, even organizations defined as socially oriented had to give up foreign funding. One of my interlocutors, Marina, leader of a very successful NGO working with vulnerable families, lamented that before the Foreign Agent Law came into effect, she raised considerable funds from the World Bank and several UK-based funders for her work with victims of domestic violence. However, when the Foreign Agent Law came into effect in 2012, she gave up all her foreign funding because she did not want to risk being put on a special registry and subjected to a convoluted audit. Although regretting the loss, Marina was quick to mention that she won a hefty presidential grant available to her as head of a socially oriented NGO. The grant and smaller donations from local businesses allowed her to continue and even expand her work, creating the largest crisis center and shelter for women victims of domestic violence in the region.

In alignment with the emerging neoliberal welfare regime, the state sought to outsource social security services to socially oriented NGOs. Focusing in particular on programs at regional and municipal levels, the 2016 law stipulated that governments at all levels must ensure small and midsize for-profit and socially oriented nonprofit organizations provide at least 15 percent of annual social services (Bogdanova and Bindman 2016; Cook, Iarskaia-Smirnova, and Tarasenko 2021; Toepler, Pape, and Benevolenski 2020). Marina, for example, with her expertise in working with vulnerable populations and foster families, won a contract with the Ministry of Social Security to conduct state-mandated courses for citizens adopting children. However, following the full-scale invasion of Ukraine and in tandem with increasing political persecution of human rights NGOs, funding opportunities and contracts from both the government and the business community for NGOs working with vulnerable populations declined in direct proportion to the rising number of those in need (Bederson 2024b; Matveev 2023).

The neoliberal model of outsourcing social services to nonprofits fosters the relationship between state and citizen that Putin's regime envisions as optimal and desirable (Hemment 2009). It asserts the role of the state as primary care provider while outsourcing the provision of social services to nonprofit and for-profit organizations, attempting to offset the high cost of social services to the most vulnerable and disadvantaged social groups—those living in poverty, children, the elderly, and people with disabilities (Cooper 2017). The model rewards those seen as socially useful and politically aligned with the state and punishes those deemed as intervening in Russia's political sphere. Thus, the alliance between neoliberal policies and socially oriented nonprofit organizations working with families has been central to providing social care and formalizing ideas about the state as a reified entity distributing it.

Traditional Family Values

During the first decade of the twentieth century, traditional family values (*traditsionnye semeinye tsennosti*) became a fixed ideological expression (Chernova 2010). Guarding these values has grown into a stable ideological imperative for protecting the Russian nation-state against so-called morally degrading external forces. Public intellectuals writing about the problem of the Russian family have presented it as the outcome of Russian society's moral and spiritual deficiency (*dukhovnoe neblagopoluchie*). This deficiency has been blamed on the paternalistic Soviet state, which changed what critics consider the natural hierarchical order within families. In this iteration of the problem, the Soviet state is presented as having taken away men's responsibilities as the main breadwinners and women's obligations to provide unpaid care for family members. In a book edited by the very reputable scholar and publicist Igor Bestuzhev-Lada titled *Why Do Russians Die: The Last Chance*, one chapter, alongside more scholarly chapters describing population trends in Russia, bemoans the destruction of Russian families caused by communist ideologies and the Soviet regime. It openly laments the loss of patriarchy and sees patriarchy's return as the only solution to the demographic crisis (Goncharov 2004). These ideas have been widespread among both demographic experts and NGO activists. I repeatedly heard them refer to patriarchy as a remedy to the problem of spiritual deficiency and thus a suitable solution to the problem of population.

Not only the Soviet past but also the porous post-Soviet present, with its Westernized and nontraditional values (*netraditsionnye tsennosti*), have been blamed for the emergence of new, unnatural family arrangements.

Social and economic reforms in capitalist Russia are frequently blamed for causing moral deficiency, seen as skewing the natural order and weakening traditional family values. Igor Gundarov, who during my fieldwork was an active member of the Duma expert committee on demography, frequently spoke about the transition to capitalism as the main culprit in the demographic crisis. Trained as a medical doctor and epidemiologist, Gundarov held Russia's economic reforms accountable for moral and spiritual deficiency, which in turn play a core role in population decline (Gundarov 2001). However, the capitalist order itself was not the main culprit. Slipping into conspiratorial thinking, he and other commentators blamed the West for scheming to limit Russia's population growth through a network of family planning clinics financed by George Soros's Open Society foundations and other similar organizations (Höjdestrand 2017; Rivkin-Fish 2024). The idea of Western imperialism weakening the moral foundations of Russian society as a weapon of demographic warfare found prominence among both conservative civic organizations and political elites. It reverberated among different platforms and set the stage for the anti-Western rhetoric that penetrated Russian society more recently, particularly following the full-scale invasion of Ukraine in 2022 (*TASS* 2022b).

The instability of the institution of marriage—evidenced by the fact that up to 70 percent of official marriages in Russia result in divorce (Krivyakina 2024; VCIOM 2019)—and changes in family arrangements such as new forms of cohabitation, blended families, and even voluntary single motherhood have all been portrayed as the result of moral decay during the Soviet and post-Soviet periods. Changing forms of kinship, conceived as a direct infringement on traditional values, have been depicted as detrimental to Russia's population growth, national identity, and political sovereignty. An argument that decline in number of registered marriages leads to decline in fertility has been advanced by a group of demographers and sociologists from Moscow State University and favored by conservative political contenders. The suggested policy solution is to actively stimulate couples to register marriages and to make divorce procedures more costly and difficult (Sinel'nikov 2016, 2018, 2019). In 2024, the government indeed increased the tax on divorce proceedings (*RBC* 2024).

Idealized family values have been presented as morally superior, with the potential to lead to an independent, self-sufficient, male-led, heterosexual household with at least two children, in which men are breadwinners and women are responsible for unpaid care work. In these socially conservative discourses, what constitutes traditional family values is never fully articulated or explained. Rather, the term *traditional values* has been used as an unmarked opposition to so-called nontraditional values (*netraditsionnye tsennosti*) associated with queer culture, new forms of heterosexual cohabitation, and single motherhood, all ostensibly brought about through destructive legacies of the Soviet past and unfavorable influences of the collective West.

Nevertheless, some new family arrangements have been tolerated more than others. Heterosexual cohabitation without registered marriage might be frowned on ideologically, but there have been very few social sanctions against it; the rate of cohabitating in Russia has grown gradually over the last decades, with an estimated two-thirds of all cohabitating couples living together without an official marriage registration (*Interfax* 2020; Lebedeva 2008; Rogacheva 2009). Thus, the offhand remark that "civil unions are evil" (*grazhdanskie braki eto zlo*) uttered to me by a city official working in an office responsible for socially oriented NGOs seemed like paying lip service to the dominant ideological imperative of protecting traditional family values. During our interview, she started counting off different kinds of family arrangements, all lumped under the category of civil union. Bending the fingers on her right hand, she listed them matter-of-factly: "seasonal marriages, weekend marriages, civil union with a registered marriage elsewhere, etcetera. We have it all." She did not seem as much concerned with the list as intrigued by the multiplicity of existing family forms.

When it comes to LGBTQ people, however, the state, aided by conservative civic organizations and the church, has construed queer relations as a clear and undeniable deviance from the norm, culminating in a 2013 federal antigay law vaguely defined as a ban on the propaganda of nontraditional sexual relations among minors (*Kommersant* 2013a). In October 2022, seven months into the brutal military invasion of Russian forces into Ukraine, as Russia was suffering clear and undeniable losses on the frontline, a new bill was submitted to the Duma and signed into law. This encompassing antigay law bans any public demonstration of "nontraditional sexual relations" among minors and adults alike (*BBC News* 2022; Golubeva and Zotova 2022).[3] Preserving imagined normative boundaries of Russian society by criminalizing certain forms of sexuality remained an issue important enough to be pursued during wartime.

Traditional Values and the Demographic Crisis

During my fieldwork, I attended dozens of federal and regional conferences, roundtables, and public events dedicated to the question of traditional family values in the context of the demographic crisis. Aligned with the goal of population growth, these exchanges were sponsored by the state in its different instantiations—chambers of the regional parliament, committees of the federal Duma, municipal departments, and, in several instances, the leading political party, United Russia. These events, attended by scholars, state officials, politicians, religious activists, and members of nongovernmental civic organizations, were important platforms for hashing out normative ideas about morality, families, gender, reproduction, and sexuality, all deemed pertinent to the problem of population decline. The general tone of these conferences, as of any other demography-oriented gathering, was of a heightened alarmism, projecting an encroaching demographic disaster. The scarcity of traditional values, causing population implosion, was presented as an immediate threat to geopolitical sovereignty and national integrity. "We are about to disappear" messages were amplified by population experts' charted forecasts, serving as a sinister and anxiety-producing background for conversations about Russia's demographic future.

In these conversations, changing family forms and the apparent postponement of first births were cast as outcomes of lost traditional values—the argument went that these social trends, if not reversed, would inevitably lead to depopulation. At a large regional conference dedicated to the demographic crisis, one demographer passionately addressed the audience with a plea: "For God's sake, don't touch the age of the first birth. It's sacred. Otherwise, they'll eventually stop giving birth" (*I radi boga, ne trogaite vozrast pervogo rozhdeniia. Eto sviatoe, a to voobshche rozhat' ne budut*). It was not clear who "they" were—presumably young women—or how the audience was supposed to operationalize this plea not to "touch the age of the first birth," but his dramatization of the problem aligned with other emotionally driven statements reiterating the need for state intervention to reverse dwindling population numbers.

The same alarmism characterized more detail-oriented panels where moral-spiritual (*nravstvenno-dukhovnye*) and psychological aspects (*psikhologicheskie aspekty*) of the demographic crisis were discussed. Conference organizers would often refer to these sessions as *psychological sessions* (*psikhologicheskie sessii*), where the term *psychological* was very broadly defined and interpreted. Conservative in tone, core discussion topics revolved around motherhood, fertility, child-rearing, and reproductive education. In contrast with the plenary sessions, which were dominated by male demographers, state officials, and politicians, these roundtables and expert sessions were led primarily by women working in civic NGOs (both secular and religious) and charity organizations (usually belonging to the church). Biomedical professionals, educators, and psychologists, also predominantly women, took part in these discussions as well.

These sessions and roundtables brought together theological discussions about families and gender offered by religious NGOs and explanations of the demographic crisis infused with the secular language of psychology and wellness. From the titles of talks alone, it was almost impossible to determine the affiliation of the speaker. One such session included the following titles: "Children and Psychological Well-Being"; "Do You Need Multiple Children to Feel Happy?"; "Spiritual and Moral Aspects of Preparing Youth for Family Life"; and "Patriotism and Children as an Important National Priority." Among these, only the first was led by a self-identified religious psychologist and antiabortion activist—none of the remaining speakers were affiliated with the church (on the phenomenon of Christian Orthodox psychologists, see Luehrmann 2016, 2019). Educators from a variety of secular NGOs and antiabortion activists from the Russian Orthodox Church were seated next to biomedical professionals promoting the importance of reproductive education, representatives of local charity groups working with women and families living in poverty, and psychologists supporting foster parents and their children. I observed surprisingly little conflict or confrontation during these sessions. The pleasant ambiance was partly the result of the frequency of these meetings; the same presenters would attend many of them, becoming familiar with each other's points of view (although of course not fully agreeing on everything).

During these discussions, I would often sit next to Marina, a local NGO leader I came to know during my fieldwork, because she would provide me with a wealth of information by whispering comments into my ear. Marina's NGO worked with women on the brink of abandoning their newborns. She and her volunteers counseled women and volunteered in a hospital where women were provided the option to entrust staff with their infants. During one of the sessions we both attended, in which a psychologist from a church-affiliated NGO took center stage, I noticed Marina doodling nervously in her notebook and looking annoyed. Herself a practicing Orthodox Christian, Marina seemed irritated by what Natalia, a hip young woman who introduced herself as a religious psychologist, had to say. In her work with a church-affiliated NGO, Natalia counseled young women who came to a clinic (*zhenskaia konsul'tatsiia*) for an abortion; her explicit mandate from the church was to persuade these women to change their minds. Natalia began the presentation with her personal story of giving birth to her first child when she was eighteen years old and single. She did not terminate her pregnancy because, in a rare instance, her ob-gyn, who in Natalia's interpretation was better educated than most, told her mother she should not. "Look at me, I tell these girls," she said, referring to her interactions with the young women she counseled, "I'm successful, God gave me a solid [*dobrotnaia*] family and a good husband because I didn't go through with it. You can do that too."

As Natalia was narrating her story of redemption, Marina whispered in my ear, "She's always talking about God, but God doesn't give to those who are always on their knees [*Bog ne daet tem, kto vse vremia na koleniakh stoit*]." We were attracting attention by chatting during the presentation, so I waited patiently until the break to probe further, hoping Marina would explain what she meant. Marina was generally supportive of Natalia's anti-abortion activism, she told me. She was, however, critical of what she called Natalia's careless behavior (*bezotvetsvennost'*). Marina had worked with some of the women Natalia had persuaded to keep their pregnancy. Some of them later came to Marina contemplating giving up their newborn. She felt that Natalia was careless because Natalia would talk young women into acting against their own interests; in doing so, she was confusing words with deeds. "She convinces them not to have an abortion, then forgets about their existence and in the end, it's me who needs to deal with their sorrow and with their newborns," Marina explained. Convincing women to continue a pregnancy without providing minimal material infrastructure to raise children is the opposite of care: "She was talking to and about God, and I was doing all the work."

Although they did not agree on what social activism should entail, both Natalia and Marina were nevertheless part of an emerging socially oriented and conservative Russian civil society. Marina's nonprofit was secular in nature, and although she was critical of Natalia's overzealous approach to religion, she nevertheless collaborated with Natalia and the church, mostly doing charity work and fundraising campaigns but also inviting Natalia and her colleagues to counsel women in vulnerable situations looking for help. Through either religious or secular language, both of them inculcated the idea of a normative family bound by traditional values, gendered family roles, and strong intergenerational relations of care and offered support to those deviating from this path.

Socially Oriented Nonprofits—A Path from Moral Deficiency to Spiritual Development

When I first introduced myself and shared my research with Larisa Niko-laevna Dokuchaeva, founding member and president of the socially ori-ented foundation 21st Century Family (Sem'ia XXI-vek), she responded, unprompted, with a question: "You want to know why people in Russia don't have more children? I can tell you why. Look around." Gesturing, she continued: "There are healthy women all around, capable of and even ready to give birth, but this doesn't happen. Why do you think that's true?" I misrecognized her rhetorical question as a real one and offered an answer, suggesting that perhaps general economic uncertainty prevents them from realizing family aspirations. Waving my response away, Dokuchaeva said that the problem is "essentially spiritual and psychological [*dukhovnaia i psikhologicheskaia*]. We've forgotten what intergenerational continuity [*preemstvennost' pokolenii*] and traditional family values are. We need to restore this foundation. Then we can move forward."

I came to know Larisa Nikolaevna Dokuchaeva as a participant in pub-lic discussions about the demographic crisis. She was a charismatic orator, well-versed in the state rhetoric of population renewal, and her authority to speak about the moral and spiritual deficiency of Russian families seemed to be trusted implicitly. Dokuchaeva has long been involved in federal and re-gional politics. In the mid-1990s, running on the fumes of an earlier women's liberal political movement known as Women of Russia (Zhenshchiny Rossii) led by her compatriot Ekaterina Lakhova,[4] she ran twice, unsuccessfully, for state and regional parliaments (Duma). In 2000, she stepped out of national and regional politics, applying her energy and political savvy toward work-ing with NGOs and registering her own public foundation in 2001.

Aside from chairing the foundation, from 2010 to 2018 Dokuchaeva was a member of the federal Duma committee on family policies and the regional (Sverdlovsk oblast) parliament's civic chamber (*obshchestvennaia palata*)—an advisory body established during Putin's second term to coordi-nate interactions between state authorities and civic organizations (Bogdan-ova and Bindman 2016; Toepler, Pape, and Benevolenski 2020). Human rights organizations and nonprofits seen as contradicting government policies were ostracized from the chamber, while the number of socially oriented NGOs within the Sverdlovsk regional civic chamber became substantial. Simi-lar to other public institutions in Putin's managed democracy, the chamber performatively acclaimed and legitimized the regime rather than acting as an instrument of public oversight (Yudin 2022b). Nevertheless, for members of socially oriented NGOs, the civic chamber has become a useful political framework for making new contacts with local policymakers and state officials as well as accumulating personal political capital (Bogdanova and Bindman 2016).

Unlike that of many religious activists in the field of family-oriented NGOs, Dokuchaeva's entry into the world of post-Soviet concern with population decline was mediated by concepts borrowed from popular psychology and a fledgling Russian self-help culture (Leykin 2015; Lerner and Zbenovich 2013; Matza 2018). Aside from her public activities, she founded, along with her husband, a popular psychological enterprise called Rodologia (from *rod*, kin, and *rodstvo*, kinship), built on the psychotherapeutic premise that social calamities experienced by previous generations manifest in the conduct of descendants/future generations. In this idea of intergenerational trauma, even though the memory of an event might disappear or be dismissed by younger generations, the trauma leaves scars on people's genes and materializes in descendants' behavior. This behavior, in turn, obstructs descendants' paths to self-realization, successful marriage, and family life (for more on Rodologia, see Leykin 2015). Therefore, in this psychotherapeutic reiteration of the crisis of family in Russia, as much as being part of a family network might cause trauma, family is also the only guaranteed path for self-realization and fulfillment.

Dokuchaeva's considerable experience and connections within a wide network of political power—both regional and national—made her an important figure for imbuing normative and idealized images of family with the language of popular psychology. Her focus on intergenerational continuity and family as a conduit for personal success resonated with both the culturally authoritative language of psychology and self-care and state discourse about traditional values as foundational to solving the demographic crisis. Dokuchaeva's ideas, although derived from a different set of epistemological assumptions, evoked socially conservative discourse about normative families and their role in demographic revival. Similar to other conservative commentators, she concluded that upholding perceived traditional family values—associated with a male-led household, two heterosexual parents, and hopefully two and more children—would lead to stable population growth, protect the normative boundaries of Russian society, and guard its political sovereignty.

One of Dokuchaeva's projects I followed during my fieldwork in 2010–2011 was a yearlong training program for college and university students preparing for family life (Fond Sem'ia XXI-vek 2010).[5] Every two months, Dokuchaeva herself or one of the foundation's employees traveled to colleges and universities in and outside of Yekaterinburg to conduct seminars and workshops about family and personal success. Helping students reconcile family life and personal growth to lead fulfilled lives (*polnotsennaia zhizn'*) was the raison d'être of these seminars, the facilitators explained to me.

Stuck in traffic on our way to a seminar in a small town just north of Yekaterinburg, Lena, a seminar convener, reminisced about her experience teaching: "Every time I entered the classroom, I got so excited about how wonderful this generation is. They always want to understand themselves better. They're really hungry to know who they are and why they do what they do." Her impression of the students was aligned with the explicit goal of the seminars as a journey toward self-realization and self-transformation. She continued: "We're simply there to help them. They all want to be successful and self-realized. We show them that to be successful they need to be in sync with their family's past. It's a powerful weapon for becoming spiritually developed beings [*dukhovno razvitymi*]." Indirectly referring to competing church-affiliated educational campaigns aimed at young couples and families, she concluded, "Religion can of course provide some form of spirituality, but it's being connected to your family past [*istoriia roda*] that gives you this spiritual foundation [*dukhovnuyu oporu*]."

Although the notion of spiritual foundation is indeed widely utilized in religious discourse about traditional family values promoted by the Russian Orthodox Church, the way Lena employed spirituality resembled Soviet discourse about the spiritual and moral development of Soviet persons. In this discourse, spiritual values were seen as fundamental to the ideological development of economically productive and socially capable communist citizens (Luehrmann 2011). In their post-Soviet reincarnation, grounded in a therapeutic idea of the self, spiritual foundations are presented as means with which to reorganize and stabilize the moral worlds of Russian citizens on the path to becoming self-realized individuals.

The idea of spiritual foundations was a refrain in all the Dokuchaeva foundation seminars I attended. In a tightly packed classroom in a local university, Lidia and Lena, two foundation employees, both consulting psychologists, conducted a seminar on effective communicative techniques in social work. It was part of a larger project training future social workers and psychologists, particularly those who plan to work with families, children, and youth. The mission of the project as it appeared on grant applications was to train knowledgeable cadres to increase the social prestige of the family as an institution in Russia. Dokuchaeva's extensive political connections and status as a long-serving member of the regional civic chamber helped her win a hefty grant and secure contracts with different city departments, regional ministries, and institutions of higher education to run these programs.

From the beginning of that particular seminar, something was not working. A group of mostly female students from the department of social work seemed uninterested and distracted. They refused to participate in one exercise after another. The seminar as planned was largely a failure. During the break, Lena and her coteacher, Lidia, attributing the students' passivity to a general disinterest in social work, decided to regroup and turn the seminar into a therapeutic session. "Let them talk about themselves," one said to the other. After the break, things seemed different. Abandoning attempts to teach practical knowledge, Lidia started off, "Who here thinks that how you live your life fully depends on you?" I saw a few hesitant hands rising. "Well, I'm going to show you that all you do is a direct result of your family's past experiences [*rodovoi opyt*]," said Lidia.

When talking about family experiences, Lidia spoke about not only students' living relatives but also the experiences of past generations in their families. Several students tried to dispute her premise about the importance of such intergenerational continuity, but Lidia skillfully navigated and debated their arguments. She used the whiteboard to chart the family history of a student who volunteered her grandparents' and great-grandparents' stories of living through wars, collectivization, and the dissolution of the Soviet Union. Emphasizing links between events in the student's familial past and her contentious relations with her mother and her boyfriend, Lidia explained that the student's familial experiences of hardship necessarily reflected on her relationships in the present. Using genealogical imagination to unite family, spirituality, and personal success under the same banner, she had the students reflect on connections between their present and their family's past. Lidia concluded the session with the following: "Knowing your family history [*istoriiu roda*] and being connected to other members of your family gives your life a spiritual foundation [*dukhovnye osnovy*]. Being spiritually grounded is crucial for your self-realization and development."

Family as an institution is an important element in this triad—it is a spiritual foundation of personal development. What undergirds many social problems in Russia, Lidia explained to the students, is that the paternalistic Soviet state destroyed family as an intergenerational form of social life. Because of that, people tend to live as if independent of their own kin (*rod*). The Soviet state, she said, almost entirely appropriated the functions traditionally associated with families. The Soviet state is no more, but this lack still haunts society. It leads to social disorientation and an inability to deal with uncertainty or difficult situations in the present. Restoring the family's "natural functions" and social prestige, Lidia suggested, helps realize one's individual goals in life.

The Soviet state had of course been far from giving up on the social institution of family as an agent of socialist and spiritual development. The Soviet family occupied an ambiguous place in communist ideology. It was, on the one hand, a microcosm of the new communist state and a socialization instrument responsible for transmitting proletarian values to future generations. On the other hand, it posed a threat to the state because familial ties could undermine people's loyalty to the communist cause (Alexopoulos 2008; Hooper 2006; Slezkine 2017). It is true that the social institution of family came under attack in the 1920s as an inherently bourgeois institution. Leading Soviet feminist Aleksandra Kollontai famously claimed, "The narrow, closed family, with its parental squabbles and its habit of thinking only about the well-being of relatives, cannot educate the New Person" (Kollontai 1918 cited in Hoffmann 2003, 91). At the same time, the social institution of family was a key object in a variety of Soviet policies. By the early 1930s, the Soviet state began introducing family policies aimed at increasing population and industrial growth (Goldman 1993; Nakachi 2021). The state also perceived the new Soviet family as an important pedagogical tool of social reproduction, capable of instilling communist values in future generations. In the new ideology, having a family was not a matter of personal desire but a social obligation to the state (Hoffmann 2000, 2003, 2011; Hooper 2006; Nakachi 2016, 2021).

However historically inaccurate Lidia's arguments about the Soviet family were, the foundation's employees repeated the idea of the destructive role of the Soviet state. Dokuchaeva used every opportunity to reiterate how lack of clear conceptualization of the social institution of family, inherited from the Soviet period, is a major problem in state efforts to overcome demographic predicaments. In one of our conversations, she went on to explain that although young people desire to build families and cherish their own, they do not know what a normal family should look like and thus, affected by what they see around them, choose family norms that do not align with the so-called universal traditional family values (e.g., cohabitation, single parenthood, etc.). The normal family, Dokuchaeva passionately explained to a group of students, consists of two heterosexual parents and at least two children, all encompassed in a larger system of kin relatedness. Obligations in a normative family are firmly gendered, with men as breadwinners and women responsible for unpaid care work around the house. In her own words: "Young people just don't know what parents should do. They don't know that fathers earn money and mothers do laundry, and that mothers can also be a shoulder to cry on."

In Dokuchaeva's view, the cure for the crisis of family is intergenerational continuity (*preemstvennost' pokolenii*). Such continuity has been presented as unique to Russian national character, a kind of panacea supposed to heal families and, by proxy, society. Between 2009 and 2011, I had lengthy conversations with Dokuchaeva and her employees about intergenerational continuity. For them, it was always mediated by ideas borrowed from popular psychological discourses, exemplified by Rodologia, their self-help enterprise. In the language of Rodologia, situating one's kinship system within a historical and cultural context (*rodovaia kul'tura sem'i*) is both a form of psychological self-care and a way to ensure the continuation of one's family. By understanding the development of their familial history, people can understand their spouses and children better and thus lead a more harmonious life. The embeddedness of personal identity within a larger structure of familial ties is supposed to make one a self-realized person able to fulfill one's potential and form healthy relations.[6]

Intergenerational continuity is not only an instrument of self-care but also a social cure for the demographic problem. Dokuchaeva explained to me once that family needs to be made a desirable institution among the youth. It is this role that socially oriented nonprofits like hers should fulfill: "We talk to young people and the majority of them want to have a family and children. If you go and read a sociological portrait of our youth in scientific research, over 60 percent of the young people in our region say that family is undeniably the most valuable thing to them. But because we live in a particularly ruptured society, no one teaches them what it means to have a normal family."

"What do you mean by ruptured?" I asked her. At this point, Dokuchaeva, a seasoned public speaker, switched from a conversational to an authoritative tone usually reserved for speeches, inserting questions as her signature rhetorical device: "Today different generations live under the same roof. They grew up in two different political orders and have different ideas about family obligations. So, what do we get?" She paused. "Political changes in our country destroyed the continuity of values." She paused again. "I ask you: Where do we prepare young people for family life? From time immemorial, it has been done within families. But what if because of the intergenerational rupture, it cannot be done?" In her view, the main mission of socially oriented civic organizations like hers is to prepare future generations for family life because "when they begin to learn about their family history, it teaches them they're not isolated beings and that they're part of a larger system of kinship. When they internalize it, they begin to understand that they're also responsible for what's going to happen after them."

Socially oriented nonprofits such as Dokuchaeva's foundation refract dominant ideas about the problem of population through a discourse of intergenerational continuity and family values stripped of any historical specificity. In this discourse, families are both the source of and cure for underpopulation, and traditional family values appear as a means for healing societal ills and increasing fertility.

Caring for Normal/Fit Families

Helping young people realize their desire for a family with established gendered and generational hierarchies has been Dokuchaeva's mission as an educator and operator in regional and federal politics. The main adjective she would use when speaking about the kind of families young people strive for can be translated into English as *fit* (*blagopoluchnaia*). Fit families (*blagopoluchnye sem'i*) should become the post-Soviet Russian state's main object of care, she would add. The way Dokuchaeva put it, "Fit families, the state completely abandoned them. The state is only interested in families when they reach some sort of a critical stage. I say, why let families reach crises at all? Wouldn't it be more prudent to care for families before they find themselves in crisis?" Referring to the state social welfare apparatus that, in her view, mistakenly invests in socially vulnerable populations at the expense of normal families, she advocated for developing programs and legislation aimed at the latter. She suggested that the social prestige of family would be raised through attention to "normal, working families,

families that despite all the hardships did not abandon their children and did not break up their families. The state and the media invest too much in pathology at the expense of investing in fit [*blagopoluchnye*] families. Wouldn't it be a more efficient investment in the long run? People should be able to see that having families is rewarded by society. It makes me happy, for example, when our politicians proudly declare that they have large families with five and more children. I see it as the emergence of a new norm of *blagopoluchnaia sem'ia*."

Blagopoluchnaia sem'ia is a common but not easily translatable phrase for describing a normal or fit family. The word *functional* could be used, though it does not capture the positive undertones of *blagopoluchie*, which variously denotes prosperity, fitness, happiness, and well-being. In Russian, as a noun, *blagopoluchie* is often collocated with the adjective *material'noe* (material) and means financially prosperous. As an adjective, *blagopoluchnyi* might also mean successful or happy. When used with family, as Dokuchaeva did, it connotes socially accepted ideas of success and normalcy and can mean prosperous, fit, successful, or happy.

However, as a cultural idiom, the adjective *blagopoluchnyi* sounds more appropriate with the negative prefix *ne-*. *Neblagopoluchnaia sem'ia* (dysfunctional, deficient, or socially vulnerable family) is more commonly used, as in "children from *neblagopoluchnye sem'i*." Curiously enough, when I tried to Google the translation of *blagopoluchnaia sem'ia* from Russian into English, Google asked me: "do you mean *NEblagopoluchnaia sem'ia*," with *ne-* indicating the negation.

Like the phrase *spiritual deficiency* (*dukhovnoe neblagopoluchie*), against which many efforts to battle the demographic crisis are aimed, *neblagopoluchnaia sem'ia* signals moral deficiency in need of a cure. Without the negative prefix, *blagopoluchie* is an unmarked category against which the marked category of dysfunctional or deficient families is defined—just as in English, where *dysfunctional family* rolls off the tongue while *functional family* sounds unidiomatic. It is almost as if the famous beginning of Tolstoy's *Anna Karenina*, "All happy families are alike; every unhappy family is unhappy in its own way," were inverted to read, "All unhappy families are alike (i.e., irresponsible and dependent on the state); every happy family is happy in its own way (i.e., available to polysemous signification)."

As a category of social differentiation, *blagopoluchie* has apparent class connotations. When I asked Dokuchaeva to describe a typical *blagopoluchnaia* family to me, she talked about self-sufficient families that can accommodate their own needs without the support of others, meaning the state. Yet the distinction cannot be reduced to material well-being alone. Although there is no clear legal definition of an unfit family (*neblagopoluchnaia sem'ia*), the term as used by the state welfare apparatus cannot be reduced to material factors only: it indicates a variety of risk factors perceived to negatively affect a child's well-being within a family. The socioeconomic status of parents is one risk factor, but state agents working with social orphans from *neblagopoluchnye sem'i* often assess it as a derivative of parents' moral qualities (Khlinovskaya Rockhill 2020). A high-ranking bureaucrat at the Ministry of Social Security I interviewed—who, similar to Dokuchaeva, spoke of the importance of introducing the concept of *blagopoluchnaia sem'ia* into the state lexicon—tried to explain the distinction at length. His test of distinguishing between fit and unfit families, or more precisely between fit and unfit parents, focused on a sense of personal responsibility and obligation of care for children. "Can I speak not as a bureaucrat for a second?" He then began his line of argument:

> I have a personal, not a scientific opinion about it. I think that what determines whether the family is fit or not is whether or not people care for their children . . . When I see a mother who is . . . she looks like . . . I don't like her when I look at her . . . but then she screams and bites the social worker who came to take her child away and I like this woman. She reminds me of my parents. After the war they didn't have much, but they cared for their children, and they would never abandon them. That's what I mean. This, I believe, is the meaning of *blagopoluchnaia sem'ia*.

The distinction between fit and unfit families seemed to be a vaguely defined moral criterion signifying middle-class values of self-sufficiency or socially accepted obligations of care. However, one benchmark seemed more important than others: the performance of eagerness to care. The bureaucrat did not like how the mother he was telling me about looked, as her class signifiers did not match his idea of a self-sufficient or normative person. She was probably a single mother living in poverty. Yet, using his own personal history, he expressed empathy and identified with the mother's economic plight. In his eyes, it was her ability to demonstrate determination to care for her children that imbued this woman's character with moral qualities classifying her as a fit parent capable of having a normal family.

There is an inherent contradiction in the concept of *blagopoluchnaia sem'ia*. As an unmarked, capacious category, it indicates an implicit norm, a kind of normalcy that both the bureaucrat and Dokuchaeva tried to convey to me. By its very essence, such a category does not require definitional precision. Yet to become a focus of state intervention, for which both of my interlocutors advocated, it would need to be properly categorized, made operational and legible to the state. Once operationalized, though, it loses its power as an unmarked category. Although both Dokuchaeva and the state official attended to the need to make *blagopoluchnaia sem'ia* an explicit, quasi-legal norm, this contradiction instilled the concept with ambivalent social meaning, preventing it from becoming a stable category for policy-makers or state institutions.

Dukhovnye Skrepy—Spiritual Bonds as a National Panacea

Emerging in the context of national concern with population decline, ideas about traditional family values, spiritual development, and intergenerational continuity reappeared as foundations for Russian state efforts to formulate a unifying national ideology. However vaguely defined, traditional values as the core of Russian national identity appeared again and again in strategic documents. In 2013, for the first time, the idea of spiritual bonds was introduced as a unifying national ideology (Kremlin.ru 2012, 2013a, 2013b, 2013c, 2021). In 2018, an amorphous list of values recognized as traditional appeared as part of the strategic plan for future national policies (*TASS* 2018). Efforts to develop this national ideology further intensified during the Putin regime's frantic search for ways to justify and legitimize the invasion of sovereign Ukraine (*Vedomosti* 2022). In the midst of a brutal war in Ukraine, Putin signed a decree on the protection of Russia's traditional values (President of Russia 2022d). The decree recognized, similarly to other documents, generational continuity, loyalty to traditional values, and robust moral guidelines as the foundation of Russia's national identity (President of Russia 2022d; *Vedomosti* 2022).

The absence of a unifying national ideology has long defined post-Soviet governments (Shevel 2011; Laruelle 2015). Following the 1996 election, President Boris Yeltsin suggested that Russia needed a new national ideology to distinguish it from both its Soviet predecessor and its imperial past. *Rossiiskaia Gazeta* announced a general competition, soliciting ideas from the public and prompting a lively but short-lived debate about what such an ideology might entail (Rostova 1996). Yeltsin's attempts to create a so-called national idea for post-Soviet Russia failed against the backdrop of perpetual ideological conflicts between political camps and Yeltsin's own reluctance to compromise with opponents (Malinova 2014; Fishman 2022).

Although Putin significantly restricted political pluralism, he remained reluctant to create a unified national idea in his first two terms, focusing instead on disconnected ideological elements such as statism and sovereign democracy. Putin's one-time alternate, Dmitry Medvedev, made modernization his calling card, but until Putin's third term and the rising opposition from within, there were no clear attempts to produce an encompassing national ideology (Malinova 2014).

My research in Russia preceded and partly coincided with the transition of power from Dmitry Medvedev as a one-time president running on what looked like a liberal agenda back to Vladimir Putin's tightening authoritative grip on Russian society. Putin's third term began in the wake of an unprecedented wave of social protests ignited by what many perceived as massive falsification of votes favoring the leading political party, United Russia, during the Duma elections of 2011 (A. O. 2011; *BBC News* 2012). The Bolotnaya protests, named after Bolotnaya Square, where one of the largest demonstrations took place in December 2011, involved protestors representing a variety of political forces demanding fair elections and immediate political reforms. The protests continued with Putin's return to the presidency after Dmitry Medvedev's one term in office but were violently repressed, with many opposition leaders arrested (*Lenta.ru* 2012b).

The national idea of spiritual bonds, introduced in 2013 and further peddling the notion of traditional values, was a direct state reaction to the social unrest caused by these massive protests. Honed during the period of heightened concern with population decline, it provided the state with a discursive framework to portray the political opposition and protestors who poured into the streets of Russian cities in 2011–2012 as the epitome of moral deficiency in Russian society: their minds had been poisoned by globalized, Western-based ideas contradictory to the traditional values of Russian society. Suppressing the opposition within, thus, was depicted as strengthening Russia's moral foundation. Moreover, in his rhetoric, Putin presented the idea that reinforcing traditional values and spiritual bonds positions Russia as a global force protecting universal traditional values that have been systematically destroyed by other, mostly Western, nations of the world (Kremlin.ru 2013b).

* * *

The notion of traditional values and spiritual bonds as a unifying national ideology has been grounded in ideological constructs developed and crystalized through heightened national concern with all things demography. Over the last twenty years, ideas about traditional values and the destructive impact of their loss on Russia's national identity have gone from dominating socially conservative discourses on the demographic crisis to being Putin's favorite rhetorical tool, feeding the regime's authoritarian aspirations.

Demographic experts have played an important part in scaling up these ideas to popular discourse about the role of family in reversing population trends. About to join others at a plenary session of a large conference, one demographer once proudly told me, only half-joking: "Look what a spectacular demographic theater [*demograficheskii teatr*] we've created here." As actors in a leading role, demographers have brought forth the discussion of social norms, indicating the kinds of families and reproductive decisions deemed socially valuable and deserving in the eyes of the state and marking behaviors outside society's normative boundaries. Socially oriented NGOs working with and around families have been natural allies of demographers and the state in tackling the problem of population. By circulating ideas about traditional family values among actual people, mostly women, these NGOs cemented the construction and formalization of the dominant meaning of population care (*narodosberezhenie*), designed to guard the moral and spiritual integrity of the nation.

The notion of a fit/normal family with gendered and generational hierarchies advanced by socially oriented conservative nonprofits served as a springboard for the ideas of traditional values and spiritual bonds, imagined as a cure for the country's social ills. It is not surprising, therefore, that Putin's third presidential term and efforts to secure those spiritual bonds began with legislative initiatives directly related to reproduction, sexuality, and the social organization of care in families, such as the antigay law effectively banning LGBTQ people in Russia, the law banning adoption by gay couples (*Kommersant* 2013b), and another infamous law banning US citizens from adopting children from Russia (*Lenta.ru* 2012a).[7] The laws established the state as a regulator of moral behavior, enshrining emerging normative boundaries of who is allowed to take care of whom, how a normative family in Russia should be imagined, and what the role of the state is in dictating these norms.

Contrary to earlier iterations of these ideas during the national obsession with demography, here the Soviet past is no longer seen as responsible for the moral deficiency of Russian society. Rather, the country's inner problems and apparent moral deficiency are presented as driven exclusively by external forces—the collective West—threatening to destroy Russia's political sovereignty and social unity (Kremlin.ru 2022). In this ideology, family, in its heteronormative form, is the bearer of traditional values, delineating and safeguarding the normative boundaries of Russian society. When used in discourse on the demographic crisis, a heterosexual procreative unit with hierarchical gender and generational roles founded on traditional values promised to bring a prosperous future to Russian citizens. Since the invasion of Ukraine, these values have been used not as a window into a better social future but as a weapon in justifying and legitimizing the regime's authoritarian policies.

While different state institutions allied with civic organizations have played an important role in defining what is thinkable and acceptable with respect to family and kinship, it is important to remember the power of ethnographic research to reveal and describe possible contradictions between normative expectations of appropriate family relations and quotidian experiences of kinship. To that, the last ethnographic chapter is dedicated.

Notes

1. Amid the war in Ukraine, Putin declared the year 2024 the Year of the Family once again, peddling the idea of traditional values as a foundation of Russia's national sovereignty. A woman who is part of a women's social movement pressing the Russian government to release their husbands, sons, and brothers from active duty on the Ukrainian front reflected on the apparent absurdity of the declaration: "What the hell is this Year of the Family, my husband has been gone for two years, when will this end?" (Belokrysova et al. 2025, 84–85).

2. The foundation's most recognizable project has been an annual, week-long antiabortion campaign called "Gift Me Life!" (Podari mne zhizn'!). Commencing on July 8—Family Day (Den' sem'i)—the stated goal of the campaign is to inform the public about the medical, moral, and ethical dangers of abortion and to "protect family values" (*sokhranit' semei'nye tsennosti*) (on Russian Orthodox antiabortion activism, see Luehrmann 2019; on the post-Soviet history of battles around abortion, see Rivkin-Fish 2024).

3. Some commentators saw the law as an attempt to distract the public from losses of Russian forces in the war in Ukraine and a quick and easy appeal to the regime's supporters

(see, for example, Golubeva 2022). It does not contradict, however, the regime's efforts to draw and solidify the moral boundaries of the body politic.

4. For two short years (1993–1995), Lakhova represented the faction Women of Russia in the Duma, running on a ticket of upholding equal rights for men and women and prioritizing legislation of family-related issues and social security (Lakhova 1995).

5. Since then, more programs preparing youth for family life have been produced, including publication of the "Guide Along the Roads of Family Life" (*Putevoditel' po dorogam semeinoi zhizni*).

6. To illustrate these ideas and introduce their therapeutic methods to the most intimate yet public domains of social life, Dokuchaeva's foundation, she told me, gave psychological consultations to people who visited the city's registry office (ZAGS) when applying for a marriage certificate. She, along with her husband, consulted interested applicants on how to prepare a genealogical map, read it, and use what they inherited from their ancestors to lead a happy family life (Leykin 2015, 2022).

7. The law banning US citizens from adopting children from Russia was a direct response to the Magnitsky Act, signed by Barak Obama in 2012. It introduced personal sanctions against state officials responsible for the death of a Russian tax lawyer who represented Hermitage Capital Management and died in prison in 2009. Later, the Magnitsky Act was expanded to include sanctions against human rights offenders worldwide and to ban their entry into the US (*Newsru* 2016).

5

MARKETIZED PRONATALISM AND DOMESTIC SPACES OF CARE

Little Alesha was pushing his stroller down the sidewalk. As Alesha practiced his new walking skills, his mom and I held the stroller steady. Nastia, Alesha's mom, was lamenting the insufficiency of day care in the city: "I know that according to a new provision, they have to offer you a slot in a municipal day care when your child turns three, but I've heard other moms telling me that their four-year-olds are still on the waiting list. What am I going to do when it's time for me to go back to work?" She told me she signed up for a nursery in anticipation of Alesha turning two, but securing a slot in a nursery was even harder than getting a place in day care. Nor could she afford or trust private day care providers. Ideally, her mother would help, but her mother lived too far away and was still working, leaving Nastia in a quandary: "I don't trust anyone else when it comes to caring for my kids [*ukhazhivat' za det'mi*]—it's either municipal day care or *babushka* [grandmother]."

By the end of the first decade of the twenty-first century, with birthrates rising, many Russian cities were suffering from a shortage of day care facilities, a phenomenon that countered the official state rhetoric encouraging women to have multiple children. Although the issue was at the center of national and regional politics, prompting social protests around the country (*FederalPress* 2009; Simonov 2011), local governments found it hard to keep pace with growing demand for day care. Even when birthrates began to decline in 2018, the problem persisted, and in 2021, for every 100 available public day care slots in the country, there were 102 three-year-old children waiting to get in (Abankina and Filatova 2018; *Argumenty i Fakty* 2013; Kiseleva 2021; Matyshin 2017). While an increasing number of private childcare services has offered some relief, their development has been slow and their reputation unstable. In 2016, only 2 percent of all day cares, nurseries, and kindergartens in the country came from the private sector (Abankina and Filatova 2018). Private facilities are not a viable alternative for the majority of the population, as the overall cost is typically four to six times higher than that of public day care (Abankina and Filatova 2018, 230).[1] Thus, parents have turned to familiar forms of kinship care to satisfy childcare needs.

As numerous studies have demonstrated, practices of kinship care are molded by broader socioeconomic transformations such as political change, transnational migration, and health crises, as well as war and conflict (Baldassar and Merla 2014; Buch 2015; Coe 2016; Drotbohm and Alber 2015; Gelsthorpe, Mody, and Sloan 2020b; Leinaweaver 2008, 2010, 2013; Pike 2019; Reece 2020; Shohet 2021; Weismantel 1995; Yarris 2020).[2] Jessaca Leinaweaver (2008) has, for example, demonstrated how growing inequality and violence in the Andes have compelled new forms of kin relations. Leinaweaver identifies the circulation of children between kin as not only an important survival strategy to move loved ones out of danger and economic difficulty but also an important form of connecting kin from different classes across time and space. In Nicaragua, Kristin Yarris (2020) has examined the effects of transnational migration on cultural models of kinship care. Studying Nicaraguan grandmothers whose daughters left the country in search of greater economic opportunity and who have been taking care of their grandchildren in the mothers' absence, she focuses on structural and gendered inequalities that shape grandmother care, which is an important moral practice and strategy that sustains the social reproduction of families (see also Coe 2016; Drotbohm 2015).

Likewise, scholars of postsocialism have highlighted the importance of kin relations and domestic care in times of political change and economic crisis. Culturally, the disappearance of state-sponsored systems of signification turned family-based histories into an important organizational logic for attributing meaning to ruptures in ongoing social and political processes (Leykin 2015, 2022; Oushakine 2004; 2019, 55).[3] Kin relations and gendered divisions of domestic labor became more visible after socialism, as changes in social and political order forced many women to turn to the domestic domain, creating forms of production based on kin relations and on female kinship in particular (Dunn 2004; Pine 2002). Within the context of privatization and economic shock therapy, postsocialist subjects learned to mobilize old networks of kin as sources of practical knowledge to navigate the uncertainty and risk inherent in the new market economy (Caldwell 2004, 2007; Shevchenko 2009; Thelen 2015; Utrata 2015).

This chapter traces emerging practices and strategies of intergenerational kinship care in the context of Russia's pronatalist efforts to increase population. Moving forward from the discussion in previous chapters of state care as an exercise of power shaped by the state's imagined demographic needs, this chapter focuses on the social meanings of the unpaid kinship care many of my interlocutors turned to for support. The analysis in this chapter is based on stories of kinship care conveyed to me by twenty women, ages twenty-four to fifty-five, with whom I spent considerable time during my fieldwork, learning their daily routines, the kinds of help and support they give and receive, their living arrangements, and their dreams and desires related to their families and loved ones.

My interlocutors' strategies of kinship care, the chapter demonstrates, have been shaped by and responded to post-Soviet state-marketized pronatalism. Marketized pronatalism is founded on rapid marketization of social policies and emerging ideals of self-reliance, both manifested in the discourse of fit families (*blagopoluchnye sem'i*) discussed in the previous chapter. However, the ideal of the self-reliant, fit family often collides with risks and social anxieties caused by the growing privatization of childbearing and child caring. As I followed women in their everyday chores and family-related practices, it became abundantly clear that even though the majority endorsed the new policy and pronatalist discourse—"it's good for the country"—personal and familial experiences related to childcare have been only tangentially associated with ideals of self-sufficient nuclear families that can absorb the risks of care. Amid economic uncertainty and change, in order to make up for the state's failure to provide adequate childcare support, women mobilize existing networks of kin, carving domestic spaces of care for themselves.

The organizing argument of this chapter is that against the logic of privatized care embedded in marketized pronatalism—through which the state aims to regulate citizens' demographic behavior—long-standing social institutions of kinship care come to prominence. Ironically, in absorbing growing expectations to respond to the state's demographic needs and the logic of privatized care embedded in the new pronatalist regime, families, but most of all women, have revitalized and reenacted two important strategies of kinship care, both with a footprint in the Soviet political economy: the *babushka* and the reshuffling and swapping of houses among relatives. The chapter focuses on how interactions between these key strategies and a new marketized pronatalist terrain produce and resignify meanings and practices of kinship care and support in contemporary Russia. It demonstrates how these networks of support are where benevolent state care clashes against state care as a burden.

Marketized Pronatalism

The backdrop of post-Soviet pronatalism requires special attention. Russia's contemporary pronatalist regime is founded on the state encouraging women to have multiple children while privatizing the risks of childbearing, compelling families to absorb the burden of care. It is fueled by socially conservative discourses and neoliberal doctrines of increased cuts in public spending. As the previous chapter demonstrated, in this new pronatalist regime, neotraditional discourses and neoliberal market logic guide a normative imaginary of a stable, self-sufficient heterosexual family unit that takes on the responsibility and economic risks of raising and caring for children. Not uniquely Russian, this marketized pronatalist regime is central to the capitalist order. In the United States, a coalition of neoliberals and neoconservatives has advocated since the 1980s for massive reforms restricting redistributive public welfare policies in favor of making the private institution of the family fully responsible for social welfare (Cooper 2017). Around the world, women have been faced with increasingly aggressive demands to grow their family size against a backdrop of cuts in public health care, childcare, and education as well as rising costs of housing and a precarious labor market (for Hungary see Glass and Fodor 2022; for Turkey see Atalay 2019; for Russia see Shpakovskaya and Chernova 2022).

In Russia, the pronatalist ideology harkens back to familiar Soviet tropes but also marks shifting conceptions of state care and obligations for social support. The Soviet pronatalist regime conceptualized women as active participants in the labor market and offered, at least nominally, expanded networks of social and childcare support built around production and service enterprises (industrial factories, state institutions, etc.), which were responsible for establishing social security funds to pay welfare benefits to their workers (Avdeyeva 2011; Nakachi 2021).[4] In post-Soviet Russia, as Michele Rivkin-Fish (2010) has argued, the state continued to acknowledge the burden of childbearing and childcare on women in general and on women's place in the labor market in particular, but it conditioned its support on fulfilling the need to increase population (see also Zdravomyslova, Temkina, and Rotkirch 2007). However, unlike its Soviet predecessor, post-Soviet pronatalism, impacted by neoliberal policy doctrines, replaced the subject of women in the labor market with monetized and individualized incentives to reproduce, narrowing the scope of women's claims and rights (Leykin 2019).

This form of pronatalism is epitomized in Russia by the Maternity Capital policy, introduced in 2007, following the political leadership's alarmist portrayal of the demographic situation.[5] The policy aims at changing the reproductive behavior of Russian women—and, by extension, men—by incentivizing them materially. Defined by the state's need to resolve its population problem, this policy targets young families, the "demographic reserve" of the country, to use a concept coined by Russian sociologist Zhanna Chernova (2010).

The launching of Maternity Capital is less surprising in the context of the monetization of social relations and policies, intensified by an exceptional advance of post-Soviet capitalism (Ovcharova and Pishnyak 2005; Oushakine 2009b). The Maternity Capital policy indeed coheres with a general trend of monetization of social policies in contemporary Russia in which neoliberal political reasoning promotes market solutions to social ills (Matza 2012, 2018). When I asked a demographer from Moscow State University serving on the Ministry of Labor's demographic policies committee about the monetary nature of the new pronatalist policy, he recounted that when preparing a set of policy measures aimed at increasing the country's birthrates, ministry officials insisted on using economic indicators of efficacy (money spent vs. absolute number of children born) instead of indicators suitable for the demographic analysis of population reproduction (see Rybakovsky 2016). The marketized logic of the Maternity Capital policy is evident: it envisions self-sufficient families absorbing the full responsibility of care and transactional relations of care with the state, weighed by rational cost and benefit calculations.

Official state rhetoric encouraging women to have multiple children has been contradicted by an acknowledged shortage of public day care facilities, many of which were shut down and appropriated for other purposes during the worst years of the demographic decline in the 1990s, when total fertility rates were barely scratching 1.2 children per woman (Savinskaya 2008). Between 2006 and 2012 fertility rates began rising, responding in a way to state pronatalist programs (Biryukova, Sinyavskaya, and Nurimanova 2016;

Frejka and Zakharov 2014) but most likely assisted by favorable oil prices, which allowed the Russian economy to thrive (World Bank Indicators 2022a, 2022b, 2022c, 2022d). This rise created a dire shortage of childcare facilities, forcing women and families to rely on other, mostly familial, networks of care.[6] The new pronatalist regime thus situated my interlocutors at the crossroads of different and often conflicting expectations of privatized and relational forms of care. The remainder of the chapter focuses on how conflicting expectations of care have interacted with rapid political economic and demographic changes in contemporary Russia and how my interlocutors worked to redistribute care in their search for support.

Grandmother Care: Invisible Signs of Expectation

I went to visit Nadia, a twenty-three-year-old mother of young twins. She and her husband were renting a place from a relative of Nadia's while waiting for the keys to the one-room apartment they had purchased some time ago. Nadia and her husband both came from a working-class background; Nadia's stepfather as well as her husband worked blue collar jobs at the city water supply company. She got married very young, right after graduating from high school, and became pregnant with twins soon after. Only recently had she found a stable job at a bank, with decent working conditions and relatively flexible hours. Because the water supply company her husband worked for had its own day care facility, Nadia and her husband were able to secure a place in a nursery and then day care for the twins before they turned three, a luxury rarely available to those on the general waiting list for day care in the city. Her husband used his days off to do odd jobs, mostly working with a construction crew renovating private apartments, allowing them to save enough money for a down payment on the one-room apartment they were supposed to move into shortly after we met.

On this particular visit, the house was uncharacteristically quiet. It was Nadia's day off, and with her husband at work and their four-year-old twins in day care, our conversation, contrary to those on my previous visits, was uninterrupted. Nadia told me a story about a teenage girl she was helping. The girl had just gone back home, and Nadia was tidying the room where the girl had slept. The girl, she said, grew up in a *neblagopoluchnaia sem'ia* (unfit family) with a mother suffering from a substance use disorder in the town where Nadia's husband had also grown up. The girl's older sister (Nadia's husband's former girlfriend) was her main caregiver, and when she needed help, the sister would bring the girl to Nadia for a few days. Nadia would also send clothes and school supplies on a regular basis. Although told with a great compassion, the story, I realized as the conversation progressed, offered Nadia an opportunity to signal a distinction between the kind of unfit family the girl's story symbolized and her own ideal of a fit, self-reliant family.

Despite dominant cultural ideals of the self-sufficient nuclear family, to which Nadia clearly aspired, Nadia's reliance on extended family networks was palpable yet easily glossed over. Although Nadia always insisted on her and her husband's full financial independence, when I asked about the relatives from whom they were renting the apartment, I learned that Nadia and her husband were not paying rent. Due to a favor this far-removed relative ("my stepfather's second cousin, if I remember the connection right," Nadia said) owed to her parents—the nature of which she did not want to reveal or did not know—they were living there free of charge while waiting to enter their newly purchased apartment. Her daily routine also relied heavily on unpaid family care. Her young and fully employed mother, whom Nadia affectionately called *nasha babushka* (our granny), picked the twins up every evening from day care: "It's a convenient arrangement [*udobno*] because my parents live within walking distance of the day care." Her mother helped with the kids on a regular basis as well: "We always call her when we need help. We never drop the kids off unannounced, mind you, but I don't remember that there was ever a time when we asked and she refused to take them."

Narratives in which grandmothers' unpaid care and familial networks were mentioned as secondary to the story of self-reliance crossed class boundaries too. Larisa, an infectious disease doctor and head of a municipal health clinic, had two children, age twenty-three and three, from two different marriages.[7] Throughout our conversations, Larisa insisted on her family's self-reliance with a certain inflection of envy toward those whose families provide unpaid care. Yet as I sought details, particulars about a grandmother's care began to emerge. As though she had never insisted "it was all on us" (*vse sami*), Larisa explained that in both of her marriages, her mothers-in-law had spent a year taking care of her children on a daily basis. When her first son was born, she wanted to go back to school, and with her second child, she wanted to go back to work because the family could not sustain its lifestyle on just one income. Importantly, Larisa did not intend to hide the fact that her mothers-in-law had provided care. Rather, the two grandmothers' unpaid care was so expected (and taken for granted) that she did not count it as help and support (see Utrata 2015 on how adult daughters take grandmothers' care for their children for granted). Similar to Nadia's and Larisa's, claims of financial and emotional independence from extended families were central to my interlocutors' personal narratives but clouded by stories about a babushka (mother or mother-in-law) collecting children from day care on a daily basis or taking care of children for their first year of life so that mothers could cut maternity leave short and go back to work (see also Utrata 2017).

The Soviet Footprint of Grandmother Care

The Soviet political economy and totality of state policies shaped the structure of kinship care and gendered nature of domestic labor (Verdery 1994). In theory, families were supported by the Soviet state in fulfilling their functions of biological and social reproduction. In reality, social life in the Soviet Union, as elsewhere in the socialist world, was practically dependent on families and intergenerational ties. The totality of the Soviet political economy molded what Katherine Verdery (1996) calls the "etatization of time," in which people's control over their time was expropriated by the state. Food lines, familiar to observers of Soviet life, are perhaps the most famous example of this process, whereby shortages of certain items were converted into a seizure of citizens' time, making people, most often women, spend hours waiting to buy basic goods and food staples (Verdery 1996). The Soviet economy of shortage, in which the monetary value of goods was less important than access to social connections useful for obtaining these goods—what in Soviet parlance became known as *blat*, a form of exchange imagined as "borrowing one's access" (*dostup*)—made relying on relatives and networks of close friends a crucial skill (Ledeneva 1998, 35; Read and Thelen 2007). Family connections in general and grandmothers in particular became the core of these networks, making up for shortages and helping women and young families make ends meet (Rotkirch, Tkach, and Zdravomyslova 2012; Shevchenko 2009; Utrata 2017).

This model of Soviet intergenerational care was also invigorated by the age and gender structure of the population of the Soviet Union. Soviet men had a much lower life expectancy than women, a problem that continues to shape Russia's age structure, creating a significant gender disbalance especially when it comes to retirement age (Sherbakova 2020). The gender imbalance, along with the relatively young age of first births—a trend that began to change in the 1990s—and early mandatory retirement for women (fifty-five), turned women in their late forties and early fifties into young, energetic grandmothers taking care of grandchildren and making household labor their primary responsibility (Ashwin et al. 2013).[8] Social reproduction of Soviet families, thus, was significantly feminized and "geriatized" insofar as women pensioners, as opposed to housewives, carried out unpaid household labor—standing in food lines, cooking, and raising grandchildren (Verdery 1994).

Grandmothers navigating the perils of Soviet food lines and taking care of grandchildren became the hallmark of Soviet existence. When recalling childhood, stories about being raised by grandmothers or sent to grandparents for extended periods of time were abundant among my interlocutors. Alisa was born in the apartment where her parents lived with her father's mother. When her parents left to work in the oil industry in the north of the Tyumen region in the 1980s, she, a kindergarten-age child, was raised by her grandmother, whom she referred to as *khoziaika* (mistress of the house).[9] Masha, another of my interlocutors, told the story of her mother, who had left a small town and moved to Yekaterinburg (then still Sverdlovsk) to study nursing and got married and pregnant before finishing her studies. Soon after Masha was born, her mother divorced Masha's father and sent Masha to live with her own mother. Masha lived with her grandmother for the first four years of her life, allowing her mother to finish nursing school uninterrupted. Only after her mother had secured a job in a hospital, gotten remarried, and received a room in a studio-like apartment (*gostinka*) did she take Masha back to live in the city. Alina, Masha's friend, was born in Perm to a young couple who had come to study at Perm State University from a small village some three hundred kilometers away. When she was born, her parents sent her to live with her grandparents on her mother's side until the first grade. Alina explained her parents' decision as an act of care, allowing her to grow up undisturbed by their ever-changing circumstances. Her parents would visit Alina during holidays "so as not to move her from one place to another [*chtoby menia ne dergali*]."

Tracing the Signs of Cultural Expectation

The cultural expectation of a babushka—poignantly dubbed by Jennifer Utrata (2015, 16) "the reserve army of feminine self-sacrifice" and considered responsible for housework and childcare as an unconditional act of love—continues to be an important feature of post-Soviet life (123–50).[10] Grandmother care is a crucial source of support in a variety of social contexts, and its symbolic power as the focal point of feminine kinship networks cannot be exaggerated (Utrata 2015; Bloch 2017). The prominence of the babushka as a social institution is such that in 2013, when the state banned adoption of children by gay couples (*Kommersant* 2013b), the Russian internet responded with a meme representing the significance of the babushka as a cultural anchor. The viral image suggested that "the majority of children in our country have been raised by a homosexual couple: a mother and a grandmother."

Grandmother care often materializes as an important source of practical know-how, especially during crises (Shevchenko 2009, 90–96). Following the 2008 economic crisis, Matrena, a single mother of a three-year-old daughter, sent her child to live with her very young and fully employed mother, only forty-seven at the time. Matrena had lost her job during the crisis, and for the first few months, her mother used paid vacation days to go back and forth between Yekaterinburg and Dektiarsk (a nearby town) to help Matrena with childcare. After her mother ran out of paid days, she took Matrena's daughter to live with her, soliciting more family support from her sister and Matrena's adult siblings to free Matrena to look for a new job.

As the center of Katia's support network, Katia's mom helps take care of her two sons (six and twelve years old). Katia works twenty-four-hour shifts at the city dispatch, and her husband is a long-haul truck driver. Katia's husband is the only child of a single mother. He was raised by his mother, grandmother, and two grandaunts who did not have grandchildren of their own. Short of calling it a homosexual family, Katia joked that her husband "grew up in a feminine kingdom [*zhenskoe tsarstvo*]." She explained, "He was raised well. Growing up with women taught him to respect them." Qualifying her story, she proudly proclaimed, "He washes his socks and underwear by himself." Katia's sixty-five-year-old mother, who suffered a stroke not long ago, takes care of the kids, taking them to and collecting them from school, cooking dinners, and taking care of the house. Though she lives with Katia's brother and his family and helps raise his children too, she is an indispensable part of Katia's day-to-day childcare. Essentially, Katia's mother works twenty-four-hour shifts synchronized with Katia's work schedule, providing unpaid care to her children and taking care of the house.

The cultural significance of the babushka was palpable in my interlocutors' lives even when biological grandmothers were absent. Karina, for example, was a single mother of two small children. We met in 2011, just after her first son was born, and have kept in touch since. Karina shared with me some of the details of her difficult life, raising two children by herself (her husband was in prison), working odd jobs, trying to make ends meet. Her parents had died one after another when she was twenty-two years old, and only then was she told by a relative she had been adopted. She has been estranged from her extended adoptive family since.

I visited Karina in the summer of 2018, when Yekaterinburg hosted several World Cup games. Karina, excited and proud to be part of a worldwide event, had signed up to volunteer at the stadium during the games, and I accompanied her to her first training session. Although I knew she was not in touch with her adoptive family, I also knew that there was a grandmother, Babushka Vera, who lived nearby and about whom Karina often spoke. Accompanying her to the training session years after we first met, I learned that Vera was not a relative but rather Karina's neighbor; they met when Karina moved to her current apartment with her one-month-old baby. In a way, Karina had adopted Vera as a babushka. They had formed a mother-daughter relationship, helping each other out since they first met (see also Utrata 2015, 143). When Karina's first son turned two months old, she began working as a janitor, cleaning offices at night. She would drop her young son off at Vera's home in the evening before going to work and in return help Vera with household chores. Vera was a relatively young woman with no grandchildren of her own, but she had many health problems, making it difficult for her to grocery shop and look after the house. That is where Karina came in. They now celebrated holidays together and often cooked for each other.

Describing their reciprocal relations of care, Karina stressed the fact that unlike others, who always tried to get something out of her (*vse trebuiut ot menia cho-to*), Vera did not demand much in exchange for her support. I wondered why I had never suspected there was no family connection between Karina and Vera. It occurred to me that because Karina always described Vera's help as unconditional, I had assumed that her kin ties with Vera, which she always narrated through the idealized cultural symbol of grandmother care, were in fact real.

Grandmother Care and Changing Welfare Regimes

Although cultural expectations of babushkas caring for grandchildren and households unquestionably linger, the changing nature of welfare in post-Soviet Russia affects how this form of kinship care is signified and enacted.

In the context of rapid economic change and a relatively early retirement age for women, which remained fifty-five until 2019, many grandparents cannot afford or do not want to retire (Ashwin et al. 2013). As of 2014, about 35 percent of Russian pensioners continued to be employed postretirement, with no financial penalty for working while drawing pension from the state (Ashwin, Keenan, and Kozina 2021, 153).[11] Middle-class aspirations and changes in life course have also contributed to the emergence of a new character of working grandmother that, as gender scholars have argued, competes with the late-Soviet gender contract of grandmothers raising their grandchildren (Zdravomyslova 2010; Rotkirch, Tkach, and Zdravomyslova 2012).

Even when grandmothers combine unpaid care work with employment, they might set boundaries between their personal lives and helping with children and grandchildren (see, for example, Utrata 2015, 2017). Elena, a forty-seven-year-old mother of three and grandmother herself, interpreted these limits as a sign of failing expectations. With a note of regret in her voice, she told me that her mother had not wanted to care for grandchildren until very recently, when Elena's third child entered the first grade: "She's accustomed to living in grand style [*na shirokuiu nogu*]. Grandchildren have never been her priority." Elena's negotiations of support with her mother were complicated by the fact that while still in the workforce and taking care of her young children from her second marriage, Elena was providing unpaid care for her oldest daughter's child, who is the same age as Elena's youngest son.

Economic changes and new ideas about care have contributed to the commercialization of domestic labor. Over the last two decades, a service economy has sprung up offering private day cares and nannies (Rotkirch, Tkach, and Zdravomyslova 2012; Savinskaya 2008; Zdravomyslova 2010). Although rooted in transactional logic, these commercial forms of care, as Rotkirch, Tkach, and Zdravomyslova (2012) point out, are often based on quasi-family relations between employers and domestic employees. Because of the previously mentioned deficit of municipal day cares, nannies and private kindergartens were options my interlocutors seriously considered and often relied on. Yet the high cost of private childcare services along with general distrust of these services created a clear obstacle. The unease with which my interlocutors considered these services was evident. They explained their distrust by alluding to a general lack of regulation and supervision for private day cares. Stories in the media about private day cares operating without state permits and about irregularities in the private childcare sector solidified this distrust (Matveev and Salikhova 2016; *Newslab* 2019; Pashenko 2017; Zaitzev 2022).

Thus, in the absence of affordable and available day care facilities, many women expressed clear preference for having a babushka care for their child. "She's the only one I trust when my children are sick or when they're acting out," they would commonly respond to my questions about a grandmother's role in childcare. "No one knows my daughter as well as my mom," Lina said when I asked her what she would do when her maternity leave ended the following month. "She's the only one I can rely on. It's different with nannies. Even if I put a hidden camera in the flat, I can't really trust them," she concluded. I asked if Lina's mom had retired and could therefore contribute to caring for her daughter. "She's retired," Lina informed me, "but she continues to work. She just can't quit. Not yet, anyway." Although sympathetic to the motives, Lina sounded upset and mildly disappointed that her mother had chosen to stay in the workforce rather than attend to her granddaughter. In a way, Lina experienced a failed expectation, which she attenuated by combining both commercial and unpaid forms of care. Lina paid a nanny to care for her children three days a week, and she and her mother would alternate the other days. "Nothing I can do [*kuda devat'sia*]," she told me with a deep sigh.

Yulia, one of my wealthier interlocutors, had two children: a nineteen-year-old university student and an eighteen-month-old daughter. A municipal nursery was out of the question, she told me. The waiting list was too long. When her son was that age, "they barely had twelve children in his class, but it's close to impossible to get a place in a day care right now." Initially, because of a considerable age gap, Yulia's son helped care for his baby sister. When he began studying engineering at the university, Yulia wanted to relieve him of that responsibility as much as possible, although he continued to live with his parents. Yulia could afford a nanny, but she wanted her mom to help so she could go back to work. Her parents lived in a different town and were still working postretirement. After negotiating with Yulia for some time, they agreed to retire. They sold their three-room apartment in the smaller town and bought a one-room apartment in Yekaterinburg after Yulia and her husband promised to contribute to the purchase.

Right after moving to Yekaterinburg, Yulia's mom started caring for Yulia's daughter on a daily basis (six days a week). Her mother's sister, Yulia's aunt, who did not have children, helped cook for the family. "This is purely family-based help [*chisto rodstvennaia pomoshch'*]," Yulia told me when I asked whether her mother or aunt are compensated for their help. She added, "It's different from paid help. I can't just give them my daughter and run away to work; they expect me to spend time with them, to talk to them. It's a different kind of relationship." Yulia's narrative is particularly interesting insofar as it demonstrates that although grandmother care is assumed to be unconditional and sacrificial, it also entails reciprocity. It is not a transactional but a relational form of care. Receiving care makes one indebted to provide care, not necessarily in kind and or at the same time; such kinship care produces a debt of gratitude (Leinaweaver 2013). In Yulia's case, the transactional nature of commercial care was substituted by a different reciprocal logic of care, through which her mother and her aunt received Yulia's care and attention as a form of gratitude.

New state economic policies also sustained cultural expectations of grandmother care. Olga was able to cut her maternity leave short and go back to work because her still-working mother took maternity leave to take care of Olga's son. Olga's mother was an engineer with a relatively stable income, and she had heard about another woman at her firm taking maternity leave to care for her granddaughter. This provision is made possible by the relatively egalitarian Russian Labor Code (article 256), which provides families an opportunity to employ kin as primary caregivers with paid maternity leave (Trudovoii kodeks RF 2014). While Russia's maternity policies allow families to employ other relatives, including fathers, as caregivers, gendered expectations of kinship care make babushkas the most popular option.[12] The policy allowed Olga's mother to remain in the workforce and help her daughter raise her child.

Grandmothers' unpaid care work is a quintessential example of kinship care as a matter of course, an obligation, and a burden. The intersubjective and relational character of kinship care marks an older woman as good and decent. My interlocutors often experienced mothers' refusal or inability to care for their children as disrespect or even personal failure. These normative expectations of kinship care have been shaped, by and large, by the Soviet political economy. Despite the enduring cultural significance of the babushka as the core of kinship support networks, the new market economy and state pronatalist ideologies do not easily commensurate with what is considered good and decent when it comes to kinship care. Creatively converting cultural expectations of care into practice, my interlocutors' strategies revealed how the redistribution of care is not only based on persisting cultural models but also circumscribed by and responding to new marketized ideologies and ideals of a family.

The Housing Question—Spatial Dimensions of Kinship Care

"Whatever you may say, the housing question [*zhilishchnyi vopros*] is a major stumbling block [*kamen' pritknoveniia*] when it comes to families," Zoya summarized, reflecting on her family situation. Zoya, a former journalist, was the mother of two children. Just before she became pregnant with her second child, Zoya was fired from the news agency where she had worked for some years after the magazine she wrote for closed down. After her second maternity leave, Zoya found a position working for a midrange PR firm. In telling me about her family, Zoya seemed to favor planning ahead. It had been clear to her that she would have children if and only if she owned an apartment. So she had postponed having children until she did. Generalizing from her own experience, Zoya explained, "When people live in a rented apartment or with their relatives, they're rarely resolved to have children. That is, if they're reasonable [*razumnye*] people of course."

Whether this behavior is reasonable or unreasonable, according to Zoya's definition, the housing question has had a stable and enduring presence in the Soviet and post-Soviet cultural repertoire of ideas and practices of kinship care. Stories about growing up in an apartment shared with other relatives, mostly grandparents, were common—a backdrop to my interlocutors' efforts to remember who had helped whom when they were growing up. Some of the stories had a familiar Soviet tone of nostalgia for the time "when things were easier and you didn't need much because everyone wore the same clothes and ate the same food," as Zoya put it. Memories also included frictions and contentious relations leading to long-lasting family feuds and disputes. When I confronted my interlocutors with questions about relations within multigenerational households, I heard pregnant pauses, stories about quarrels between relatives living together, or tales of despotic fathers and grandfathers who dominated the household. When I talked with Alisa about what it was like growing up with her grandparents while her parents worked in the far north for seven years, her initial narrative of a household dominated by her grandmother, the absolute and undisputable *khoziaika*, shifted into stories about her grandfather's drunken and violent sprees.

The sharing of living space has been central to anthropological investigations of kin making. Anthropologists have demonstrated that managing shared living spaces simultaneously produces and contests intergenerational practices of kinship care (Carsten 1995; Reece 2020; Tkach 2015). For former Soviet citizens, the home as a place where intergenerational practices of care are produced, enabled, and contested has been informed by a long history of housing shortages—an enduring and recognizable feature of Soviet life. The centralized structure of housing distribution and chronic shortages in the public housing market throughout the Soviet period led many citizens to live in multigenerational households (Attwood 2010). Intergenerational forms of coresidence, in turn, facilitated certain practices of social and material support, strengthening expectations of grandparents—mostly grandmothers—providing emotional and material care to adult children and grandchildren (Caldwell 2007; Utrata 2015, 2017).

Multigenerational forms of living are part of what Russian sociologist Simon Kordonsky (2000) has called a "distributive lifestyle" (*raspredelennyi obraz zhizni*), through which Russian families manage material and social resources (see also Cherkaev 2023). Indeed, sharing living space with relatives, swapping and exchanging apartments among family members, and dividing time between a city dwelling and a *dacha* or a city apartment and a relative's house in a village were long-standing features of my interlocutors' lives, shaping practices of kinship care past and present (see also Tkach 2015). Essentially, all stories involving the distributive lifestyle included recollections of moving in and out of grandparents' apartments, swapping houses between sets of relatives, and participating in complicated chains of apartment exchanges through which my interlocutors or their parents could eventually get their own, separate place. Housing stories spanned two political periods with very different conceptual understandings of property and ownership rights. They originated in the centralized state housing distribution system, when apartments could not be bought or sold but could be exchanged among citizens living in state-owned houses.[13] The stories stretched into the post-Soviet period, in which ideas of individual private property took root and apartments could be bought and sold for profit.

Soviet Housing Policies

The promises and failures of Soviet mass housing have been well documented in historical research (Attwood 2010; Harris 2013; Meerovich 2008;

2018; Smith 2010; Varga-Harris 2015). The expropriation and distribution of private apartments following the Bolshevik Revolution of 1917 failed to provide sufficient living spaces. In the first few decades of the Soviet Union, although separate apartments were built for state and party nomenclature, the majority of urban dwellers lived in barracks and czarist-era expropriated apartments, popularly known as communal apartments (*kommunalki*) (Meerovich 2008). *Kommunalka* occupants—whose number would sometimes hit double digits—lived in separate rooms but shared a communal kitchen, bathroom, and storage space with their neighbors.[14] Russian anthropologist Ilya Utekhin's (2004) comprehensive account of Soviet communal apartments shows how sharing physical spaces with others shaped Soviet cultural ideas about responsibility and obligation and distinctions between the shared and the personal.

The housing crisis was exacerbated during Stalin's industrialization era and World War II, dragging shortages into the postwar period. In 1957, following Stalin's death, the new Soviet leader, Nikita Khrushchev, launched a comprehensive housing reform, promising to move ordinary citizens from overcrowded communal apartments and barracks to separate apartments inhabited by single families, envisioned as enabling the "communist way of life" (*kommunisticheskii byt*) (Harris 2013; Lebina 2024; Varga-Harris 2015). Soviet distribution norms (8.25 meters per person) and economic constraints of implementing reform on a massive scale became the foundational aesthetic principles of these standardized, small-dimensioned (*malogaboritnye*) separate apartments, popularly named, in association with their creator, *khrushchevki* (Harris 2013). In the first two years of its existence, Khrushchev's reform improved housing conditions for over sixty-five million individuals, but the construction pace eventually stalled without resolving the crisis (Lebina 2024, 18; Varga-Harris 2015, 2). Khrushchev's housing campaign became an important point of contact between the state and its citizens insofar as it was a domain where Soviet ideological prescriptions on family matters, material desires, and domestic ideals interacted with intimate personal relations and practices (Harris 2013; Lebina 2019; Meerovich 2008; Varga-Harris 2015).[15]

Other housing programs and promises followed Khrushchev's removal from leadership. The last time the Soviet state attempted to solve the housing crisis, under the slogan "to each family its own apartment" (*kazhdoi sem'e otdel'nuiu kvartiru*), was in 1986. During the XXVII Party Congress, Mikhail Gorbachev announced his sweeping housing reform, Domicile 2000 (*Zhil'e 2000*), which pledged to provide every family its own apartment by the year 2000 (Attwood 2010, 207). Ultimately, the Soviet state failed to deliver on its famous promise. In fact, the continual ideological presence of the slogan "to each family its own separate apartment" in party campaigns and reforms against the backdrop of perpetual housing shortages symbolized the promise's chronic failure.

Soviet standardized apartments, built for separate nuclear families, could hardly accommodate changes in family size over the life course. Because of perpetual shortages in allocated housing, grown-up and now married children, although entitled to their own apartment by law in most cases, often continued to live with their parents, turning de jure single-family apartments into de facto multigenerational ones, with at least three generations sharing space. These intergenerational households blurred boundaries between communal and separate living, affecting domestic divisions of labor and forms of care (Attwood 2010). Complaints about congested spaces, fraught family relations, and especially conflicts between family members of different generations all occupying single-family apartments were a rich source of material for fiction writers and publicists (see, for example, Attwood 2010, 187–88; Harris 2005; Lebina 2019). Intergenerational residences were a gold mine for Soviet jokes, in particular about mothers-in-law; the wife's mother was a perpetual object of ridicule and verbal abuse, making shared living arrangements a space where gender inequalities were cemented and normalized (Lialenkova 2007).

In these separate-cum-multigenerational apartments, geriatric and gendered expectations of women to manage domestic labor made older women a focal point of households. During the period of mass housing campaigns in the early 1970s that promised to move Soviet families away from communal living toward separate apartments, Boris Davydov, a regional artist from Saratov, painted a three-generation family. In the painting, called *Family Portrait*, family members with identical, *American Gothic*-like facial expressions look at an observer from the balcony of an apartment in an easily recognizable, newly erected Soviet residential neighborhood. The painting's socialist realist aesthetic encapsulates both the materiality and multigenerational reality of the Soviet family. If the Soviet housing policy envisioned a nuclear family consisting of two parents and their children, the portrait depicts a more realistic version of the apartment's occupants. It includes a babushka standing next to her adult daughter or perhaps daughter-in-law. The way she is painted, the babushka is not a tangential but rather an inextricable element of the family portrait, giving the painting its compositional unity.[16]

Intergenerational coresidency was at the center of my interlocutors' stories about child and intergenerational care. "I was born when my father was still a student in medical school and my mother just finished the Ural Polytechnic Institute," Sofia told me. She remembered growing up in an apartment where her parents, older brother, grandparents, and uncle's family lived. Her grandfather had moved to Yekaterinburg from Kazakhstan to work at a Soviet Sverdlovsk heavy industrial factory, where he met and married her grandmother. Sofia's family occupied one room in her mother's parents' three-room apartment, assigned by the factory. In Sofia's story, both her grandmothers played a primary role in not only taking care of grandchildren but also dealing with the housing question. Because apartments could not be bought and sold, for Soviet citizens, dealing with the housing question meant exchanging apartments with other state-housing dwellers through convoluted chains of apartment swaps. Usually, a larger apartment would be exchanged for two smaller ones, allowing adult children to move out (Attwood 2010, 184–87).[17]

When Sofia was in the seventh grade, her uncle, now an army officer, moved out because he received an army accommodation. To help Sofia's parents get their own place, her grandparents participated in a complex chain of apartment swapping, exchanging their three-room apartment for two one-room apartments. Sophia's family then moved to a one-room, more centrally located khrushchevka. Her father's mother took part in a no-less-complicated exchange. To be able to help with childcare, Sofia's grandmother moved from a private house (*chastnyi dom*) in a provincial town in Kazakhstan to a small one-room khrushchevka in Sverdlovsk, a property Sofia's father later inherited and moved into after divorcing Sofia's mother. During the altogether different property regime of the early 1990s, Sofia's mother was able to swap her one-room ground-floor khrushchevka for a larger two-room apartment because during that period, ground-floor apartments, highly desired by the booming retail industry, held higher value than larger apartments on higher floors. Sofia's mother still lives there, sharing the apartment with Sofia's brother, his wife, and their child.

The Post-Soviet Housing Question

Managing shared living spaces and swapping houses remains an important strategy of kinship care in post-Soviet Russia. Elena has three children. Her twenty-seven-year-old daughter from her first marriage is married and has two children of her own. Elena's younger children, sixteen and nine years old, live with her and her new husband in a three-room apartment. All of her children live in the same building, Elena told me proudly. Elena has been working as a nurse in the same clinic for over thirty years. After six years of working there, she received a very small studio-like one-room apartment (*gostinka*) from the state, and when it became possible, she privatized it. She then swapped with her mother, moving to her two-room apartment in a different neighborhood and sending her mother to live in her now privatized studio. Elena moved there with her two children and new husband. Elena's third child was born in 2009, which made her eligible for Maternity Capital. They used the payment and a bank loan to buy a three-room apartment in a brand-new neighborhood in the city.

Elena's oldest daughter, from her first marriage, gave birth to her first child not long after Elena herself gave birth to her third child, making Elena a very young grandmother and a mother of a newborn at the same time. To help her oldest daughter, Elena found a one-room apartment directly underneath her flat, then took out another bank loan and helped her daughter purchase that apartment. Although they agreed that her daughter and son-in-law would pay the mortgage, Elena nevertheless had to occasionally pay it. Because her youngest son and her granddaughter are approximately the same age, Elena took maternity leave to care for both children, freeing her daughter to go back to college after a short leave of absence. Living in the same building helped enormously, Elena assured me. It also helped that Elena's mother had sold her studio and moved to the same neighborhood so that, as Elena put it jokingly, "we can exploit her better [*chtoby my ee luchshe ekspluatirovali*]." The labor of care, thus, is distributed between Elena, her adult daughter, and Elena's mother. The babushka, whom Elena herself embodies, remains at the core of this triad of support.

Resolving the housing question is a family project, a process in which both properties and care are redistributed. Another interlocutor, Svetlana, lives in a two-room apartment her husband inherited from his family. In the early 1980s, her husband's grandmother received a two-room apartment from a large chemical factory where she had worked her whole life. She exchanged it with a family working in the same factory and moved to a two-room apartment that shared a wall with the one-room apartment in which her adult daughter lived with her son, Viacheslav—Svetalana's husband. When Viacheslav was a boy, Svetlana told me, he would knock on his grandmother's wall if he wanted her to visit him. After Svetlana married Viacheslav, she moved in with her husband and his mother in this one-room flat. After their children were born, they swapped apartments with Viacheslav's grandmother, moving to her two-room flat and relocating the grandmother to a smaller apartment next door. After the grandmother died, Svetlana's mother-in-law moved to the smaller apartment, leaving the two-room apartment to Svetlana, Viacheslav, and their children. Rather than knocking on the wall, they installed a wireless bell to communicate with Svetlana's mother-in-law. Eventually, Viacheslav inherited both apartments and built a movable wall between them, essentially combining the two. Resolving the housing question allowed Svetlana and her mother-in-law to manage their shared living space more efficiently, Svetlana told me. Viacheslav's mom helps with childcare, and Svetlana gives her mother-in-law a hand with other forms of domestic labor.

The housing question also intersects with monetized welfare policies in interesting ways, affecting how kinship care is "housed" (Reece 2020). Aside from the anticrisis provision that allows families to draw a small percentage of their Maternity Capital payment for immediate use, Maternity Capital has most frequently been used toward improving living conditions (Borozdina et al. 2016). While Russia's monetized welfare policy may help some individuals avoid falling into poverty during difficult times or buy larger apartments to accommodate growing families, many of my interlocutors, although eligible for the Maternity Capital payment, could not qualify for bank loans. Yet the existence of the monetized social policy helped revitalize some traditional expectations and practices of kinship care.

Masha, a single mother of two, was struggling to make ends meet when we first met in 2011. She was in her mid-twenties, divorced, raising a toddler, and working at a market research firm. She had moved to the city from a much smaller provincial town to study at the university, where the father of her daughter was a fellow student. Soon after her daughter was born, they got divorced; he moved to a different city and has not been present in his daughter's life since. Masha got married a second time when her daughter was four years old, and soon after, her second daughter was born. Throughout this period, Masha's mother, who lived in a small town some two hours away from the city, would come and visit for extended periods of time to help Masha raise her two children. Masha's mother received disability benefits from the state because of her extremely high blood pressure and was not working; however, she was very busy cultivating her home garden, offering a steady food supply for Masha and her children.

When I met Masha again in 2018, she was divorced for the second time, living with her mother and two children in a small apartment she had bought on the outskirts of the city. Even before divorcing her second husband, Masha had been looking for a small apartment she could buy using the Maternity Capital when the state amended the law and allowed families to use the voucher toward a mortgage before the second child turned three. Real estate prices in the city, even in the most remote neighborhoods, were far from affordable and made the purchase virtually impossible. Masha's mother was practically living with her by then, caring for the children, especially the younger daughter, who was still on a waiting list to be placed in municipal day care. In the end, Masha's mother sold her apartment in the small town and contributed, along with the Maternity Capital, to the down payment on a flat in what looked like a dilapidated apartment complex on the outskirts of the city.

Masha's story reveals an important spatial dimension of kinship care emerging through existing expectations of care, changing welfare regimes, and new forms of ownership (see also Reece 2020; Tkach 2015). In effect, in Masha's family, monetized welfare benefits in the form of Maternity Capital contributed to the reenactment of existing cultural expectations of kinship care. Yet again, through state-marketized pronatalism, the so-called Russian homosexual family—the mother and the babushka—rather than an idealized *blagopoluchnaia sem'ia*, had reaffirmed itself.

* * *

Cultural practices of kinship care in post-Soviet Russia have been shaped by the legacy of Soviet economic policies, demographic changes, emerging lifestyles, and new family ideologies. The transactional pronatalist regime envisioning self-sufficient families absorbing the risks of childcare has shaped relations of care between the state and its citizens as well as obligations of care within families. It became clear in my ethnographic explorations of kinship care practices that the new pronatalist regime, while seemingly failing in its explicit efforts to change established childbearing patterns (Frejka and Zakharov 2014), has been rather influential in how intergenerational kinship care is perceived, enacted, and distributed in post-Soviet Russia.

In Russia, practices of care—either the social institution of the babushka or the distribution of living spaces—materialize in the "distributive lifestyle," through which people manage social and familial relations and sustain their everyday lives amid economic and social uncertainty (Kordonsky 2000). These practices shed light on how people in Russia make sense of competing understandings of social responsibility by reinterpreting the idea of self-reliance embedded in the state pronatalist discourses. Against the backdrop of ideologies of self-sufficient nuclear families, marketized social policies, and new property regimes, my interlocutors resignified existing cultural models of kinship care to support themselves and their families and, to use Morris's language (2015), to make their shared and personal lives "habitable." Their revitalized strategies of kinship care, grounded in the Soviet political economy, helped manage shared lives and properties within dramatically different sociopolitical conditions. These strategies had little to do with emerging ideologies of self-sufficient and autonomous family units, but they did reemphasize official expectations expressed in state discourses and programs and revealed conflicting understandings of the nature of social support and care in contemporary Russia.

Notes

1. Abankina and Filatova (2018) further demonstrate that even though the difference between costs of private and public day cares has been getting smaller, it is not because private day cares have become more affordable but because costs associated with public day cares have been rising (voluntary parents' payments, etc.).

2. Anthropologists have begun to deploy the concept of care in relation to kinship, turning from a long-standing analytical tradition of comparative kinship studies to an understanding of kinship as a symbolic system (Kuper 2018). Set in motion by David Schneider's work on American kinship and fueled by theoretical developments in feminist anthropology, new kinship studies in anthropology have been concerned with the ways kinship is created, negotiated, reconfigured, and dismissed through practices of care (Carsten 2004; Franklin and McKinnon 2001; McKinnon and Cannell 2013). In this direction, kinship serves as an imaginary matrix through which to define and articulate different forms of belonging and relatedness (Borneman 1992; Sahlins 2011a; Weston 1991). However influential this approach has been, the idea of kinship and care as shaped by amity and diffused solidarity, advanced by Marshall Sahlins's famous account of mutuality of being (Sahlins 2011a, 2011b), often fails to account for the constraints of kinship ties and the obligations and coercion that often inform these relations of care (for this critique, see, for example, Mody 2020; Shryock 2013).

3. In postsocialist societies, relations between kin, living and dead, have been transformed through restitution of property confiscated by socialist states. In Romania, for example, while presocialist owners claimed properties through genealogical idioms of blood relations and descent, current tenants, in an attempt to deemphasize the "blood" idiom, mix definitions of kin relations with a sense of place (Chelcea 2003, 2016). New restrictive

memory laws in many postsocialist states (Gutman 2016; Koposov 2022) have played a role in shaping the meanings and lived experiences of intergenerational family relations as well (Leykin 2022).

4. Steven Kotkin (1991) describes Soviet industrial enterprises as a sort of welfare agency, distributing benefits to employees.

5. See introduction for more information on Maternity Capital.

6. The rise in fertility reached its peak in 2015 and then reversed. The timing of the renewed decline coincided with the beginning of the reproductive phase for a small cohort of women born in the 1990s, during a period of dramatic fertility decline. The effect of this fertility decline on general population growth could not be remedied even by the annexation of Crimea in 2014 (Popova 2016).

7. Larisa was not the only interlocutor whose children had such a large age difference. The changing age of natality and improved economic conditions in the late 2000s, as well as the state support that likely stimulated deferred births among older women who had their first child at a much younger age, have contributed to the age difference among children within Russian families (Popova 2016).

8. The retirement structure in post-Soviet Russia remained intact until the 2018 pension reforms. In 2018, the age of retirement for both men and women was set to rise gradually over ten years to sixty and sixty-five, respectively (*RIA* 2021).

9. On the Russian concept of *khoziain* in the context of post-Soviet market reforms, see Cherkaev 2023; Rogers 2006. On the gendered character of the concept, see Rogers 2005.

10. Grandmothers' assistance has been naturalized as an unpaid and unreciprocated form of care in other postsocialist contexts too (see, for example, Ghodsee and Bernardi 2012; Thelen and Leutloff-Grandits 2010; Thelen, Thiemann, and Roth 2014).

11. The situation shifted slightly in 2016, when a new law introduced penalties for working while drawing pension (Ashwin, Keenan, and Kozina 2021).

12. Interestingly enough, during my fieldwork, the option of a father taking maternity leave instead of the mother came up only once—and even then, it was as a joke between a husband and a wife meant to offset anxieties in anticipation of a new baby. According to the statistics published by the Social Insurance Fund of the Russian Federation, the share of fathers who took paternity leave in 2019 was 2 percent (Bagirova, Blednova, and Neshataev 2023).

13. The Soviets abolished private property and created a legal construct of socialist property, managed by city soviets, cooperatives, and departments (*vedomstva*). However, the state did have a concept of personal property (*lichnaia sobstvennost'*), justified by the fact that such ownership could not lead to profit (could not be sold or bought) and had as its source the worker's income in the socialist economy (Smith 2010). In effect, personal property was "theorized as each individual citizen's stake in the inviolable commons," which was the Soviet state-led economy (Cherkaev 2023, 20).

14. The *kommunalka* was valorized in Soviet literature and popular culture, and it remains an object of fascination in post-Soviet culture (Vepreva and Osminkin 2022; Vorobyova 2015; Utekhin 2004). Russian anthropologist Ilya Utekhin and his colleagues have created a museum of the *kommunalka* that offers virtual tours through different facets of communal living in the Soviet Union: https://kommunalka.colgate.edu/cfm/about.cfm?Open.

15. For historians of the Soviet Union and the post-Stalin period in particular, studying housing policies and their materialization opens a window to understanding the Soviet

concept of the communist way of life (*kommunisticheskii byt*). Focusing on the relationship between the state and its citizens, this research is particularly attentive to the gap between what was promised and what was delivered. The gap, the research demonstrates, opened a space where residents could express dissatisfaction and challenge policymakers' and architects' cultural authority to dictate an appropriate socialist way of life (Harris 2013; Smith 2010; Varga-Harris 2015).

16. Boris Davydov, *Family Portrait*, 1972–1974. http://artkatalog.radmuseumart.ru/ru /fullsearch/48535. The painting is part of the collection held in the Radischev Museum in Saratov. Despite multiple requests for permission to use a reproduction of the painting in the book, my requests were denied, as the museum was reluctant to grant permission to a foreign institution or individual.

17. Attwood (2010) gives several dramatic examples of just how convoluted and fragile these exchange chains could be.

CONCLUSION

Caring Like a State in a Time of War

The Brutality of State Care

*C*ARING *LIKE A STATE* HAS OFFERED THE NATIONAL preoccupation with demography in Russia as a lens through which to understand relations of care between state and citizens. The study has focused on what it means, to paraphrase James Scott (1998), to care like a state, but it has also considered how efforts to care for population resonate and clash with existing cultural models of care and support in contemporary Russia. By linking the distinct worlds of population experts, state and nonstate actors, and ordinary citizens, the book has examined diverse meanings of care produced by Russia's population problem.

Population experts, whose presence in public discourse during Russia's years of heightened preoccupation with demography was unprecedented, placed ideas about the behavior of individuals at the core of state discourse about reversing unfavorable population trends. Interactions between population experts and state bureaucrats provided ideological orientations and assumptions that shaped the dominant understanding of the problem of population, as well as possible solutions to it. These paradigms, in turn, determined which state programs were seen as capable of altering population dynamics and made the Maternity Capital program—aimed at facilitating individual change through marketized means—the state's flagship policy.

Interactions among population experts, state agents, and nonstate organizations have also been influential in the process by which so-called traditional values became dominant in popular and state discourses about the demographic crisis. Portrayed as a self-sufficient, autonomous unit absorbing the risks of raising children, the fit or normal family (*blagopoluchnaia sem'ia*) became the target of demographic policies and the anticipated driver of positive population change, the entity in which the state invested its caring efforts.

State discourse on the demographic crisis in Russia underscores the fusing between neoconservative and neoliberal ideas about population and state care; widely circulated conservative ideas about traditional family values and therapeutically imbued ideas about the self have been incorporated into the monetization of social welfare policies (e.g., the Maternal Capital policy) and the outsourcing of social support to nonprofit and for-profit organizations. Russian citizens responded to these family ideologies and marketized social policies by tapping into cultural models of kinship care institutionalized under the Soviet political regime and its economic policies. They also utilized the logic of privatized care embedded in marketized pronatalist policies and family ideologies to sustain personal networks of care and support.

* * *

The Russian invasion of Ukraine on February 24, 2022, prompted me to reflect once again on the idea of care as a framework through which to understand the demographic crisis in Putin's Russia. In the days and weeks following the invasion, I watched the news incessantly, listening with horror to reports of tens of thousands dying, Ukrainian women and children fleeing the country, and Russian soldiers perpetrating atrocities and sexual violence.[1] Russian soldiers quickly became cannon fodder, their death toll during the first year of the war exceeding the official number of Soviet soldiers killed over nine years of war in Afghanistan (*Mediazona* 2023a).[2] Hundreds of thousands of Russian citizens left the country either in protest or to avoid being drafted (*Novaya Gazeta* 2024).[3] The unfolding tragedy made me question the use of the word *care* because of its typically positive meaning. At the same time, I was acutely aware of how the new population tragedy unraveling in both Ukraine and Russia accentuated the malevolent aspects of state care described here.

Since the invasion of Ukraine, mortality rates have continued to rise, most likely due to Russian men dying on the battlefield. Already declining birthrates fell even further, intensifying the general population decline (*Moscow Times* 2023, 2024c; Sergeev 2024). Politicians continue to lament Russian women's refusal to follow the state's imperative of raising the birthrate. The state continues to criminalize sexuality and advance conservative ideologies of so-called traditional values. Despite the regime's recurrent campaigns to promote traditional values, divorce rates have been rising, and in 2024, eight out of ten marriages ended in divorce (*TASS* 2024b). State programs continue to offer welfare incentives to reproduce but also advance more repressive means, such as restricting women's rights to abortion, erroneously insisting that doing so will increase fertility (Preobrazhensky 2023). In the regime's political rhetoric, these restrictive initiatives are a form of benevolent care, protecting Russian citizens from the forces threatening their values and virtuous way of life.

As I have shown in this book, the language of demography as the vernacular of state care has played a crucial role in determining what behaviors and social aspirations are considered worthy of state support and protection. Since Putin's ascendance to power, one of the most important conditions for receiving state care has been staying away from anything that can be interpreted as remotely political. Those unwilling to accept the rules of the game are not only prevented from receiving care but also likely punished for their disobedience. The depoliticization of citizenship has thus been central to the Russian state's vision of state care.

In this open-ended concluding chapter, I discuss the depoliticization of citizenship as foundational to the relations of care between the Russian state and its citizens. I also sketch preliminary thoughts about how the invasion of Ukraine, the occupation of several regions in Ukraine, and the effects of prolonged war mark a new stage in the relations of care between the Russian state and its citizens. Further militarization of the language of demography and political rhetoric of expanding territorial borders, I suggest, have infused the state's thinking about population with a new imperial imagination and changed the parameters of which population the state is willing to care for and protect. These processes foreground the benevolent-malevolent nature of state care personified in Putin's image as chief care provider, willing to grant care to those who accept the regime's ideological imperatives.

The Depoliticization of Citizenship as a Foundation for Providing State Care

I collected the majority of my ethnographic data about the Russian state's endeavor to solve its population problem during the period in which, along with visibly autocratic components of contemporary Russian political culture, the post-Soviet state made extensive use of scientific expertise and democratic tools as foundations for its social policies. Thus, the work practices of population experts were pulled directly from the political democracy playbook. As experts, they responded to the moral demands of the political regime by providing a scientific foundation for administrative efforts to improve the country's population dynamics while claiming relatively independent authority grounded in scientific objectivity (Porter 1995, 2009).

For me, the production of knowledge about population in post-Soviet Russia presents a telling variation on the tension between politics and expertise in democracy. Unlike in modern liberal democracies, where, at least in theory, scientific expertise fulfills the political system's need for transparency and participation, in post-Soviet Russia, scientific expertise (in this case, socio-demographic knowledge of polity) has been separated from the issue of informed participation of citizenry. The abundance and transparency of statistical data pertaining to population dynamics, as well as their frequent use in public discussions, are examples of how scientific knowledge can be displayed for public consumption in a more or less transparent manner without creating a basis for popular political participation.

The invasion of Ukraine on February 24, 2022, and the ensuing war further crystalized the limits of post-Soviet democratization, accentuating lack of citizen participation as a major component in the state's approach to providing care. As the country was thrown into full-fledged authoritarian mode, the role of social knowledge and relative autonomy of scientific expertise were undeniably reduced to serving the regime's authoritarian machine.[4] Quite literally as I was first writing this paragraph in 2023, a news alert popped up on my screen informing me that the state Duma had passed a law authorizing the government to conceal from the public, at its full discretion, statistical data of any kind, thus putting an end to a period of relative transparency of statistical knowledge in Russia (*RBC* 2023). In 2024, in its annual report, the Russian central statistical agency (Rosstat) for the first time in post-Soviet history concealed information on categories of external causes of deaths, which independent journalists had previously used to estimate the number of Russian soldiers killed in the war (*Meduza* 2024b, 2024c).[5]

The regime's fusing of authoritarian political agendas with neoliberal economic policies enabled the depoliticization of citizenship long before the invasion of a neighboring country was even imaginable, leading to what Jeremy Morris (2021) has called "neoliberal authoritarianism" (see also Ishchenko and Zhuravlev 2022). Since the completion of my fieldwork and the beginning of the war, processes of disengagement have become even more prominent. Following the invasion, the regime, building on general political apathy, has tried to communicate that everything is going according to plan. Yet already in March 2022—save for compulsory military conscription, which did not begin until late September 2022—the country was under de facto martial law. A first wave of protests against the war was brutally quashed, and repressive laws criminalizing criticism of Russian troops and government were quickly introduced, leading to thousands of arrests (Human Rights Watch 2022b; OVD-Info 2022; *Reuters* 2022a). Human rights organizations were banned, and many socially oriented NGOs lost funding, while NGOs loyal to the government and supporting the war received unprecedentedly large grants (*Re: Russia* 2023a). Although the squelching of independent media and investigative journalism had begun much earlier, it reached a decisive phase during the first months of the invasion (Greene 2022; Troianovski and Safronova 2022).[6] Russian authorities effectively outlawed any form of social or political protest. In fact, even spontaneous and unsanctioned acts of support were not particularly welcomed, signaling the citizenry to stay away from any kind of politics—loyal or oppositional (Zagovora 2022).

Watching it all, I was at a loss for words. I texted and called my friends and interlocutors in Russia. I did not hear enthusiastic support for the invasion, as the Russian state-owned opinion poll agencies claimed (VCIOM 2022), but some spoke in half sentences, not quite fearing the authorities but also not wanting to take chances (*ne ispytyvat' sud'bu*), as one of them told me. I myself was not sure whether I was endangering them by speaking openly about the war, the use of the word *war* itself having been banned (AFP 2022). In a feeble attempt to justify the invasion, some of my interlocutors, while acknowledging the tragedy, used popular cultural clichés, some of them deliberately promoted by state propaganda: "we'll never know the whole truth [about the war]" (*my vsei pravdy nikogda ne uznaem*) and "those in charge must know what they're talking about" (*naverkhu ved' ne duraki sidiat, oni znaiut, cho govoriat*).[7] Others, although generally critical of the invasion, suggested that losing the war would bring Russia to its knees (*postavit Rossiiu na koleni*), which the country cannot afford; it has no choice but to continue fighting and win. Those expressing shame about what their country is doing to its neighbors tried to distance themselves from the atrocities done in their name, relying on another popular cliché: "I'm just a simple person, what can I do?" (*Ia chelovek malen'kii, chto ia mogu sdelat'?*)

Jeremy Morris (2022) describes these reactions as a form of "defensive consolidation" that, unlike the concept of "rally around the flag," is "not directly connected to expressions of patriotism, or nationalism, or enthusiasm for either the 'special military operation' or the Russian government" (260). Supporting the war, he claims, might be giving Russian citizens recognition of a more general sense of despair, frustration, and disappointment (Morris 2022). Recent independent studies based on ethnographic research and hundreds of interviews conducted in the first two years of the war have examined how Russian citizens express support for the invasion, voice dissent, or claim ambiguity. The studies have convincingly demonstrated that the majority of Russian citizens simultaneously support and do not support the war. Their position is best described as passive nonresistance to the war (Erpyleva, Kappinen, and PS LAB Team 2022, 2024; Erpyleva and Savelyeva 2023; Kappinen and Zhuravlev 2024). The regime's deliberate efforts to mold Russian citizens as uninterested in and indifferent to politics played an important role in shaping these reactions to the war (Greene 2017; Ishchenko and Zhuravlev 2022; Yudin 2017).

In the public imagination, Putin's ascendance to power in 2000 is associated with his promise to care for citizens by improving the standard of living. For my interlocutors who lived through the nineties, the transition of power from Boris Yeltsin to Vladimir Putin was associated with a new and relatively stable economy. They spoke of employment opportunities, bank credits, and summer vacations abroad becoming available during this period. The common denominator in these conversations was that the state (*vlast'*) was taking care of them by making their lives normal (*normal'naia zhizn'*). Enabled by favorable macroeconomic trends in relation to the Russian extractive economy, these new and improved social and economic conditions played a part in compensating for the chaos and empty pockets of "the wild 1990s" (*likhie devianostye*) (Levada Center 2014). The state was finally taking care of its citizens.

However, these developments came with a price—conditions that comprised the transactional relations of care I describe in the book. Simply put, in return for increasing economic stability, Russian citizens were expected not to interfere in the broadly defined political sphere. Sanctions against those who dared to intervene, whether financial elites, journalists, or ordinary citizens, came fast and heavy. Mikhail Khodorkovsky, CEO of Yukos Oil Company, was believed in 2003 to be one of the richest men in Russia; he paid a heavy price for his political ambitions, spending ten years in prison (Sakwa 2014).[8] From the beginning of Putin's first term in 2000, any media outlet that criticized him or the government's policies became a target of persecution (Roudakova 2017).[9]

The crackdown on political and civil activism intensified in the wake of the Bolotnaya social protests against the falsification of elections, culminating with the introduction of the Foreign Agent Law in 2012 (Flikke 2016, 2018; Moser and Skripchenko 2018).[10] The state was initially cautious in implementing the law, mostly using it to outlaw foreign NGOs; in later years, however, and increasingly since the invasion, the definition of *foreign influence* has become much more expansive, and the law is now explicitly used to simply mark dissent (Human Rights Watch 2022a; *TASS* 2023).[11] The depoliticization of citizenship has been further institutionalized through a new political culture in which quintessential tools of democracy, such as elections, referenda, and opinion polls, are reduced to a performative function of validating the regime's legitimacy. As Gregory Yudin (2020, 2022b) has convincingly argued, rather than representing popular opinion or popular will, polls are used to assert the legitimacy of the regime's predetermined political decisions.

Thus, for over twenty years, Putin's political machine has been working tirelessly, through both positive and repressive means, to create depoliticized subjects who do not interfere in the political sphere but are dependent on the state as a main caregiver (Kolesnikov 2023; Shulman 2022; Yudin 2022a). These processes of disengagement are at the heart of how people in post-Soviet Russia sustain themselves and their social relations in an increasingly neoliberal market economy. Russians have constructed various means of capitalizing on state institutions as a resource without engaging with the state politically (Kordonsky 2016). Neoliberal forms of exchange at the heart of new social policies, manifested in the Maternity Capital policy, have become a technology through which state institutions govern disengaged and depoliticized subjects. Russian citizens are compelled to relinquish political demands in exchange for certain forms of state care; their ability to care for themselves and their families depends on their depoliticized and disengaged citizenship.

My interlocutors' responses, neither actively supporting nor openly opposing the war, illustrated a detached engagement with the state (Erpyleva and Savelyeva 2023; *Re: Russia* 2023c). One of my interlocutors confessed that since the invasion, her family has spent more time in the dacha they bought in a nearby village during more economically prosperous times: "I'm so glad we bought this house ten years ago," she told me. "We use any spare moment to go there, just us, even if it means we have to spend a lot of time commuting to work." Essentially a form of "internal migration" (*vnutrenniaia emigratsiia*) (Filipova 2022), the dacha provides a shelter from the reality of the war. The war has intensified both the retreat from state omnipresence and reliance on networks of personal relationships (Yaffa 2023), rendering practices of disengagement Russian citizens have been honing for over twenty years reliable instruments for coping with uncertainty.

The results of popular opinion polls conducted by several polling companies that show overwhelming approval of the invasion can also be refracted through depoliticized citizenship. When analyzed through the lens of disengaged relations with the state, rates of approval look more like lip service to the regime. That is, polls indicate the level of support Russian citizens know the regime expects them to express, and by demonstrating approval (i.e., what is expected of them), they expect the state to leave them alone; their relations with the state remain disengaged from personal and familial relations of care and support.

When I spoke with my long-term interlocutors, usually on WhatsApp or Telegram,[12] through many awkward silences indicating efforts to make sense of the brutal new reality, one thing was absolutely clear—relying on personal networks of support had become a very important and yet precarious strategy for managing reality. The war and the deep social, political, and economic crisis it has engendered have foregrounded the importance but also the fragility of relations of care and support between individuals, in which families, friends, neighbors, and the state have all been entangled. One interlocutor relayed with horror a story of her friend whose husband supports the war, whereas she and her son do not: "Can you imagine what it means to be part of this family?" she exclaimed (for similar stories about conflicts within families, see Gorin 2023).

In addition to disengagement molded by Putin's regime, many of my interlocutors invoked Soviet-era practices for surviving shortages when international sanctions began to deepen the economic crisis. Over a WhatsApp call, Vika, a fifty-seven-year-old mother of two adult daughters, complained offhandedly about rising prices. Having recently retired from her job as a kindergarten music teacher, Vika spends a significant amount of time helping her daughters raise their children. When I asked how they were managing, she assured me it was not that bad: "So we won't be buying a new shirt or a new dress. We know how it works." Now that she has retired, she told me half-jokingly, she has more time to go back to "our good old Soviet tradition of pickling everything" (*nasha dobraia sovetskaia traditsiia vse konservirovat'*) in preparation for winter. Although she had not used them recently, she still has recipes her mother gave her a long time ago.[13]

Nikolai Travkin, who in 1990 founded the Russian Democratic Party and was a member of Yeltsin's government and of the Duma, has been a prolific and sharp-tongued commentator on Russia's domestic politics. In a post on Telegram, he reflects on reports describing the impact of international sanctions on the Russian economy.[14] He imagines a dialogue with a friend who says, with a note of sadness, "We've lived our lives, but it's the youth I feel sorry for." Travkin disagrees. Unlike the younger generations, his own "generation of pensioners," who lived through the Soviet planned economy, with its perpetual shortages, knows how to adapt to new economic conditions. This expertise will soon be seen as useful and valuable, and their grandchildren will appreciate what the older generations can teach: "By the time the youth realize what 'no more than one kilo [of something] to a pair of hands' [*v odni ruki bol'she kilogramma ne davat'*] even means, you and I have already been standing in three different queues to get that thing . . . our life experience, Misha, will finally be in demand [*vostrebovan*]. Our grandchildren will stop addressing us as if we were some sort of relic and will begin to respect us" (Travkin 2023). If the war has accelerated the transformation of relations of care between state and citizens into relations of disengagement, it has also turned relations of care based on personal and familial networks into a prominent yet fragile social resource, vulnerable to the uncertainty and potential cruelty of the state.

Weaponizing Demography During the War

As the war escalated the rate of population decline, the threat of underpopulation again became a touchstone of domestic and international debate about Russia's uncertain future. During my research, when speaking about the demographic situation, population experts and political contenders alike did not shy away from using militarized metaphors of foreign invasion and direct threats to sovereignty. Depending on the speaker, these threats took the form of imagined migrants replacing the dying-out Russian men or of a conspiracy on the part of other nations to overpower Russia (see chapter 3). Since February 2022, discussions about population dynamics have been further militarized, and the imagined external threat to Russia's sovereignty has been exercised as a central justification for the invasion of Ukraine. Prompting anxiety over dwindling population numbers or evoking fear of foreign others overpowering the country, the projected demographic hell became a major rhetorical device employed by both supporters of the war and those who openly opposed it.

Presenting Russia's demographic dynamics, an article in *The Economist* depicted "Russia's population nightmare" (*The Economist* 2023). Written in the genre of "demodystopia" (Domingo 2008), it presented the country's demographic dynamics as sinister, leading inevitably to near collapse of the state.[15] In domestic discussions in Russia, as the war was ravaging Ukraine, fear of population implosion and its threat to the country's sovereignty shaped the rhetoric of politicians and state officials. Conservative ideologies about family, gender, and sexuality as well as criminalization of the LGBTQ community were seen as necessary to reverse troubling population trends. The idea of creating a state-sponsored think tank dedicated to demographic policymaking—a proposal familiar to many post-Soviet demographers—reemerged (Polnomochnyi predstavitel' Prezidenta v Tsentral'nom federal'nom okruge 2022). Putin's propagandists and political contenders demanded a proactive approach to encouraging families to have more children. Putin himself called for programs to establish families with three to four children as "the new normal" (*Izvestiia* 2022; *Moscow Times* 2024b).[16]

After signing the presidential decree on so-called traditional values as the foundation of Russia's sovereignty, the state Duma created a special working group dedicated to policies aimed at protecting these values. During one of its meetings, Dmitry Gusev, representing the Just Russia Party, described the demographic problem: "We're dying out. Maternity Capital is good, but it's not enough. It was helpful in encouraging women to have children at all, but now our goal should be to urge them to give birth to multiple children [*chtoby rozhali mnogo*]" (Mukhametshina 2023). He estimated that for Russia's population to grow, each family must have at least four children. After a short pause and likely a few gasps of disbelief, he spoke about the importance of balancing women's reproductive careers with careers outside the home: "Take for instance Anna Karenina. By the age of 30, she had a school-age son, but her story ended badly. Had she had a chance to build a career like a modern woman can, it would have had a different ending" (Mukhametshina 2023). In other words, women need to realize their reproductive potential but also be economically independent and self-fulfilled. It is unclear from the journalistic report whether Gusev was being intentionally funny or was aware of the irony of his suggestions. Nevertheless, he encapsulated the marketized pronatalism enmeshed with conservative ideologies I have described in the book, fortified by a sense of urgency and a heightened fear of population implosion.

Many emergency measures to fight population decline suggested since the beginning of the war in Ukraine have roots in Stalin-era population policies discussed in the first chapter of the book. During a meeting organized by the Presidium of the Russian Academy of the Sciences, Robert Nigmatulin, an eighty-two-year-old applied mathematician and former candidate for president of the Russian Academy of the Sciences, suggested that the severity of the situation requires resurrecting measures from the Soviet period. In order to boost birthrates, he argued, the state must reintroduce the bachelor tax (*Interfax* 2022). The tax on bachelors and small families, known in late-Soviet vernacular as the "tax on testicles," was introduced in 1941, as World War II was ravaging the country. It sought to incentivize childbirth by penalizing childless single men and married couples with fewer than three children. Later amendments canceled the penalty for married couples with children, but until the dissolution of the Soviet Union in 1991, the tax applied to single men and childless married couples (Ironside 2017). Proposals to reinstate the tax were introduced several times during my fieldwork but never legislatively enacted (Filippova 2017; see also Ironside 2017, 876).

In August 2022, in a highly symbolic act, Putin signed a decree reviving the Soviet-era honorary title of Mother Heroine, introduced by Stalin in 1944, bestowed on women with ten or more living children. The title qualifies such women to receive one million Russian rubles when their tenth child turns one (*TASS* 2022a). Given the very small number of families with ten or more children in Russia, the decree seems performative, symbolically empowering the state to benefit those who fulfill its demographic needs. The state also sought to make divorce more expensive, raising the tax on divorce from 650 RUB to 5000 RUB (*RBC* 2024), another measure that bears the legacy of Stalin-era family policies initiated in 1944 (Nakachi 2021). Invoking penalty-oriented taxes as an instrument for facilitating childbirth demonstrates the urgency of the situation and the sacrifice required of Russian citizens in this demographic battle.

The language of demography has become an important rhetorical tool in the revanchist politics of the current regime. Tapping into anti-Western sentiments and xenophobia, political contenders invoke demography as a weapon with which anti-Russian forces are endeavoring to destroy Russian sovereignty. Thus, one of the main reasons for urgently protecting traditional values and mores has been the impact "of the destructive ideological influence on Russia's citizens that threatens the demographic situation in the country" (President of Russia 2022d, 4). To fight this destructive influence, conservative values have been presented as a positive force capable of protecting Russia's population, political sovereignty, and national unity (President of Russia 2022d; *TASS* 2022b). Large families (i.e., families with more than three children) have been championed as the foundation of such traditional values. Once they become the social norm, it has been argued, these families will be effective weapons in the country's battle against demographic challenges (*Izvestiia* 2022).

In the summer of 2022, at a meeting organized by the United Russia Party, participants—none of whom had any professional qualifications related to demography—discussed vaguely defined proactive measures to facilitate childbirth. Favored by Putin and his propaganda machine, the alarmist language of the meeting was grounded in familiar anti-Western rhetoric justifying the military invasion of Ukraine as necessary to protect Russia's sovereignty and special path (*osobyi put'*). One senator, Margarita Pavlova, called demography "a soft weapon, used by our geopolitical enemies in their mental war against the Russian world [*Russkii mir*]."[17] To win this war, Pavlova continued, there is an urgent need to fight enemies with strategies that motivate women to have more children, combating the invasion of "values foreign to us" (*chuzhdykh nam tsennostei*) (Katrenko 2022). Without specifying what such strategies might entail, Pavlova invoked the distinction between the good and bad use of demography. *They* use demography to destroy *us*. We use it to defend and protect our traditional values and beliefs, defining our special path to sovereignty (Dmitriev 2022). In this us versus them reiteration of Russia's population drama, a familiar form of demodystopia emerges: the West is threatened by Russia's commitment to traditional values and is thus out to get Russia, but for Russia to combat the West, its population must grow by any and all means.

Anxiety over dwindling population numbers and fear of being overrun by the growing world population—the ultimate form of demodystopia—have been particularly visible in the myth of the golden billion (*zolotoi milliard*), which has gained traction and become increasingly popular among Russian political elites since the invasion of Ukraine. The golden billion has come to signify certain nations in the global North conspiring to expropriate wealth and resources, including human resources, from the rest of the world, particularly from Russia.[18] Similar to a more sociological distinction between the global North and South, this conspiracy theory accentuates a shared will and a secret, coordinated plot between actors of the golden billion, whose endgame is to make everyone outside the golden billion powerless and impotent.

Nikolai Patrushev, secretary of the Security Council and former director of the Federal Security Service of Russia (FSB), favors conspiracy theories about the destructive influence of the West in general and the golden billion in particular. In an interview, he claimed that under the guise of struggling for democracy, freedom, and human rights, "'Anglo-Saxons' [part of the conspiracy] have embarked on the project of implementing their 'golden billion doctrine'. . . . Because only a limited number of people can prosper, in this struggle for resources, they [Anglo-Saxons] are after us [Russia]" (Efimov 2022). Addressing the international economic forum in Saint Petersburg, Putin accused Western elites of being "trapped in their own illusions about the countries outside of the so-called golden billion, . . . considering everyone else . . . as their backyard . . . and themselves as exceptional. If they are exceptional, then everyone else is second rate" (President of Russia 2022a).

Using the image of the golden billion interchangeably with that of the collective West, Putin warned Russians that the expansionist logic of the West and its harmful influence threaten the sovereignty of the country. Using language reminiscent of the Nazis, he suggested that a "self-cleansing" (*samoochishchenie*) is necessary to free Russia from Western influences perpetrated by the so-called local fifth column of national traitors (President of Russia 2022c; see also Shchipkov 2022). The Russian people, he assured his audience, would know how to distinguish between real patriots and national traitors and would "simply spit them out like a small fly that accidently flew into their mouth" (President of Russia 2022c). Recognizing traitors and distinguishing between them and patriots is necessary for determining who deserves the state's care and who should be excluded from it.

Whether or not Putin and his inner circle sincerely believe in this conspiracy theory or are using it opportunistically is irrelevant. More important is that Western conspiracies against Russia have become a legitimate point of reference for a general revanchist political ideology of us versus them, the embodiment in Russian popular culture of which Eliot

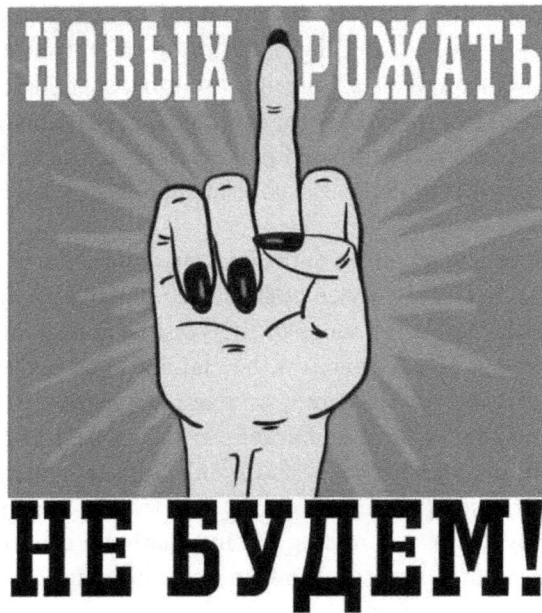

Figure 6.1. A call to refuse conscription following the announcement of partial mobilization in September 2022 with a caption: "We refuse to give birth to new ones." Credit: Roman Super.

Borenstein (2019) wrote about so eloquently.[19] Conspiracies serve as proof that the West is working tirelessly to destroy Russia, to extricate its wealth through material as well as human resources. The discourse of over- and underpopulation (the two sides of demodystopia) and population numbers themselves, far from statistically dry (Kravel-Tovi 2016), provide a plethora of symbolic instruments to feed the regime's political appetite for resentment and revanchist politics.

Those opposing the military invasion have used demography as a political rhetorical device as well. Use of popular tropes from the discourse on the demographic crisis especially intensified following the announcement of partial mobilization and annexation of eastern Ukrainian territories in late September 2022. In a public appeal, a Russian Orthodox priest criticized women for helping their sons avoid conscription and suggested that if Russian women had more children, and if they followed God's command to "be fruitful and multiply" rather than having abortions, they would have an easier time allowing their children to sacrifice themselves in the war in Ukraine (Malyutin 2022). In response, critics of the invasion satirized the priest's approach to human life, cynically employing a popular phrase of unclear provenance: "No worries, chicks will give birth to new ones" (*baby novykh narozhaiut*) (Maysuryan 2022). This popular saying has been ridiculed in antiwar statements, becoming a popular meme on social media. For example, after the announcement of partial mobilization in September 2022, Russian journalist Roman Super employed a variation of the saying on Telegram, publishing a call to refuse conscription: "tear up your conscription notices" (*rvite povestki*). Under a meme of a hand with painted nails and a raised middle finger, he wrote: "we refuse to give birth to new ones" (*novykh rozhat' ne budem*) (Super 2022) (fig. 6.1). His play on the saying "No worries, chicks will give birth to new ones" demonstrates both its absurdity and the creative resistance the Russian domestic opposition to the war has become known for.

Imperial Scaling of the Population Problem

Following the same conscription announcement, Andrey Desnitsky, a publicist and humanities scholar who quit his position at the Russian Academy of Sciences and left Russia in 2022 in opposition to the war, wrote on Telegram, "For a long time, the leader claimed demography to be the major issue facing the country. What an unusual way to solve the problem" (Desnitsky 2022). The majority of his followers seemed to be in on the joke, and some responded with a similar level of sarcasm: "Not a big deal. Chicks will give birth to new ones" (*Da ladno, baby novykh narazhaiut*) or "No population— no problem" (*net naseleniia—net problem*). One response stood out, though. Referring to the popular referendum, a poll haphazardly conducted in four Ukrainian regions under Russian military rule, a follower named Ksena replied, "The population of Russia will increase by about 5–6 million people." Someone else replied, "These territories belong to Ukraine, so no, it won't." To that, Ksena responded, "These territories will become Russia. Very soon. If you don't like it, there's nothing I can do about it."

Likely supporting the invasion, Ksena communicated Putin's expansionist and imperialist ambitions of waging war on sovereign Ukraine. The comment echoed an ideological premise Putin and his supporters have forwarded to justify the invasion: Ukraine became an independent state by an unfortunate historical mistake made by the Bolsheviks, who turned an inseparable part of historic Russia into a made-up state (President of Russia 2021). Justified by this particular iteration of the region's history and comparing himself to Peter the Great, Putin described the invasion of Ukraine as his historic mission to recapture what was rightfully Russian (*Meduza* 2022b). Tapping into his image as the main consolidator of Russian society (Sharafutdinova 2020), Putin presented Ukraine as having always belonged to Russia and the people who live there as Russians.

These imperial imaginaries inform the ways in which population and its problems have been discussed in Russia since the war. The increasing personalization of political power and crackdown on anyone who criticizes the government go hand in hand with the growing imperial appetite of Putin's regime. Prior to the invasion of Ukraine, the imperial appetite materialized in the second Chechen war—which boosted Putin's consolidation of power—and became entrenched through the Russian-Georgian war in 2008, the annexation of Crimea in 2014, and the ensuing military conflict in eastern Ukraine (Herpen 2015; Matveev 2021). Scholars have addressed these imperial aspirations, analyzing the growing popularity of neo-Eurasianism as a new imperial ideology (Laruelle 2012; Shlapentokh 2007); the ingrained idea of Russia as savior and liberator of others (Kassymbekova and Laruelle 2022); the idea of the Russian world (*Russkii Mir*) as politically and geographically exceeding the boundaries of the nation-state (Beissinger 2015; Suslov 2018); the capitalist logic of Russia's new imperialism (Matveev 2021); and the regime's expansionist tactics in relation to its close neighbors, such as Belarus, Ukraine, and the Central Asian states (Herpen 2015).

When it came to state discourse on population care (*narodosberezhenie*), these imperial tendencies were less evident prior to the invasion of Ukraine in 2022. During my decade of research, expert and popular debate about the population problem as well as pronatalist policies with which the state purported to care for its population were circumscribed by the territorial boundaries of the nation-state—the Russian Federation. Having said that, the idea of restoring national sovereignty beyond Russia's territorial borders did become more prominent in the regime's rhetoric after the annexation of Crimea. At a public event in 2016, when war in Ukraine still seemed unfathomable, Putin asked a nine-year-old student about the territorial borders of the Russian Federation. The student began to answer, "The border goes across the Bering Strait . . ." But Putin cut his answer short: "Wrong. Russia's borders stop nowhere [*granitsy Rossii nigde ne zakanchivaiutsia*]" (*BBC News* 2016). What in 2016 seemed to be just another one of Putin's pugnacious remarks became reality in 2022—a palpable threat of expansion to other neighboring nations, not only Ukraine.

Putin's tendency to deploy the idea of national sovereignty to generate support for imperial expansion has shaped the ways in which the boundaries of population—and more importantly, the relationship between population and national territory—have been imagined in popular and expert discourses about Russia's demographic problem. Following the annexation of Crimea and especially the invasion of Ukraine, the scaling of population, to borrow anthropologist Michal Kravel-Tovi's (2023) concept, through the idiom of forever expanding territorial borders has infused a statistical artifact of population with a new imperial imagination and political poignancy.

This imperial scaling of population has laid bare the question of territorial boundaries that define population as an object of state biopolitical care. The very concept of population—a reified entity driven by a certain set of rules and patterned behaviors that can be statistically disaggregated and made an object of state intervention—was born in the context of the modern nation-state and founded on the conceptualization of population as delineated by clear-cut territorial boundaries (Foucault 2009). In other words, to identify, isolate, and act on the categories, rates, and trends that constitute the statistical construct of population, people must be localized within particular territorial borders (Curtis 2001). Localized in space, the concept of population makes existing social relations observable and legible to the administrative authority of the modern state (Scott 1998; Curtis 2001).

The alignment of population with a specific territory has been a necessary governing tool for nation-states just as for modern empires. Thus, the British project of census making expanded to its colonies in nineteenth-century South Asia. The empire's capacity to produce knowledge about population in its colonies was heavily dependent on the administrative ability to define clear territorial borders populated by different people (Cohn 1987, 1996; Mamdani 1996).The alignment between territory and population was also relevant when the Russian regime materialized its imperial aspirations in the annexation of Crimea in 2014. To efficiently render those living in the peninsula an object of state intervention, an early major administrative project realigned territory with population through a comprehensive census conducted the same year. Through the census—an important political instrument of the state—Crimea became part of the Russian political entity, making it possible to execute state power in the new territory. Indeed, as early as January 2015, Crimea had been incorporated into all national calculations conducted by the Central Statistical Bureau (Rosstat) (Surinov 2014). Measuring Crimea's population and thus making it legible constituted one of the state's first power performances, localizing its new political subjects and enclosing the population within new and expanded territorial borders.

Despite the Soviet state's complex relations with the theory of population (see chapter 1), its capacity to govern depended on an elaborate system of population measurements defined by national territorial borders. The Russian Federation inherited this administrative and conceptual apparatus as well as its practices. The official Russian name for demography, inherited from the Soviet period, is *nauka o narodonaselenii*: the science of people residing in a specific territory. The name clearly denotes the territorial component inherent in the concept of population. Population as an object of state care is delineated by the boundaries of the nation-state—the Russian Federation. In post-Soviet Russia before the invasion of Ukraine, despite the growing imperial appetite of Putin's regime, this localized conceptualization of population informed discussions about Russia's demographic problem. When concerns about falling birthrates or low life expectancy were raised, assertions were based on numerical expressions and codifications of concerns within the boundaries of the nation-state. State policies were invoked as having a primary responsibility for turning those trends around. When speaking about caring for the population, state policies were imagined as applying to people residing within the borders of the nation-state.

The war and haphazard annexation of new provinces in Ukraine have unleashed an increasingly capacious definition of the country's population as exceeding the territorial boundaries of the Russian nation-state. It impacted how the state identifies the boundaries of the population it purports to care for and protect. In February 2022, several days prior to the invasion, when observers were still trying to convince themselves and others that the buildup of troops was only a power play and that Putin would not dare invade Ukraine, Putin held a televised meeting of the state Security Council during which the recognition (or annexation) of two separatist states in the east of Ukraine (DNR and LNR) was at stake (President of Russia 2022b). In this carefully crafted televised performance of power, participants talked about concerns for the population living in these territories. Viacheslav Volodin, speaker of the state Duma, spoke about the urgency of the decision because of the state's responsibility to protect more than a million citizens in Donbass who had already applied to become Russian citizens. Valentina Matviyenko, a seasoned politician and the only woman on the council, urged members to immediately recognize the independence of these political entities because "for Ukraine, it [the Donbass region] is just a territory, and for Russia, it's about people, and it doesn't matter if they're Russians or Ukrainians." The recognition should be immediate, she continued, because only Russia cares about the people living in those territories (Mukhametshina and Grobman 2022). In a topsy-turvy manner, the objective of the occupation and resulting territorial expansion were presented as an act of state care—for the population residing in the territories that should be, but were not yet, part of Russia.

On September 30, 2022, in the midst of the brutal war, Putin announced the annexation of new eastern and southern Ukrainian territories. After a bogus referendum conducted by pollsters accompanied by soldiers going door to door to collect votes, Putin signed an accord annexing four occupied provinces in eastern and southern Ukraine—Donesk, Luhansk, Kherson, and Zaporizhzhia oblasts (Kirby 2022). Addressing international audiences, he said, "I want the authorities in Kyiv and their real masters in the West to hear this and everyone else to remember: people living in Lugansk, Donetsk, Zaporozhie and Kherson oblasts are becoming ours forever" (President of Russia 2022b). Repeating his claim that the population of independent Ukraine has been "historically Russian" (*naselenie istoricheskoi Rossii*), unlawfully given by the Bolshevik government to the new Soviet republic of Ukraine, Putin presented the occupation and war as acts of consolidating Russia and restoring historical justice (Sharafutdinova 2020). In this rhetoric, Russia's population exceeds its territorial borders, and Putin's mission has been to realign the two by returning to Russia its rightfully owned territories. People in these provinces were "becoming ours" not by moving into Russia but rather by having territorial borders moved to include them.

However, the annexation of these provinces challenges the conceptualization of population as a territorially bounded object of state intervention, insofar as population and territory could not be easily aligned when it came to the new occupied provinces. Large parts of these provinces, although declared Russian, remained under Ukraine's de facto control (Harding, Koshiw, and Beaumont 2022; Smirnov 2022). Early in the war, Russia began losing its territorial grip over parts of all annexed provinces except Zaporizhzhia, and in November 2022, Ukrainian forces regained control over the administrative capital of the Kherson region, the only capital captured by the Russian forces since the beginning of the war (Gutiérrez and Kirk 2023). The status of the occupied provinces in both political rhetoric and state administrative decisions remains decidedly vague, oscillating between Russian territories and Russian ex-territories.

The occupation and annexation of these provinces not only revealed Putin's imperial motivations but also highlighted the limits of his intentions in relation to population as an object of state intervention and control. Forged in the political settings of modern nation-states, statistical administration is ill equipped to count populations and measure their movement when territorial borders and populations do not align. In other words, these provinces' political limbo poses a considerable challenge to the work of the modern state statistical apparatus. With the question of borders unclear and undecided, the Russian state cannot conduct a census in the occupied territories as it did in Crimea. The indeterminate status of these territories has also caused population experts in Russia to deliberate whether movement between the territories and the rest of Russia should be considered internal or international migration (Starostina 2022). There are no reliable numbers about Ukrainian refugees in Russia; those published tend to be manipulated by the propaganda machine.[20] Even less is known about Ukrainian refugees who found themselves in Russia in fleeing the war but whose cities and towns of origin have been declared Russian. Should they be considered refugees or internal migrants moving from one part of Russia to another? The state administration's statistical tools cannot account for the movement of a population undefined by territorial borders. In the meantime, the state simply abstains from counting refugees.

I raised the question of occupied territories and population counting with one of my former interlocutors, who retired several years ago from her position at the institute where I conducted a large portion of my fieldwork. I refrained from asking about the war, but I did ask about the status of people living in the annexed territories (*prisoedinennye territorii*). She was acutely aware of the problem of counting the population, wondering why the state had not conducted a census to estimate who and how many are living there. Looking at the numbers of Ukrainian refugees published in official channels, she estimated that around 3.5 million people live in these provinces but said that there is no way to know for sure—no way to know who they are or whether they are on the move. In James Scott's (1998) terms, they remain illegible to the state. To illustrate the practical side of the problem, she suggested I think about the Maternity Capital policy. Although women living in these provinces are now eligible because they are Russian citizens, there is no way to determine or even estimate how many women might apply. "Imagine an economist," she said, "sitting in his office and trying to estimate how much additional money needs to be put in the state budget to accommodate all the requests. Based on what? There are no numbers. And that's only one welfare policy among many."

It is clear that the state statistical apparatus does not have the conceptual or practical tools to deal with the political limbo of these territories, rendering the population there illegible. This conceptual inconsistency limits the state's capacity to execute power through either welfare or repression and prevents state institutions from practically turning the population into a full-fledged object of state power.

Even though the limbo of the occupied regions of Ukraine restricts the regime's political grip on residents of these territories to a certain extent, the Russian state nevertheless finds ways to care for those living in them. Perhaps the most pernicious manifestation of such care is the regime's forcible deportations of Ukrainian children to Russia and their resocialization into "Russia-loving" subjects (Landay and Lewis 2023; Yapparova 2024).[21] Still, the relative illegibility of the population in the occupied regions restricts Putin's imperial aspirations. It is unclear how state institutions will cope with the imperial scaling of the population—in which the population the state claims to execute its power over is not aligned with a specific territory—and how imperial scaling will affect the development of the war and the state's political grip on the occupied territories in Ukraine. Ultimately, it remains to be seen how Russia will exercise its care for the occupied population.

Notes

1. In February 2023, the Office of the High Commissioner for Human Rights at the United Nations reported that over seven thousand civilians had been killed in Ukraine (OHCHR 2023). Perhaps even more staggering for a country of about forty-three million people before the war was the number of Ukrainian refugees: over eight million were recorded across Europe in late 2022 (UNHCR 2023).

2. Russia has not been disclosing its war casualty numbers. Using publicly available media sources (posts on social media, regional media alerts, and reports from local authorities) and available statistical data, a group of independent Russian journalists and data scientists has been estimating Russian military casualties since the beginning of the war. The group

estimates that over the two first years of the war, at least 75,000 Russian soldiers have been killed, about 120 per day (*Meduza* 2024a, 2024c). These numbers are likely underestimated because they do not include the death toll of those recruited by paramilitary organizations, such as the Wagner private military group. Before the group was dismantled, Russian prisoners constituted up to 80 percent of its mercenary forces; the group essentially used them as cannon fodder (Limaye 2023; Treshchanin 2024). In June 2024, Putin suggested for the first time that over 130,000 Russian soldiers might have been killed in the war (*Moscow Times* 2024a).

3. It is estimated that over 600,000 Russian citizens left the country following the invasion of Ukraine (*Novaya Gazeta* 2024).

4. For a discussion of the fate of academia's relative autonomy in post-Soviet Russia, see Dubrovsky 2022; Sokolov 2022.

5. On the accessibility of information to the public in post-Soviet Russia, see Begtin 2024.

6. Reports about censorship of independent news outlets poured in: TV Rain, the only independent Russian TV news channel, and Echo of Moscow, a liberal radio station, were taken off the air in the very first months of the war (*Reuters* 2022b, 2022d). Following the invasion and the introduction of laws criminalizing anything contradicting the official line, *Novaya Gazeta*, a highly reputable independent newspaper whose editor-in-chief, Dmitry Muratov, was that year's Nobel Prize laureate, was shut down (*Reuters* 2022c). *Meduza*, the largest independent news site, was blocked in Russia and in early 2023 declared an "undesirable organization," its operation within Russia punishable by law (Seddon 2023). Banning investigative journalism and social media platforms such as Facebook and Instagram was also part of the crackdown. The courts labeled the technology conglomerate Meta as extremist and the use of its social media platforms (aside from WhatsApp) as participation in extremist activities (Sauer 2022b). Seeking to circumvent the ban, many turned to VPN services, but the go-to social network for news outside of the official Kremlin TV and print news became the messaging app Telegram (*Nezavisimaia Gazeta* 2022).

7. Anthropologist Alexandra Arkhipova and her colleagues have amassed a relatively long list of cultural clichés used to justify the war since the invasion (Focht 2022). Other popular examples are "we were left with no choice" or "we weren't given a chance" (*nam ne ostavili vybora/nam ne ostavili shansov*). These clichés became popular during the occupation of Crimea and gained prominence after Putin's announcement of the invasion on February 24, 2022 (*Fontanka.ru* 2022).

8. Ahead of the 2014 Winter Olympics in Sochi, Khodorkovsky was exonerated by a special presidential decree, left Russia, and has not returned (*BBC News* 2013; Zhegulev 2019).

9. In 2001, after producing a variety of content critical of Putin's leadership and policies, NTV, the largest independent TV channel, was effectively dismantled, its owner arrested and forced to flee the country (Golubeva and Morozov 2021; Lipman and McFaul 2001; Traynor 2001).

10. For more information on the Foreign Agent Law, see chapter 4.

11. In the updated version of the law, it is enough to claim that a person or an organization is "under the influence" of a foreign institution to declare someone a foreign agent (*TASS* 2023). A new law on "undesirable organizations" (*nezhelatel'nye organizatsii*), enacted in 2015, further intensified the persecution of human rights NGOs and other civil organizations deemed as undermining the state's political interests (Peremitin 2015).

12. The messaging app Telegram was founded by Pavel and Nikolai Durov. Pavel Durov, the founder of VKontakte, the largest Russian social media platform, was ousted from his

post as CEO of the company and left Russia in 2014 after allegedly refusing to cooperate with the authorities when asked to disclose opposition activists' information. Durov created Telegram not long after selling his share in VKontakte and leaving Russia for good (Bryzgalova 2014). The app became increasingly popular following the invasion.

13. Preserving food at home during periods of crisis is a popular and well-known strategy across the post-Soviet space. On the relations among the Soviet modernizing project, food preservation, and the disintegration of the state, see Dunn 2008.

14. Independent media outlets, journalists, political activists, and publicists opposing the war as well as state propagandists and nationalist zealots who believe Russia should be even more aggressive all use Telegram to post content (Bergengruen 2022; *Nezavisimaia Gazeta* 2022; Scott 2022).

15. For more on demodystopia, see introduction.

16. As part of this trend, the government designed a course in family studies to be taught in high schools across the country (Gabdullina 2024).

17. As Rivkin-Fish (2024) has demonstrated, this type of argumentation was extensively employed before the war by Russian political contenders opposing family planning and supporting abortion restrictions.

18. This conspiracy theory appears to be uniquely Russian. It is most likely a reaction to popular 1970s Western discourse about overpopulation in the context of limited environmental resources (Meadows, Randers, and Meadows 1972; Ehrlich 1968) and was indeed a topic of interest among late Soviet publicists and public intellectuals (Efimov 2022).

19. On the popularity of conspiratorial thinking in post-Soviet Russia, see also Oushakine 2009a.

20. Demographer Igor Efremov estimated that as of September 2022, 800,000 to 1,000,000 refugees arrived in Russia. His estimate is based on the Russian state reporting that around 7.6 billion rubles were paid to Ukrainian refugees, with 10,000 rubles paid by the state to each refugee. How many stayed and how many left for Europe remains unknown (Starostina 2022).

21. For a discussion of these deportations, see introduction.

BIBLIOGRAPHY

Abankina, Irina, and Ludmila Filatova. 2018. "Dostupnost' doshkol'nogo obrazovaniia." *Voprosy Obrazovaniia* [Educational Studies Moscow], no. 3 (September): 216–46. https://doi.org/10.17323/1814-9545-2018-3-216-246.

AFP. 2022. "Russia Bans Media Outlets from Using Words 'War,' 'Invasion.'" *Moscow Times*, February 26, 2022. https://www.themoscowtimes.com/2022/02/26/russia-bans-media-outlets-from-using-words-war-invasion-a76605.

Ahlburg, Dennis A., and Wolfgang Lutz. 1998. "Introduction: The Need to Rethink Approaches to Population Forecasts." *Population and Development Review* 24 (January): 1–14. https://doi.org/10.2307/2808048.

Ahlburg, Dennis A., Wolfgang Lutz, and James W. Vaupel. 1998. "Ways to Improve Population Forecasting: What Should Be Done Differently in the Future?" *Population and Development Review* 24 (January): 191–98. https://doi.org/10.2307/2808056.

Alber, Erdmute, and Heike Dobohm, eds. 2015. *Anthropological Perspectives on Care*. New York: Palgrave Macmillan.

Alexopoulos, Golfo. 2008. "Stalin and the Politics of Kinship: Practices of Collective Punishment, 1920s–1940s." *Comparative Studies in Society and History* 50 (1): 91–117. https://doi.org/10.1017/S0010417508000066.

Alonso, William, and Paul Starr, eds. 1987. *The Politics of Numbers*. New York: Russell Sage Foundation. https://www.russellsage.org/publications/politics-numbers.

Andersson, Hilary. 2023. "Missing Ukrainian Child Traced to Putin Ally." *BBC News*, November 23, 2023. https://www.bbc.com/news/world-europe-67488646.

Andreev, Andrey. 2014. "Matkapital povysil rozhdaemost' vtorykh detei na 40 protsentov." *Rossiiskaia Gazeta*, September 11, 2014. https://rg.ru/2014/09/11/reg-cfo/rozhdaemost-anons.html.

Andreev, Evgenii. 2011. "Ozhidaemaia prodolzhitel'nost' zhizni 70 let, ili déjà vu otechestvennoi demografii" [Expected life expectancy of seventy years, or déjà vu of the national demography]. *Demoscope Weekly*, December 4, 2011. http://www.demoscope.ru/weekly/2011/0487/tema01.php.

Andreev, Evgenii, and Tatiana Kharkova. 2002. "Can We Believe Demographic Projections?" *Demoscope Weekly*, February 4, 2002. http://www.demoscope.ru/weekly/2002/053/tema01.php.

Anekdot.ru. "Anekdot No. 475376." 2010. Anekdot.ru. October 22, 2010. https://www.anekdot.ru/id/475376/.

Antonov, Anatoly. 1980. *Sotsiologiia rozhdaemosti* [Sociology of fertility]. Moskva: Statistika.

———. 2005. *Mikrosotsiologiia sem'i* [Microsociology of the family]. Moskva: Infra-M.

———. 2006. "Demograficheskaia i semeinaia politika: Zabluzhdenia, mify i istina" [Demographic and family policy: Misconceptions, myths and truth]. Demografia.ru Institut demograficheskikh issledovanii. June 7, 2006. http://www.demographia.ru/articles_N/index.html?idR=19&idArt=389.

———. 2009. *Demograficheskie issledovaniia* [Studies in demography]. Moskva: KDU.

Antonov, Anatoly, and A. A. Avdeev. 1990. *Zhiznedeiatel'nost' sem'i: Tendentsii i problemy* [Family life: Trends and problems]. Voprosy demografii. Moskva: Nauka.

Antonov, Anatoly, and Vladimir Borisov. 2006. *Dinamika naseleniia Rossii v XXI veke i prioritety demograficheskoi politiki* [Russian population dynamics in the 21st century and priorities of demographic policy]. Moskva: Kluch-S.

Antonov, Anatoly, and Vladimir Medkov. 1996. *Sotsiologiia sem'i* [Sociology of the family]. Moskva: Mezhdunarodnyi Universitet.

Antonov, Anatoly, Vladimir Medkov, and Vladimir Arkhangelsky. 2002. *Demograficheskie protsessy v Rossii XXI veka* [Demographic processes in Russia in the 21st century]. Moskva: Graal.

A. O. 2011. "A Russian Awakening." *The Economist*, December 11, 2011. https://www.economist.com/eastern-approaches/2011/12/11/a-russian-awakening.

Aptekar, Pavel. 2017. "Prem'er stimuliruet rozhdaemost'" [Prime minister stimulates birthrates]. *Vedomosti*, January 31, 2017. https://www.vedomosti.ru/opinion/articles/2017/01/31/675515-premer-stimuliruet.

Arab-Ogly, Edvard. 1999. "'Togda kazalos', chto koe-chto udavalos'" [We were under the impression that some things work well]. In *Rossiiskaia sotsiologiia shestidesiatykh godov v vospominaniiakh i dokumentakh* [Russian sociology in the 1960s: Memories and documents], edited by Gennadii Batygin, 358–70. Saint Petersburg: Russian Christian Academy for Humanities.

Argumenty i Fakty. 2013. "Detskie sady: Kto rabotat' budet?" *AiF*, October 23, 2013. https://ural.aif.ru/society/1006774.

Arkhangelsky, Vladimir, Justislav Bogevolnov, Jack Goldstone, Daria Khaltourina, and Andrey Korotayev. 2015. *Critical 10 Years: Demographic Policies of the Russian Federation: Successes and Challenges*. Moscow: Russian Presidential Academy of National Economy and Public Administration (RANEPA).

Arkhangelsky, Vladimir, and Valerii Elizarov. 2016. "Demograficheskie prognozy v sovremennoi Rosii: Analiz rezul'tatov i vybor gipotez." In *Nauchnye trudy: Institut narodnokhoziaistvennogo prognozirovaniia RAN*, edited by Andreii Korovkin, 524–45. Moskva: MAKS Press.

Ashwin, Sarah, Katherine Keenan, and Irina M. Kozina. 2021. "Pensioner Employment, Well-Being, and Gender: Lessons from Russia." *American Journal of Sociology* 127 (1): 152–93. https://doi.org/10.1086/715150.

Ashwin, Sarah, Irina Tartakovskaya, Marina Ilyina, and Tatyana Lytkina. 2013. "Gendering Reciprocity: Solving a Puzzle of Nonreciprocation." *Gender and Society* 27 (3): 396–421.

Atalay, Zeynep. 2019. "Partners in Patriarchy: Faith-Based Organizations and Neoliberalism in Turkey." *Critical Sociology* 45 (3): 431–45. https://doi.org/10.1177/0896920517711488.

Attwood, Lynne. 2010. *Gender and Housing in Soviet Russia: Private Life in a Public Space*. Manchester, UK: Manchester University Press.

Avdeev, Alexandre, and Alain Monnier. 1995. "A Survey of Modern Russian Fertility." *Population: An English Selection* 7:1–38.

Avdeyeva, Olga A. 2011. "Policy Experiment in Russia: Cash-for-Babies and Fertility Change." *Social Politics: International Studies in Gender, State & Society* 18 (3): 361–86.

Babül, Elif M. 2012. "Training Bureaucrats, Practicing for Europe: Negotiating Bureaucratic Authority and Governmental Legitimacy in Turkey." *PoLAR: Political & Legal Anthropology Review* 35 (1): 30–52. https://doi.org/10.1111/j.1555-2934.2012.01178.x.

———. 2015. "The Paradox of Protection: Human Rights, the Masculinist State, and the Moral Economy of Gratitude in Turkey." *American Ethnologist* 42 (1): 116–30. https://doi.org/10.1111/amet.12120.

———. 2017. *Bureaucratic Intimacies: Translating Human Rights in Turkey.* Stanford, CA: Stanford University Press.

Bagirova, Anna, Natalia Blednova, and Aleksandr Neshataev. 2023. "The Right of Russian Fathers to Parental Leave: Is a Transformation of an Established System Necessary?" *International Journal of Sociology and Social Policy* 44 (1/2): 267–85. https://doi.org/10.1108/IJSSP-08-2023-0190.

Baklanov, Alexander. 2014. "Programmu materinskogo kapitala mogut zakryt'" [Maternity capital program may be closed]. *snob.ru*, October 1, 2014. https://snob.ru/selected/entry/81701/.

Baldassar, Loretta, and Laura Merla. 2014. *Transnational Families, Migration and the Circulation of Care: Understanding Mobility and Absence in Family Life.* Edited by Loretta Baldassar and Laura Merla. New York: Routledge.

Ballestero, Andrea. 2012. "Transparency Short-Circuited: Laughter and Numbers in Costa Rican Water Politics." *PoLAR: Political and Legal Anthropology Review* 35 (2): 223–41. https://doi.org/10.1111/j.1555-2934.2012.01200.x.

Barazgova, Evgenia. 2007. "Riski budushchego: Regional'nyi aspekt issledovaniia problemy." In *Sud'ba Rossii: Vektor peremen*, edited by Rudolf Pikhoia, 317–37. Yekaterinburg: Akademicheskii Proekt.

Barth, Fredrik. 2002. "An Anthropology of Knowledge." *Current Anthropology* 43 (1): 1–18. https://doi.org/10.1086/324131.

Bashford, Alison. 2007. "Nation, Empire, Globe: The Spaces of Population Debate in the Interwar Years." *Comparative Studies in Society and History* 49 (1): 170–201. https://doi.org/10.1017/S0010417507000448.

Bashford, Alison, and Joyce E. Chaplin. 2016. *The New Worlds of Thomas Robert Malthus: Rereading the Principle of Population.* Princeton, NJ: Princeton University Press. https://press.princeton.edu/books/hardcover/9780691164199/the-new-worlds-of-thomas-robert-malthus.

Batygin, Gennadii, ed. 1999. *Rossiiskaia sotsiologiia shestidesiatykh godov v vospominaniiakh i dokumentakh* [Russian sociology in the 1960s: Memories and documents]. Saint Petersburg: Russian Christian Academy for Humanities.

BBC News. 2012. "Oppozitsionery v Moskve vstali v 'Bol'shoi belyi krug.'" *BBC News Russian*, February 26, 2012. https://www.bbc.com/russian/russia/2012/02/120226_big_white_circle.

———. 2013. "Russia Frees Khodorkovsky after Putin Signs Pardon." *BBC News*, December 20, 2013, sec. Europe. https://www.bbc.com/news/world-europe-25460427.

———. 2016. "Putin: 'Granitsy Rossii nigde ne zakanchivaiutsia.'" *BBC News Russian*, November 24, 2016. https://www.bbc.com/russian/news-38093222.

———. 2019. "Kak zapisyvali poslednee obrashchenie Borisa El'tsina? Vspominaet Valentin Iumashev." *BBC News Russian*, December 23, 2019. https://www.bbc.com/russian/media-50751300.

———. 2022. "Zapret 'gei-propagandy' dazhe sredi vzroslykh i 'otritsaniia traditsionnykh tsennostei': Novyi zakonoproekt v Gosdume." *BBC News Russian*, July 18, 2022. https://www.bbc.com/russian/news-62146549.

———. 2023. "Vyvoz Rossiei ukrainskikh detei iavliaetsia voennym prestupleniem—komissiia OON." *BBC News Russian*, March 16, 2023. https://www.bbc.com/russian/news-64983782.

Bederson, Vsevolod. 2024a. "Ispytanie politikoi: Kak rossiiskie grazhdanskie organizatsii pytalis' naiti politicheskuiu strategiiu v postsovetskoe vremia" [Tested by politics: How Russian civil organizations tried to find a political strategy in post-Soviet times]. *Moscow Times*, June 12, 2024, sec. news. https://www.moscowtimes.ru/2024/06/12 /ispitanie-politikoi-kak-rossiiskie-grazhdanskie-organizatsii-pitalis-naiti -politicheskuyu-strategiyu-v-postsovetskoe-vremya-a133775.

———. 2024b. "Prokliatie 'chernoi metki': Diffuziia statusa 'inostrannogo agenta' v Rossii i Kazakhstane" [The curse of the 'black mark': Diffusion of the 'foreign agent' status in Russia and Kazakhstan]. *Riddle Russia* (blog). February 9, 2024. https://ridl.io/ru /proklyatie-chernoj-metki-diffuziya-statusa-inostrannogo-agenta-v-rossii-i -kazahstane/.

Bederson, Vsevolod, and Andrey Semenov. 2020. "Politicheskie osnovaniia gosudarstvennoi podderzhki nekommercheskogo sektora: Analiz raspredeleniia prezidentskikh grantov v Rossii." *Mir Rossii* 29 (3): 96–120. https://doi.org/10.17323/1811-038X-2020-29-3-96-120.

———. 2022. "Knut, prianik i ne tol'ko: Upravlenie grazhdanskim obshchestvom v putinskoi Rossii" [Carrots, sticks and more: Governance of civil society in Putin's Russia]. *Riddle Russia* (blog). January 9, 2022. https://ridl.io/ru/knut-prjanik-i-ne-tolko-upravlenie -grazhdanskim-obshhestvom-v-putinskoj-rossii/.

Begtin, Ivan. 2024. "Ot tsifrovogo pravitel'stva do tsifrovogo kamufliazha. Dostupnost' informatsii: Ogranicheniia kosnutsia i ee potrebitelei, i rasprostranitelei" [From digital government to digital camouflage. Availability of information: Restrictions will affect both its consumers and distributors]. *Novaya Gazeta*, March 20, 2024. https://novayagazeta .ru/articles/2024/03/20/ot-tsifrovogo-pravitelstva-do-tsifrovogo-kamufliazha.

Beissinger, Mark R. 2015. "Self-Determination as a Technology of Imperialism: The Soviet and Russian Experiences." *Ethnopolitics* 14 (5): 479–87. https://doi.org/10.1080 /17449057.2015.1051810.

Belokrysova, Aida, Masha Birk, Sasha Kappinen, and Natalia Savelyeva. 2025. "NEPOKORNYE: Kak zhenshchiny boriutsia za blizkikh, okazavshikhsia v Rossiiskoi armii" [The Rebels: How women fight for their loved ones in the Russian army]. Public Sociology Laboratory. https://publicsociologylab.com/assets/reports/PS-lab .nepokornye_1.2.pdf.

Belova, Valentina. 1975. *Chislo detei v sem'e* [Number of children in a family]. Moskva: Statistika.

Belova, Valentina, Galina Bondarskya, and Leonid Darsky. 1983. "Dinamika i differentsiatsiia rozhdaemosti v SSSR" [The dynamics and differentiation of birthrates in the USSR]. *Vestnik Statistiki* 12:14–24.

Belova, Valentina, and Leonid Darsky. 1972. *Statistika mnenii v izuchenii rozhdaemosti* [The statistics of opinions in the study of fertility]. Moskva: Statistika.

Bergengruen, Vera. 2022. "Telegram Becomes a Digital Battlefield in Russia-Ukraine War." *Time*, March 21, 2022. https://time.com/6158437/telegram-russia-ukraine-information-war/.

Berishvili, Natalia. 2018. "Rossianki otlozhili materinstvo." *Izvestiia*, January 22, 2018, sec. obshchestvo. https://iz.ru/696411/nataliia-berishvili/rossiianki-otlozhili-materinstvo.

Bestuzhev-Lada, Igor V. 1976. "Sotsialnye problemy sovetskogo obraza zhizni" [The social problems of the Soviet way of life]. *Novyi Mir* 7:208–21.

Bindman, Eleanor. 2017. *Social Rights in Russia: From Imperfect Past to Uncertain Future*. London: Routledge. https://doi.org/10.4324/9781315731919.

Biryukova, Svetlana, Oxana Sinyavskaya, and Irina Nurimanova. 2016. "Estimating Effects of 2007 Family Policy Changes on Probability of Second and Subsequent Births in Russia." SSRN Scholarly Paper. Rochester, NY. https://doi.org/10.2139/ssrn.2727130.

Bloch, Alexia. 2017. "'Other Mothers,' Migration, and a Transnational Nurturing Nexus." *Signs: Journal of Women in Culture and Society* 43 (1): 53–75. https://doi.org/10.1086/692441.

Blum, Alain. 2001. "Social History as the History of Measuring Populations: A Post-1987 Renewal." *Kritika: Explorations in Russian and Eurasian History* 2 (2): 279–94.

———. 2005. *Rodit'sia', zhit' i umeret' v SSSR. 1917–1991.* Moskva: Novoe izdatel'stvo.

———. 2021. "Anatoly Vishnevsky – uchenyii, sozidatel', chelovek tverdykh ubezhdenii" [Anatoly Vishnevsky – Scientist, doer, a man of conviction]. *Russian Sociological Review* 20 (1): 324–33.

Blum, Alain, and Martine Mespoulet. 2006. *Biurokraticheskaia anarkhiia. Statistika i vlast' pri Staline.* Moskva: ROSSPEN.

Bockman, Johanna, and Michael A. Bernstein. 2008. "Scientific Community in a Divided World: Economists, Planning, and Research Priority during the Cold War." *Comparative Studies in Society and History* 50 (3): 581–613. https://doi.org/10.1017/S0010417508000261.

Bogdanova, Elena, and Eleanor Bindman. 2016. "NGOs, Policy Entrepreneurship and Child Protection in Russia: Pitfalls and Prospects for Civil Society." *Demokratizatsiya* 24 (2): 143–71.

Bogdanova, Elena, Linda J. Cook, and Meri Kulmala. 2018. "The Carrot or the Stick? Constraints and Opportunities of Russia's CSO Policy." *Europe-Asia Studies* 70 (4): 501–13. https://doi.org/10.1080/09668136.2018.1471803.

Boletskaya, Ksenia. 2018. "Kirill Kleimanov bol'she ne budet vesti programmu 'Vremia'" [Kirill Kleimenov will no longer host the Vremia program]. *Vedomosti*, May 10, 2018. https://www.vedomosti.ru/technology/articles/2018/05/10/769074-kleimenov-bolshe-ne-budet-vesti-vremya.

Bondarskaya, Galina A. 1971. "Vliianie etnicheskogo faktora na uroven' rozhdaemosti v SSSR i v nekotorykh sotsialisticheskikh stranakh Evropy" [The effects of the ethnic factor on birthrates in the USSR and several socialist countries in Europe]. In *Faktory rozhdaemosti* [Indicators of fertility trends], edited by Andrey Volkov, 52–62. Moskva: Statistika.

———. 1976. "Etnicheskaia differentsiatsiia rozhdaemosti v SSSR i ee sushchnost'" [Ethnic differentiation of fertility in the USSR and its essence]. In *Rozhdaemost'*, edited by Leonid E. Darsky, 106–20. Moskva: Statistika.

———. 1977. *Rozhdaemost' v USSR (Etnodemograficheskii aspekt)* [Natality in the USSR (Ethno-demographic aspects)]. Moskva: Statistika.

Bondarskaya, Galina A., and Viktor I. Kozlov. 1971. "Natsional'nyi sostav naseleniia kak faktor differentsiatsii rozhdaemosti" [Nationality as a differentiating factor]. In *Faktory Rozhdaemosti* [Indicators of fertility trends], edited by Andrey Volkov, 63–76. Moskva: Statistika.

Borenstein, Eliot. 2019. *Plots against Russia: Conspiracy and Fantasy after Socialism.* Ithaca, NY: Cornell University Press.

Borisov, Vladimir. 1976. *Perspektivy rozhdaemosti* [Perspectives on fertility trends]. Moskva: Statistika.

Borisov, Vladimir, and Anatoly Vishnevsky. 2001. "Boris Tsezarevich Urlanis, demograf." *Demoscope Weekly*, September 9, 2001. https://www.demoscope.ru/weekly/031/nauka01.php.

Borneman, John. 1992. *Belonging in the Two Berlins: Kin, State, Nation*. Cambridge: Cambridge University Press.

——. 2001. "Caring and Being Cared For: Displacing Marriage, Kinship, Gender, and Sexuality." In *The Ethics of Kinship: Ethnographic Inquiries*, edited by James D. Faubion, 29–46. Lanham, MD: Rowman & Littlefield.

Borozdina, Ekaterina, Anna Rotkirch, Anna Temkina, and Elena Zdravomyslova. 2016. "Using Maternity Capital: Citizen Distrust of Russian Family Policy." *European Journal of Women's Studies* 23 (1): 60–75. https://doi.org/10.1177/1350506814543838.

Boyarsky, Aron Ya. 1959. "K voprosu o vzaimosviazi pokazatelei vosproizvodstva naseleniia" [On the question of the interactions between different indicators of population replacement]. In *Problemy demograficheskoi statistiki* [Problems of demographic statistics], edited by Vasily S. Nemchinov, 7–18. Moskva: Gosstatizdat.

——. 1968. "K probleme demograficheskogo optimuma" [On the theory of population optimum]. In *Izuchenie vosproizvodstva naseleniia* [Studies in population reproduction], edited by Andrey G. Volkov, 47–63. Moskva: Nauka.

——. 1975a. "Demografiia kak nauka" [Demography as science]. In *Naselenie i metody ego izucheniia* [Population and the methods of population research], 13–19. Moskva: Statistika.

——. 1975b. "K probleme naseleniia" [On the question of population]. In *Naselenie i metody ego izucheniia* [Population and the methods of population research], 64–78. Moskva: Statistika.

Boyer, Dominic. 2008. "Thinking through the Anthropology of Experts." *Anthropology in Action* 15 (2): 38–46. https://doi.org/10.3167/aia.2008.150204.

Boym, Svetlana. 2002. "Stil' PR." *Neprikosnovennyi zapas* 26 (6): 78–84.

Brada, Betsey Behr. 2016. "The Contingency of Humanitarianism: Moral Authority in an African HIV Clinic." *American Anthropologist* 118 (4): 755–71. https://doi.org/10.1111/aman.12692.

Brenneis, Don. 2009. "Anthropology in and of the Academy: Globalization, Assessment and Our Field's Future." *Social Anthropology* 17 (3): 261–75. https://doi.org/10.1111/j.1469-8676.2009.00077.x.

Briggs, Charles. 2004. "Malthus' Anti-rhetorical Rhetoric, or, on the Magical Conversion of the Imaginary into the Real." In *Categories and Contexts: Anthropological and Historical Studies in Critical Demography*, edited by Simon Szreter, Hania Sholkamy, and A. Dharmalingam, 57–78. Oxford: Oxford University Press.

Broome, André, and Leonard Seabrooke. 2015. "Shaping Policy Curves: Cognitive Authority in Transnational Capacity Building." *Public Administration* 93 (4): 956–72. https://doi.org/10.1111/padm.12179.

Bryzgalova, Ekaterina. 2014. "Durov ne obeshchal vernut'sia." *Gazeta.Ru*, April 22, 2014. https://www.gazeta.ru/business/2014/04/22/6002397.shtml.

Buch, Elana D. 2015. "Anthropology of Aging and Care." *Annual Review of Anthropology* 44 (1): 277–93. https://doi.org/10.1146/annurev-anthro-102214-014254.

Bulgakov, Mikhail. 1968. *Heart of a Dog*. New York: Grove Press.

Caldwell, Melissa L. 2004. *Not by Bread Alone: Social Support in the New Russia*. Berkeley: University of California Press.

———. 2007. "Elder Care in the New Russia: The Changing Face of Compassionate Social Security." *Focaal* 2007(50): 66–80.

Camic, Charles, Neil Gross, and Michèle Lamont, eds. 2011. *Social Knowledge in the Making*. Chicago: University of Chicago Press.

Carr, E. Summerson. 2010. "Enactments of Expertise." *Annual Review of Anthropology*. 39:17–32. https://doi.org/10.1146/annurev.anthro.012809.104948.

Carsten, Janet. 1995. "The Substance of Kinship and the Heat of the Hearth: Feeding, Personhood, and Relatedness among Malays in Pulau Langkawi." *American Ethnologist* 22 (2): 223–41.

———. 2004. *After Kinship*. New Departures in Anthropology. Cambridge: Cambridge University Press.

Chelcea, Liviu. 2003. "Ancestors, Domestic Groups, and the Socialist State: Housing Nationalization and Restitution in Romania." *Comparative Studies in Society and History* 45 (4): 714–40. https://doi.org/10.1017/S0010417503000331.

———. 2016. "Kinship of Paper: Genealogical Charts as Bureaucratic Documents." *PoLAR: Political and Legal Anthropology Review* 39 (2): 294–311. https://doi.org/10.1111/plar .12195.

Chepovskya, Anastasia. 2017. "Tablitsa razmnozheniia." *Izvestiia*, November 29, 2017, sec. Obshchestvo. https://iz.ru/676843/anastasiia-chepovskaia/tablitca-razmnozheniia.

Cherkaev, Xenia. 2018. "Self-Made Boats and Social Self-Management: The Late-Soviet Ethics of Mutual Aid." *Cahiers Du Monde Russe* 59 (2/3): 289–310.

———. 2023. *Gleaning for Communism: The Soviet Socialist Household in Theory and Practice*. Ithaca, NY: Cornell University Press.

Chernova, Natalya. 2023. "Marketologi chuzhoi zhizni. Prinuzhdenie k materinstvu putem ogranicheniia prava na abort stalo odnoi iz samykh aktual'nykh tem dlia zakonodatelei" [Technologists of other people's lives. Coercing motherhood through restrictions on abortion rights has become one of the most pressing issues for legislators]. *Novaya Gazeta*, November 18, 2023, sec. Obshchestvo. https://novayagazeta.ru/articles /2023/11/18/marketologi-chuzhoi-zhizni.

Chernova, Zhanna. 2010. "'Demografiicheskii reserv': Molodaia sem'ia kak ob"ekt gosudarstvennoi politiki" ['Demographic reserve': Young family as an object of state policies]. *Zhenshchina v rossiiskom obshchestve* [Woman in a Russian society] 1 (54): 23–42.

Chua, Liana. 2009. "To Know or Not to Know? Practices of Knowledge and Ignorance among Bidayuhs in an 'Impurely' Christian World." *Journal of the Royal Anthropological Institute* 15 (2): 332–48.

Clowes, Edith W. 2011. *Russia on the Edge: Imagined Geographies and Post-Soviet Identity*. Ithaca, NY: Cornell University Press.

Coe, Cati. 2016. "Orchestrating Care in Time: Ghanaian Migrant Women, Family, and Reciprocity." *American Anthropologist* 118 (1): 37–48.

Cohn, Bernard S., ed. 1987. "The Census, Social Structure and Objectification in South Asia." In *An Anthropologist among the Historians and Other Essays*, 224–54. Delhi: Oxford University Press.

———. 1996. *Colonialism and Its Forms of Knowledge: The British in India*. Princeton Studies in Culture/Power/History. Princeton, NJ: Princeton University Press.

Collier, Stephen J. 2011. *Post-Soviet Social: Neoliberalism, Social Modernity, Biopolitics*. Princeton, NJ: Princeton University Press.

Collins, H. M., and Robert Evans. 2002. "The Third Wave of Science Studies: Studies of Expertise and Experience." *Social Studies of Science* 32 (2): 235–96. https://doi.org/10.1177/0306312702032002003.

———. 2007. *Rethinking Expertise.* Chicago: University of Chicago Press.

Connelly, Matthew James. 2008. *Fatal Misconception: The Struggle to Control World Population.* Cambridge, MA: Belknap Press of Harvard University Press.

Cook, Joanna, and Catherine Trundle. 2020. "Unsettled Care: Temporality, Subjectivity, and the Uneasy Ethics of Care." *Anthropology and Humanism* 45 (2): 178–83. https://doi.org/10.1111/anhu.12308.

Cook, Linda J., Elena Iarskaia-Smirnova, and Anna Tarasenko. 2021. "Outsourcing Social Services to NGOs in Russia: Federal Policy and Regional Responses." *Post-Soviet Affairs* 37 (2): 119–36. https://doi.org/10.1080/1060586X.2020.1853454.

Cooper, Melinda. 2017. *Family Values: Between Neoliberalism and the New Social Conservatism.* New York: Zone Books.

Curtis, Bruce. 2001. *The Politics of Population: State Formation, Statistics, and the Census of Canada, 1840–1875.* Toronto: University of Toronto Press. https://www.degruyter.com/document/doi/10.3138/9781442682108/html.

Dashkov, Igor. 2009. "V Moskve proshel s"ezd novogo obshchestvennogo dvizheniia 'Za sberezhenie naroda.'" *Rossiiskaia Gazeta*, December 18, 2009. https://rg.ru/2009/12/18/narod.html.

Davis, Kingsley. 1945. "The World Demographic Transition." *Annals of the American Academy of Political and Social Science* 237 (1): 1–11.

Dean, Mitchell. 2015. "The Malthus Effect: Population and the Liberal Government of Life." *Economy and Society* 44 (1): 18–39. https://doi.org/10.1080/03085147.2014.983832.

Demographia.ru. 2014. "Demograficheskii Likbez i demograficheskaia azbuka." Demographia.ru. January 23, 2014. http://demographia.ru/node/97.

Demoscope Weekly. 2003. "Vernite nashi dushi!" [Bring back our souls!]. *Demoscope Weekly*, February 16, 2003. http://www.demoscope.ru/weekly/2003/099/lisa01.php.

———. 2016. "Likbez bezlik" [The eradication of illiteracy is faceless]. *Demoscope Weekly*, March 20, 2016. http://www.demoscope.ru/weekly/2016/0677/lisa01.php.

———. 2017. "Iubilei stat'i 'Skol'ko zhe nas bylo?'" [Anniversary of the article 'How Many of Us Were There?']. *Demoscope Weekly*, December 31, 2017. https://www.demoscope.ru/weekly/2017/0753/nauka02.php.

Denezhkina, Elena, and Adrian Campbell. 2009. "The Struggle for Power in the Urals." In *Federalism and Local Politics in Russia*, edited by Cameron Ross and Adrian Campbell, 207–26. New York: Routledge.

Denisenko, Mikhail, and Valery Elizarov, eds. 2014. *Razvitie naseleniia i demograficheskaia politika. Pamiati A. Ia. Kvasha* [Population development and demographic policies. In memory of A.Ya. Kvasha]. Moskva: Prospekt.

Derluguian, Georgi M. 2005. *Bourdieu's Secret Admirer in the Caucasus: A World-System Biography.* Chicago: University of Chicago Press.

Desfosses, Helen. 1981. *Soviet Population Policy: Conflicts and Constraints.* Pergamon Policy Studies on International Politics. New York: Pergamon Press.

Desnitsky, Andrey. 2022. "Desnitsky." *Desnitsky* (blog). September 26, 2022. https://t.me/desnitsky.

Desrosières, Alain. 1998. *The Politics of Large Numbers: A History of Statistical Reasoning.* Cambridge, MA: Harvard University Press.

Dik, Sergey. 2023. "Demograf: My ne znaem chislo pogibshikh rossiian na voine." *Dw.com*, March 12, 2023. https://www.dw.com/ru/rossijskij-demograf-my-nikogda-ne -uznaem-tocnoe-cislo-pogibsih-na-vojne/a-64950560.

Dilley, Roy. 2010. "Reflections on Knowledge Practices and the Problem of Ignorance." *Journal of the Royal Anthropological Institute* 16 (2010): S176–92. https://doi.org/10.1111 /j.1467–9655.2010.01616.x.

DiMaio, Alfred J., Jr. 1981. "Evolution of Soviet Population Thought: From Marxism-Leninism to the Literaturnaya Gazeta Debate." In *Soviet Population Policy: Conflicts and Constraints,* edited by Helen Desfosses, 157–78. Pergamon Policy Studies on International Politics. New York: Pergamon Press.

"Diti viini" [Children of war]. 2024. Children of War. April 14, 2024. https://childrenofwar .gov.ua/.

Dmitriev, Denis. 2022. "Minkul't Rossii sostavil reestry traditsionnykh tsennostei i chuzhdykh idei." *Meduza*, January 24, 2022. https://meduza.io/feature/2022/01/24 /minkult-rossii-sostavil-reestry-traditsionnyh-tsennostey-i-chuzhdyh-idey.

Domingo, Andreu. 2008. "'Demodystopias': Prospects of Demographic Hell." *Population and Development Review* 34 (4): 725–45. https://doi.org/10.1111/j.1728–4457.2008.00248.x.

Douglass, Carrie B., ed. 2005. *Barren States: The Population "Implosion" in Europe.* Oxford and New York: Berg.

Drotbohm, Heike. 2015. "Shifting Care among Families, Social Networks, and State Institutions in Times of Crisis: A Transnational Cape Verdean Perspective." In *Anthropological Perspectives on Care: Work, Kinship, and the Life-Course,* edited by Erdmute Alber and Heike Drotbohm, 93–115. New York: Palgrave Macmillan. http://ebookcentral .proquest.com/lib/cam/detail.action?docID=4716843.

Drotbohm, Heike, and Erdmute Alber. 2015. "Introduction." In *Anthropological Perspectives on Care,* edited by Erdmute Alber and Heike Drotbohm, 1–19. New York: Palgrave Macmillan.

Dubrovina, Evgenia. 2023. "Oplata uslug ZHKKH materinskim kapitalom mozhet obestsenit' ego ideiu" [Paying for housing and communal services with Maternity Capital may devalue his idea]. *Vedomosti*, January 16, 2023. https://www.vedomosti.ru/society /articles/2023/01/16/959242-oplata-uslug-zhkh.

Dubrovsky, Dmitry. 2022. "Academic Rights and Freedom in Russia: Researchers' Views Introduction to the Special Issue." *Demokratizatsiya: Journal of Post-Soviet Democratization* 30 (1): 3–10.

Duma. 2006. *Federal'nyi zakon ot 10.01.2006 N 18-FZ "O vnesenii izmenenii v nekotorye zakonodatel'nye akty Rossiiskoi Federatsii"* [Federal law of January 10, 2006 N 18-FZ "On amendments to certain legislative acts of the Russian Federation" (with amendments and additions)]. https://base.garant.ru/12144310/.

———. 2010. *Federal'nyi zakon ot 5 aprelia 2010 g. N 40-NZ "O vnesenii izmenenii v otdel'nye zakonodatel'nye akty Rossiiskoi Federatsii po voprosu podderzhki sotsial'no orientirovannykh nekommercheskikh organizatsii"* [Federal law of April 5, 2010 N 40-FZ "On amendments to certain legislative acts of the Russian Federation on the issue of supporting socially oriented non-profit organizations"]. https://base.garant.ru/12174777/.

———. 2012. *Federal'nyi zakon ot 20 iiulia 2012 g. N 121-FZ "O vnesenii izmenenii v otdel'nye zakonodatel'nye akty Rossiiskoi Federatsii v chasti regulirovaniia deiatel'nosti nekommercheskikh organizatsii, vypolniaiushchikh funktsii inostrannogo agenta"* [Federal law of July 20, 2012 N 121-FZ "On amendments to certain legislative acts of the Russian

Federation regarding the regulation of the activities of non-profit organizations performing the functions of a foreign agent"]. https://base.garant.ru/70204242/.

———. 2013. *Federal'nyi zakon ot 28 dekabria 2013 g. N 442-FZ "Ob osnovakh sotsial'nogo obsluzhivaniia grazhdan v Rossiiskoi Federatsii"* [Federal law of December 28, 2013 N 442-FZ "On the fundamentals of social services for citizens in the Russian Federation"]. https://base.garant.ru/70552648/.

———. 2015. *Federal'nyi zakon "O vnesenii izmenenii v otdel'nye zakonodatel'nye akty Rossiiskoi Federatsii" ot 23.05.2015 N 129-FZ* [Federal law "On amendments to certain legislative acts of the Russian Federation" dated May 23, 2015 N 129-FZ]. https://www.consultant.ru/document/cons_doc_LAW_179979/.

———. 2016. *Federal'nyi zakon ot 3 iiulia 2016 g. № 287-FZ "O vnesenii izmenenii v federal'nyi zakon 'O nekommercheskikh organizatsiiakh' v chasti ustanovleniia statusa nekommercheskoi organizatsii – ispolnitelia obshchestvenno poleznykh uslug"* [Federal law of July 3, 2016 No. 287-FZ "On amendments to the federal law 'On Non-Profit Organizations' in terms of establishing the status of a non-profit organization – a provider of socially useful services"]. http://www.garant.ru/products/ipo/prime/doc/71335072/.

Dunn, Elizabeth C. 2004. *Privatizing Poland: Baby Food, Big Business, and the Remaking of Labor.* Culture and Society after Socialism. Ithaca, NY: Cornell University Press. http://www.loc.gov/catdir/toc/ecip0411/2003024996.html.

———. 2008. "Postsocialist Spores: Disease, Bodies, and the State in the Republic of Georgia." *American Ethnologist* 35 (2): 243–58.

Dzenovska, Dace. 2020. "Emptiness: Capitalism without People in the Latvian Countryside." *American Ethnologist* 47 (1): 10–26. https://doi.org/10.1111/amet.12867.

The Economist. 2023. "Russia's Population Nightmare Is Going to Get Even Worse." *The Economist*, March 4, 2023. https://link.gale.com/apps/doc/A739541675/AONE?u=cambuni&sid=bookmark-AONE&xid=c84d39c2.

Edwards, Jeanette. 2000. *Born and Bred: Idioms of Kinship and New Reproductive Technologies in England.* Oxford Studies in Social and Cultural Anthropology. Oxford: Oxford University Press.

Efimov, Artem. 2022. "Zolotoi milliard. Pochemu im vse, a nam nichego?" *Signal, Meduza* (blog). November 8, 2022. https://us10.campaign-archive.com/?u=ff4a009ba1f59d865f0301f85&id=8a07623eea.

Ehrlich, Paul R. 1968. *The Population Bomb.* New York: Ballantine Books.

Elder, Miriam. 2013. "Russia Raids Human Rights Groups in Crackdown on 'Foreign Agents.'" *The Guardian*, March 27, 2013, sec. world news. https://www.theguardian.com/world/2013/mar/27/russia-raids-human-rights-crackdown.

Elizarov, Valery. 1980. "Model' upravleniia reproduktivnym povedeniem sem'i" [Model for the regulation of family's reproductive behavior]. In *Upravlenie demograficheskimi protsessami* [The regulation of demographic processes], edited by Dmitry Valentei, 89–103. Moskva: Statistika.

———. 2014. "Demograf s bol'shoi bukvy" [Demograph with a capital D]. In *Razvitie naseleniia i demograficheskaia politika. Pamiati A.Ia. Kvashi* [Population development and demographic policies. In memory of A.Ya. Kvasha], edited by Mikhail Denisenko and Valery Elizarov, 33–44. Moskva: Prospekt.

Ellison, Susan Helen. 2018. *Domesticating Democracy: The Politics of Conflict Resolution in Bolivia.* Durham, NC: Duke University Press.

Erpyleva, Svetlana, Sasha Kappinen, and PS LAB Team. 2022. "Resigning Themselves to Inevitability: How Russians Justified the Military Invasion of Ukraine (Fall-Winter 2022)." Public Sociology Laboratory. https://therussiaprogram.org/ps_lab_1.

———. 2024. "'We Need to Carry On': Ethnography of Russian Regions During Wartime." 5. Academic Policy Papers Series. The George Washington University. https://therus siaprogram.org/ps_lab_ethnography.

Erpyleva, Svetlana, and Natalia Savelyeva, eds. 2023. *The War Near and Far: How Russians Perceive the Invasion of Ukraine February 2022 through June 2022.* Berlin: lmverlag.

Evans, Robert. 2005. "Introduction: Demarcation Socialized: Constructing Boundaries and Recognizing Difference." *Science, Technology, & Human Values* 30 (1): 3–16.

FederalPress. 2009. "Nekhvatka detskikh sadov vyvela sverdlovchan na ulitsu." *FederalPress,* June 11, 2009. https://fedpress.ru/news/russia/society/641994.

Fedorov, Evgenii. 1975. "Ekologicheskii krizis i sotsial'nyi progress" [The Ecological Crisis and Social Progress]. *Novyi Mir* 9:175–201.

Feshbach, Murray. 1986. "The Soviet Population Policy Debate: Actors and Issues." N-2472-AF. Santa Monica, California: RAND Corporation.

Field, Deborah A. 2007. *Private Life and Communist Morality in Khrushchev's Russia.* New York: Peter Lang International Academic.

Filipova, Anna. 2022. "Eta voina 'pobedoi' zakonchit'sia ne mozhet." *Meduza,* April 25, 2022. https://meduza.io/feature/2022/04/25/eta-voyna-pobedoy-zakonchitsya-ne-mozhet.

Filippova, Daria. 2017. "V Rossii predlagaiut vvesti nalog na malodetnost'" [A new proposal to tax families with fewer children was introduced in Russia]. *Izvestiia,* May 10, 2017, sec. Obshchestvo. https://iz.ru/news/699494.

Firat, Bilge. 2014. "The Accession Pedagogy: Power and Politics in Turkey's Bid for EU Membership." *Anthropological Journal of European Cultures* 23 (1): 99–120. https://doi.org/10 .3167/ajec.2014.230106.

———. 2016. "Political Documents and Bureaucratic Entrepreneurs: Lobbying the European Parliament during Turkey's EU Integration." *PoLAR: Political and Legal Anthropology Review* 39 (2): 190–205. https://doi.org/10.1111/plar.12189.

Fishman, Mikhail. 2022. *Preemnik: Istoriia Borisa Nemtsova i strany, v kotoroi on ne stal prezidentom* [Successor: The story of Boris Nemtsov and the country in which he didn't become president]. Moskva: Corpus.

Fitzpatrick, Sheila. 2002. *The Commissariat of Enlightenment: Soviet Organization of Education and the Arts Under Lunacharsky, October 1917–1921.* Cambridge: Cambridge University Press.

Flikke, Geir. 2016. "Resurgent Authoritarianism: The Case of Russia's New NGO Legislation." *Post-Soviet Affairs* 32 (2): 103–31. https://doi.org/10.1080/1060586X.2015.1034981.

———. 2018. "Conflicting Opportunities or Patronal Politics? Restrictive NGO Legislation in Russia 2012–2015." *Europe-Asia Studies* 70 (4): 564–90. https://doi.org/10.1080/0966813 6.2018.1455806.

Focht, Elizaveta. 2022. "'Gde vy byli vosem' let' i 'ne vse tak odnoznachno.' Antropolog Arkhipova o tom, kak i pochemu rossiiane opravdyvaiut voinu v Ukraine." *BBC News Russian,* April 27, 2022, sec. features. https://www.bbc.com/russian/features-61235671.

Fond Sem'ia XXI-vek. 2010. "Molodezh'-sem'ia-Razvitie - Fond Sem'ia XXI – vek." Fond Sem'ia XXI-Vek. 2010. http://xn--21-flcjd4aj2b3g4a.xn--p1ai/proekty-fonda-1/molodezh -semya-razvitie/.

———. 2022. "Fond 'Semia XXI-Vek'" [Foundation 'The 21st Century Family']. 2022. http:// xn--21-flcjd4aj2b3g4a.xn--p1ai/o-fonde-semya---xxi-vek/.

Fond sotsial'no-kul'turnykh initsiativ. 2008. "Fond sotsial'no-kul'turnykh initsiativ" [Foundation for socio-cultural initiatives]. 2008. https://fondsci.ru/about/.

Fontanka.ru. 2022. "'Nam ne ostavili shansov.' Na zhitelei Peterburga s bol'shikh ekranov teper' smotrit Putin." *Fontanka.ru*, February 25, 2022. https://www.fontanka.ru/2022 /02/25/70471553/.

Foucault, Michel. 2003. *"Society Must Be Defended": Lectures at the Collège de France, 1975–1976.* New York: Picador.

———. 2009. *Security, Territory, Population: Lectures at the Collège de France, 1977–78.* Edited by Michel Senellart. New York: Palgrave Macmillan.

Franklin, Sarah, and Susan McKinnon. 2001. *Relative Values: Reconfiguring Kinship Studies.* Durham, NC: Duke University Press. http://www.loc.gov/catdir/toc/fy031/2001040472.html.

Frejka, Tomas, Tomáš Sobotka, Jan M. Hoem, and Laurent Toulemon. 2008. "Childbearing Trends and Policies in Europe." *Demographic Research* 19 (2): 5–14.

Frejka, Tomas, and Sergei Zakharov. 2014. "Evolutsiia rozhdaemosti v Rossii za polveka: Optika uslovnykh i real'nykh pokolenii" [Fertility trends in Russia during the past half century: Period and cohort perspectives]. *Demograficheskoe obozrenie* 1 (1): 106–43.

Fuller, Steve. 1991. "Disciplinary Boundaries and the Rhetoric of the Social Sciences." *Poetics Today* 12 (2): 301–25.

Gabdullina, Emilia. 2024. "Shkoly poluchat programmy kursa 'Sem'evedenie' v blizhaishee vremia" [Schools will receive the program for teaching 'family studies' in the near future]. *Kommersant*, June 18, 2024. https://www.kommersant.ru/doc/6773642.

Gal, Susan, and Gail Kligman. 2000. *The Politics of Gender after Socialism: A Comparative-Historical Essay.* Princeton, NJ: Princeton University Press.

Gall, Carlotta, Oleksandr Chubko, Cora Engelbrecht, and Daniel Berehulak. 2023. "Ukraine's Stolen Children." *New York Times*, December 27, 2023, sec. world. https://www .nytimes.com/interactive/2023/12/26/world/europe/ukraine-war-children-russia.html.

Garcia, Angela. 2010. *The Pastoral Clinic: Addiction and Dispossession along the Rio Grande.* Berkeley: University of California Press.

Gelsthorpe, Loraine, Perveez Mody, and Brian Sloan. 2020a. "Introduction: Spaces of Care: Concepts, Configurations, and Challenges." In *Spaces of Care*, edited by Loraine Gelsthorpe, Perveez Mody, and Brian Sloan, 1–14. Oxford: Hart.

———, eds. 2020b. *Spaces of Care.* Oxford: Hart.

Gershon, Ilana. 2000. "How to Know When Not to Know: Strategic Ignorance When Eliciting for Samoan Migrant Exchanges." *Social Analysis: The International Journal of Social and Cultural Practice* 44 (2): 84–105.

Gershon, Ilana, and Dhooleka Sarhadi Raj. 2000. "Introduction: The Symbolic Capital of Ignorance." *Social Analysis: The International Journal of Social and Cultural Practice* 44 (2): 3–14.

Ghodsee, Kristen, and Laura Bernardi. 2012. "Starting a Family at Your Parents' House: Multigenerational Households and Below Replacement Fertility in Urban Bulgaria." *Journal of Comparative Family Studies* 43 (3): 439–59.

Gieryn, Thomas F. 1983. "Boundary-Work and the Demarcation of Science from Non-science: Strains and Interests in Professional Ideologies of Scientists." *American Sociological Review* 48 (6): 781–95.

———. 1999. *Cultural Boundaries of Science: Credibility on the Line*. Chicago: University of Chicago Press.

Glass, Christy, and Éva Fodor. 2022. "Risk, Reward, and Resistance: Navigating Work and Family under Hungary's New Pronatalism." *Social Politics: International Studies in Gender, State & Society* 29 (4): 1425–48. https://doi.org/10.1093/sp/jxac033.

Gluckman, Max. 1949. "The Village Headman in British Central Africa." *Africa: Journal of the International African Institute* 19 (2): 89–106. https://doi.org/10.2307/1156514.

Gohain, Swargajyoti. 2019. "Selective Access: Or, How States Make Remoteness." *Social Anthropology/Anthropologie Sociale* 27 (2): 204–20. https://doi.org/10.1111/1469-8676.12650.

Goldman, Wendy Z. 1993. *Women, the State, and Revolution: Soviet Family Policy and Social Life, 1917–1936*. Cambridge Russian, Soviet and Post-Soviet Studies. Cambridge: Cambridge University Press.

Golub, Ekaterina. 2018. "Nauka na prodazhu: Kak vuzy Peterburga monetiziruiut svoiu nauchnuiu deiatel'nost'." *dp.ru*, February 5, 2018. https://www.dp.ru/a/2018/02/02 /Nauka_na_prodazhu_kak_vuz.

Golubeva, Anastasia. 2022. "Dukhovnaia voina protiv satanizma. Kak v Dume obsuzhdali polnyi zapret 'gei propogandy'" [Spiritual warfare against Satanism. How the Duma discussed a complete ban on 'gay propaganda']. *BBC News Russian*, October 17, 2022. https://www.bbc.com/russian/news-63291777.

Golubeva, Anastasia, and Natalia Zotova. 2022. "Gosduma priniala zakon o zaprete 'gei-propogandy.' Chem on grozit i chto zapreshchaet?" *BBC News Russian*, November 23, 2022. https://www.bbc.com/russian/news-63714632.

Golubeva, Anna, and Alexander Morozov. 2021. "'Razdrom-Media': Postscriptum k odnomu iubileiu." *OpenSpace.ru* (blog). April 18, 2021. https://os.colta.ru/media/air/details/21853/.

Goncharenko, Oksana. 2011. "Sberezhenie natsii." *Aktual'nye kommentarii*, April 13, 2011. http://actualcomment.ru/sberezhenie_natsii.html.

Goncharov, A. G. 2004. "Est' i takaia tochka zreniia. Matriarkhat." In *Pochemu vymiraiut russkie. Poslednii shans*, edited by Igor V. Bestuzhev-Lada, 259–64. Moskva: Eksmo.

Gorham, Michael S. 2014. *After Newspeak: Language, Culture and Politics in Russia from Gorbachev to Putin*. Ithaca, NY: Cornell University Press. https://www.cornellpress .cornell.edu/book/9780801452628/after-newspeak/.

Gorin, Vladislav, dir. 2023. "Kak prisposablivaiutsia k zhizni v Rossii te, kto ne soglasen s politikoi Putina." *Chto sluchilos'?* 2023. https://meduza.io/episodes/2023/04/28 /govorim-s-sotsiologom-annoy-kuleshovoy-ona-provela-issledovanie-togo-kak -prisposablivayutsya-k-zhizni-v-rossii-te-kto-ne-soglasen-s-politikoy-putina.

Gosudarstvennaia Duma. 2023. "Vse, chto nuzhno znat' o materinskom kapitale v 2023 godu" [Everything you need to know about maternity capital in 2023]. Gosudarstvennaia Duma. February 1, 2023. http://duma.gov.ru/news/56275/.

Graham, Loren R. 1993. *Science in Russia and the Soviet Union: A Short History*. Cambridge: Cambridge University Press.

Graham, Loren R., and Irina Dezhina. 2008. *Science in the New Russia: Crisis, Aid, Reform*. Bloomington: Indiana University Press.

Greene, Samuel. 2017. "From Boom to Bust: Hardship, Mobilization & Russia's Social Contract." *Daedalus* 146 (2): 113–27. https://doi.org/10.1162/DAED_a_00439.

———. 2022. "The Informational Dictator's Dilemma: Citizen Responses to Media Censorship and Control in Russia and Belarus – PONARS Eurasia." *PONARS Eurasia: New*

Approaches to Research and Security in Eurasia (blog). June 12, 2022. https://www
.ponarseurasia.org/the-informational-dictators-dilemma-citizen-responses-to-media
-censorship-and-control-in-russia-and-belarus/.

Greenhalgh, Susan. 2008. *Just One Child: Science and Policy in Deng's China.* Berkeley: University of California Press.

Greenhalgh, Susan, and Edwin A. Winckler. 2005. *Governing China's Population: From Leninist to Neoliberal Biopolitics.* Stanford, CA: Stanford University Press.

Gritsuk, Marina. 2010. "Tut lishnikh net: Demograf Anatoly Vishnevsky ubezhden: Rossii pomogut molodye migranty." *Rossiiskaia Gazeta*, April 7, 2010, 5151 (72) ed.

Gundarov, Igor. 2001. *Probuzhdenie: Puti preodoleniia demograficheskoi katastrofy v Rossii.* Moskva: Tsentr tvorchestva "Belovodiie."

Guskova, Anastasia. 2022. "Golikova rasskazala o starenii naseleniia Rossii." *Izvestiia*, May 25, 2022, sec. Obshchestvo. https://iz.ru/1339984/2022-05-25/golikova-rasskazala-o
-starenii-naseleniia-rossii.

Gusterson, Hugh. 1996. *Nuclear Rites: A Weapons Laboratory at the End of the Cold War.* Berkeley: University of California Press.

Gutiérrez, Pablo, and Ashley Kirk. 2023. "A Year of War: How Russian Forces Have Been Pushed Back in Ukraine." *The Guardian*, February 21, 2023. https://www.theguardian
.com/world/ng-interactive/2023/feb/21/a-year-of-war-how-russian-forces-have-been
-pushed-back-in-ukraine.

Gutman, Yifat. 2016. "Memory Laws: An Escalation in Minority Exclusion or a Testimony to the Limits of State Power?" *Law & Society Review* 50 (3): 575–607.

Han, Clara. 2012. *Life in Debt: Times of Care and Violence in Neoliberal Chile.* Berkeley: University of California Press.

Harding, Luke, Isobel Koshiw, and Peter Beaumont. 2022. "Russia No Longer Has Full Control of Any of Four 'Annexed' Ukrainian Provinces." *The Guardian*, October 4, 2022, sec. world news. https://www.theguardian.com/world/2022/oct/03/russia-has-no-full
-control-of-any-of-four-annexed-ukrainian-provinces.

Harris, Steven. 2005. "'We Too Want to Live in Normal Apartments': Soviet Mass Housing and the Marginalization of the Elderly under Khrushchev and Brezhnev." *Soviet and Post-Soviet Review* 32 (1): 143–74. https://doi.org/10.1163/187633205X00041.

———. 2013. *Communism on Tomorrow Street: Mass Housing and Everyday Life after Stalin.* Washington, DC: Woodrow Wilson Center Press, Johns Hopkins University Press.

Heleniak, Tim, and Albert Motivans. 1991. "A Note on Glasnost' and the Soviet Statistical System." *Soviet Studies* 43 (3): 473–90.

Hemment, Julie. 2009. "Soviet-Style Neoliberalism?: Nashi, Youth Voluntarism, and the Restructuring of Social Welfare in Russia." *Problems of Post-Communism* 56 (6): 36–50. https://doi.org/10.2753/PPC1075-8216560604.

Herpen, Marcel H. Van. 2015. *Putin's Wars: The Rise of Russia's New Imperialism.* Lanham, MD: Rowman & Littlefield.

Herrera, Yoshiko M. 2004. "The 2002 Russian Census: Institutional Reform at Goskomstar." *Post-Soviet Affairs* 20 (4): 350–86. https://doi.org/10.2747/1060-586X.20.4.350.

———. 2010. *Mirrors of the Economy: National Accounts and International Norms in Russia and Beyond.* Ithaca, NY: Cornell University Press.

Hirsch, Francine. 2000. "Toward an Empire of Nations: Border-Making and the Formation of Soviet National Identities." *Russian Review* 59 (2): 201–26.

———. 2005. *Empire of Nations: Ethnographic Knowledge & the Making of the Soviet Union.* Culture and Society after Socialism. Ithaca, NY: Cornell University Press.

Hodžić, Saida. 2013. "Ascertaining Deadly Harms: Aesthetics and Politics of Global Evidence." *Cultural Anthropology* 28 (1): 86–109.

Hoffman, Steve G. 2011. "The New Tools of the Science Trade: Contested Knowledge Production and the Conceptual Vocabularies of Academic Capitalism." *Social Anthropology* 19 (4): 439–62. https://doi.org/10.1111/j.1469-8676.2011.00180.x.

Hoffmann, David L. 2000. "Mothers in the Motherland: Stalinist Pronatalism in Its Pan-European Context." *Journal of Social History* 34 (1): 35–54.

———. 2003. *Stalinist Values: The Cultural Norms of Soviet Modernity, 1917–1941.* Ithaca, NY: Cornell University Press.

———. 2011. *Cultivating the Masses: Modern State Practices and Soviet Socialism, 1914–1939.* Ithaca, NY: Cornell University Press.

Höjdestrand, Tova. 2016. "Social Welfare or Moral Warfare?: Popular Resistance against Children's Rights and Juvenile Justice in Contemporary Russia." *International Journal of Children's Rights* 24 (4): 826–50. https://doi.org/10.1163/15718182-02404007.

———. 2017. "Nationalism and Civicness in Russia: Grassroots Mobilization in Defense of 'Family Values.'" In *Rebellious Parents: Parental Movements in Central-Eastern Europe and Russia*, edited by Katalin Fábián and Elzbieta Korolczuk, 31–60. Bloomington: Indiana University Press.

Holmes, Douglas R., and George E. Marcus. 2005. "Cultures of Expertise and the Management of Globalization: Toward the Re-functioning of Ethnography." In *Global Assemblages: Technology, Politics, and Ethics as Anthropological Problems*, edited by Aihwa Ong and Stephen J. Collier, 235–52. Malden, MA: Blackwell.

Holquist, Peter. 2003. "New Terrains and New Chronologies: The Interwar Period through the Lens of Population Politics." *Kritika: Explorations in Russian and Eurasian History* 4 (1): 163–75.

———. 2010. "'In Accord with State Interests and the People's Wishes': The Technocratic Ideology of Imperial Russia's Resettlement Administration." *Slavic Review* 69 (1): 445–68.

Hooper, Cynthia. 2006. "Terror of Intimacy: Family Politics in the 1930s Soviet Union." In *Everyday Life in Early Soviet Russia: Taking the Revolution Inside*, edited by Christina Kiaer and Eric Naiman, 61–91. Bloomington: Indiana University Press.

Human Rights Watch. 2022a. "Rossiia: Novye ogranicheniia dlia 'inoagentov.'" *Human Rights Watch* (blog). December 1, 2022. https://www.hrw.org/ru/news/2022/12/01/russia-new-restrictions-foreign-agents.

———. 2022b. "Russia Criminalizes Independent War Reporting, Anti-war Protests." *Human Rights Watch* (blog). March 7, 2022. https://www.hrw.org/news/2022/03/07/russia-criminalizes-independent-war-reporting-anti-war-protests.

Huskey, Eugene. 2004. "From Higher Party Schools to Academies of State Service: The Marketization of Bureaucratic Training in Russia." *Slavic Review* 63 (2): 325–48. https://doi.org/10.2307/3185731.

Interfax. 2020. "VCIOM uznal, skol'ko rossiian zhivut v nezaregistrirovannom brake" [VCIOM found out how many Russians live in unregistered marriages]. *Interfax.ru*, March 5, 2020. https://www.interfax.ru/russia/697849.

———. 2022. "Problema demografii v Rossii: Spetsialisty RAN - o putiakh razresheniia krizisa." *Interfax.ru*, May 18, 2022. https://www.interfax.ru/russia/841475.

Ipsen, Carl. 2002. *Dictating Demography: The Problem of Population in Fascist Italy*. Cambridge: Cambridge University Press.

Ironside, Kristy. 2017. "Between Fiscal, Ideological, and Social Dilemmas: The Soviet 'Bachelor Tax' and Post-War Tax Reform, 1941–1962." *Europe-Asia Studies* 69 (6): 855–78. https://doi.org/10.1080/09668136.2017.1344189.

Ishchenko, Volodymyr, and Oleg Zhuravlev. 2022. "Imperialist Ideology or Depoliticization? Why Russian Citizens Support the Invasion of Ukraine." *HAU: Journal of Ethnographic Theory* 12 (3): 668–76. https://doi.org/10.1086/723802.

Ivanov, Alexei. 2010. *Khrebet Rossii*. Sankt-Peterburg: Azbuka.

Ivanov, Sergey F. 2006. "Chetvert' veka spustia" [Quarter of the century later]. In *D. I. Valentei v vospominaniiakh kolleg i uchenikov* [D. I. Valentei as remembered by his colleagues and students], edited by Raisa S. Rotova and Mikhail B. Denisenko, 14–18. Moskva: MAKS Press.

Ivanov, Sergey, Anatoly Vishnevsky, and Sergey Zakharov. 2006. "Population Policy in Russia." In *Demography: Analysis and Synthesis. Volume 4*, edited by Graziella Caselli, Jacques Vallin, and Guillaume Wunsch, 407–33. New York and London: Academic Press.

Ivushkina, Anna. 2017. "Prioritet detiam." *Izvestiia*, December 29, 2017, sec. Obshchestvo. https://iz.ru/688592/anna-ivushkina/prioritet-detiam.

Izvestiia. 2009. "Natalia Estemirova byla poslednei nadezhdoi na zashchitu ot proizvola" [Natalya Estemirova was the last hope for protection from arbitrariness]. *Izvestiia*, July 16, 2009, sec. Obshchestvo. https://iz.ru/news/350776.

———. 2017. "Gosduma prodlila programmu materinskogo kapitala do kontsa 2021 goda." *Izvestiia*, December 21, 2017, sec. Obshchestvo. https://iz.ru/686193/2017-12-21/gosduma-prodlila-programmu-materinskogo-kapitala-do-kontca-2021-goda.

———. 2022. "Putin nazval mnogodetnye sem'i otvetom na demograficheskie vyzovy." *Izvestiia*, May 25, 2022, sec. Obshchestvo. https://iz.ru/1339950/2022-05-25/putin-nazval-mnogodetnye-semi-otvetom-na-demograficheskie-vyzovy.

Jasanoff, Sheila. 1990. *The Fifth Branch: Science Advisers as Policymakers*. Cambridge, MA: Harvard University Press.

Johnson-Hanks, Jennifer. 2007. "What Kind of Theory for Anthropological Demography?" *Demographic Research* 16 (1): 1–26.

———. 2008. "Demographic Transitions and Modernity." *Annual Review of Anthropology* 37: 301–15.

Kalutzkova, N. N., M. D. Goryachko, and A. V. Speransky. 2004. "Sverdlovskaia oblast' 2004–2007." In *Bol'shaia rossiiskaia entsiklopediia*, edited by Sergey Kravets, 29:514–25. Moskva: Ministerstvo kul'tury RF. https://old.bigenc.ru/geography/text/3539838.

Kamakin, Andrey. 2013. "Lozh' i statistika" [Lying and statistics]. *Itogi*, December 23, 2013.

Kappinen, Sasha, and Oleg Zhuravlev. 2024. "Nenarodnaia voina: Rossiiskie protivniki i ne-protivniki vtorzheniia v Ukrainu" [Non-people's war: Russian opponents and non-opponents of the invasion of Ukraine]. *Re: Russia* (blog). July 10, 2024. https://re-russia.net/expertise/0173/.

Karpenko, Oksana. 2010. "Teaching 'Ethnic' and 'National' Differences: The Concept of 'Narod' in Russian School Textbooks." In *Dilemmas of Diversity after the Cold War: Analyses of "Cultural Difference" by U.S. and Russia-Based Scholars*, edited by Michele Rivkin-Fish and Elena Trubina, 193–219. Washington, DC: Woodrow Wilson Center Press.

Kassymbekova, Botakoz, and Marlène Laruelle. 2022. "The End of Russia's Imperial Innocence." *Russia.Post* (blog). May 25, 2022. https://russiapost.info/politics/the_end_of_russias_imperial_innocence.

Katrenko, Semen. 2022. "'Edinaia Rossiia' napravit rekomendatsii po realizatsii proaktivnogo podkhoda v sfere narodosberezheniia i povysheniia effektivnosti demograficheskoi politiki" ["United Russia" will send recommendations on the implementation of a proactive approach to population care and increasing the efficiency of demographic policy]. Edinaia Rossiia. July 21, 2022. https://er.ru/activity/news/edinaya-rossiya-napravit-rekomendacii-po-realizacii-proaktivnogo-podhoda-v-sfere-narodosberezheniya-i-povysheniya-effektivnosti-demograficheskoj-politiki.

Kertzer, David I., and Dominique Arel, eds. 2002. "Censuses, Identity Formation, and the Struggle for Political Power." In *Census and Identity: The Politics of Race, Ethnicity, and Language in National Censuses*, 1–42. New Perspectives on Anthropological and Social Demography. Cambridge: Cambridge University Press.

Keyfitz, Nathan. 1981. "The Limits of Population Forecasting." *Population and Development Review* 7 (4): 579–93. https://doi.org/10.2307/1972799.

———. 1982. "Can Knowledge Improve Forecasts?" *Population and Development Review* 8 (4): 729–51. https://doi.org/10.2307/1972470.

Khalturina, Daria A., and Andrey V. Korotaev. 2013. *Russkii krest: Faktory, mekhanizmy i puti preodoleniia demograficheskogo krizisa v Rossii* [The Russian Cross: The demographic crisis's factors and mechanisms and plans to overcome it]. Moskva: URSS. http://urss.ru/104378.

Khlinovskaya Rockhill, Elena. 2020. "'All Children Are Our Children': Care and Kinship in Residential Children's Homes in the Russian Federation." In *Spaces of Care*, edited by Loraine Gelsthorpe, Perveez Mody, and Brian Sloan, 1st ed., 77–98. Oxford: Hart.

Kirby, Paul. 2022. "What Russian Annexation Means for Ukraine's Regions." *BBC News*, September 30, 2022, sec. Europe. https://www.bbc.com/news/world-europe-63086767.

Kiseleva, Anna. 2021. "Issledovanie VSHE: Na 100 mest v detskikh sadakh prikhoditsia 102 rebenka." *Vedomosti*, October 8, 2021. https://www.vedomosti.ru/society/articles/2021/10/07/890269-issledovanie-detskih.

Knorr-Cetina, K. 1999. *Epistemic Cultures: How the Sciences Make Knowledge*. Cambridge, MA: Harvard University Press.

Kolesnikov, Andrei. 2023. "How Russians Learned to Stop Worrying and Love the War." *Foreign Affairs*, February 1, 2023. https://www.foreignaffairs.com/ukraine/how-russians-learned-stop-worrying-and-love-war.

Kommersant. 2013a. "Putin podpisal zakon o zaprete gei-propagandy sredi detei." *Kommersant*, June 30, 2013. https://www.kommersant.ru/doc/2223504.

———. 2013b. "V Rossii vveden zapret na usynovlenie odnopolymi parami." *Kommersant*, July 3, 2013. https://www.kommersant.ru/doc/2225475.

Konstantinova, Alla. 2023. "'Papa, nas khotiat usynovit'" [Dad, they want to adopt us]. *Mediazona*, June 21, 2023. https://zona.media/article/2023/06/21/report.

Koposov, Nikolay. 2022. "Populism and Memory: Legislation of the Past in Poland, Ukraine, and Russia." *East European Politics and Societies* 36 (1): 272–97. https://doi.org/10.1177/0888325420950806.

Kordonsky, Simon. 2000. "V real'nosti i 'na samom dele.'" *Logos* 26 (5/6): 53–64.

———. 2016. *Socio-economic Foundations of the Russian Post-Soviet Regime: The Resource-Based Economy and Estate-Based Social Structure of Contemporary Russia.* Stuttgart: Ibidem-Verlag.

Kotkin, Stephen. 1991. *Steeltown, USSR: Soviet Society in the Gorbachev Era.* London: Weidenfeld and Nicolson.

———. 2007. "Mongol Commonwealth?: Exchange and Governance across the Post-Mongol Space." *Kritika: Explorations in Russian and Eurasian History* 8 (3): 487–531.

KPSS. 1986. "Materialy XXVII s''ezda partii Sovetskogo Soiuza" [Materials from the XXVII Soviet Union's Party Congress]. KPSS. S''ezd 26. 1986. Moskva.

Krause, Elizabeth L. 2005. *A Crisis of Births: Population Politics and Family-Making in Italy.* Case Studies on Contemporary Social Issues. Belmont, CA: Thomson/Wadsworth.

Krause, Monika. 2021. *Model Cases: On Canonical Research Objects and Sites.* Chicago, IL: University of Chicago Press.

Kravel-Tovi, Michal. 2016. "Wet Numbers: The Language of Continuity Crisis and the Work of Care among the Organized American Jewish Community." In *Taking Stock: Cultures of Enumeration in Contemporary Jewish Life*, edited by Michal Kravel-Tovi and Deborah Dash Moore, 141–63. Bloomington: Indiana University Press. http://www.iupress.indiana.edu/isbn/9780253020574.

———. 2018. "Accounting of the Soul: Enumeration, Affect, and Soul Searching among American Jewry." *American Anthropologist* 120 (4): 711–24. https://doi.org/10.1111/aman.13123.

———. 2020. "The Specter of Dwindling Numbers: Population Quantity and Jewish Biopolitics in the United States." *Comparative Studies in Society and History* 62 (1): 35–67. https://doi.org/10.1017/S0010417519000409.

———. 2023. "Ambivalences of Smallness: Population Statistics and Narratives of Scale among American Jewry." *Theory and Society* 52 (2): 293–331. https://doi.org/10.1007/s11186-022-09473-5.

Kreager, Philip. 2004. "Objectifying Demographic Identities." In *Categories and Contexts: Anthropological and Historical Studies in Critical Demography*, edited by Simon Szreter, Hania Sholkamy, and A. Dharmalingam, 33–56. International Studies in Demography. Oxford: Oxford University Press.

Kremlin.ru. 2006. "Poslanie federal'nomu sobraniiu Rossiiskoi Federatsii." Prezident Rossii. May 20, 2006. http://kremlin.ru/events/president/transcripts/23577.

———. 2012. "Poslanie Prezidenta Federal'nomu Sobraniiu." Prezident Rossii. December 17, 2012. http://kremlin.ru/events/president/news/17118.

———. 2013a. "Interv'iu Pervomu Kanalu i agenstvu Assossiated Press." Prezident Rossii. September 4, 2013. http://kremlin.ru/events/president/news/19143.

———. 2013b. "Poslanie Prezidenta Federal'nomu Sobraniiu." Prezident Rossii. December 16, 2013. http://kremlin.ru/events/president/news/19825.

———. 2013c. "Press-konferentsiia Vladimira Putina." Prezident Rossii. December 20, 2013. http://kremlin.ru/events/president/news/19859.

———. 2020. "Poslanie Prezidenta Federal'nomu Sobraniiu." Prezident Rossii. January 15, 2020. http://kremlin.ru/events/president/news/62582.

———. 2021. "Zasedanie diskussionogo kluba 'Valdai.'" Prezident Rossii. October 25, 2021. http://kremlin.ru/events/president/news/66975.

———. 2022. "Soveshchanie o merakh sotsial'no-ekonomicheskoi podderzhki regionov." *Prezident Rossii*. March 19, 2022. http://kremlin.ru/events/president/news/67996.

Krivyakina, Elena. 2024. "Raspadaiutsia sem' iz 10 brakov: Pochemu v Rossii rezko vyroslo chislo razvodov" [Seven out of 10 marriages break up: Why the number of divorces has sharply increased in Russia]. *kp.ru*, November 13, 2024, sec. Ekonomika. https://www.kp.ru/daily/27659/5010058/.

Kuper, Adam. 2018. "We Need to Talk about Kinship." *Anthropology of This Century* (blog). October 2018. http://aotcpress.com/articles/talk-kinship/.

Kurakin, Dmitry. 2017. "The Sociology of Culture in the Soviet Union and Russia: The Missed Turn." *Cultural Sociology* 11 (4): 394–415. https://doi.org/10.1177/1749975517728625.

Kuznetsova, Irina. 2017. "Dangerous and Unwanted: Policy and Everyday Discourses of Migrants in Russia." *E-International Relations* (blog). April 28, 2017. https://www.e-ir.info/2017/04/28/dangerous-and-unwanted-policy-and-everyday-discources-of-migrants-in-russia/.

Kvasha, Alexander Ya. 1971. "Etapy demograficheskogo razvitiia SSSR" [Stages of demographic development in the USSR]. In *Faktory rozhdaemosti* [Factors of fertility], edited by Andrey G. Vokov, 77–87. Moskva: Statistika.

———. 1973. "Problemy demograficheskogo optimuma" [Problems of population optimum]. In *Narodonaselenie* [Population], edited by Dmitry I. Valentei, 13–26. Moskva: Statistika.

Lakhova, Ekaterina. 1995. *Zhenskoe dvizhenie v gody reform: Problemy i perspektivy*. Moskva: Informatik. https://a-z.ru/women/texts/lahova3r.htm.

Landay, Jonathan, and Simon Lewis. 2023. "U.S.-Backed Report Says Russia Has Held at Least 6,000 Ukrainian Children for 'Re-education.'" *Reuters*, February 15, 2023, sec. Europe. https://www.reuters.com/world/europe/us-backed-report-says-russia-has-held-least-6000-ukrainian-children-re-education-2023-02-14/.

Laruelle, Marlène. 2012. *Russian Eurasianism: An Ideology of Empire*. Baltimore, MD: Johns Hopkins University Press.

———. 2015. "Russia as a 'Divided Nation,' from Compatriots to Crimea: A Contribution to the Discussion on Nationalism and Foreign Policy." *Problems of Post-Communism* 62 (2): 88–97. https://doi.org/10.1080/10758216.2015.1010902.

Latour, Bruno. 1987. *Science in Action: How to Follow Scientists and Engineers through Society*. Cambridge, MA: Harvard University Press.

Lave, Jean. 1991. "Situating Learning in Communities of Practice." In *Perspectives on Socially Shared Cognition*, edited by Lauren B. Resnick, John M. Levine, and Stephanie D. Teasley, 63–82. Washington, DC: American Psychological Association.

———. 2011. *Apprenticeship in Critical Ethnographic Practice*. Chicago: Chicago University Press.

Lebedev, Alexander. 2007. "Vybit' 'dur'." *Novaya Gazeta*, September 10, 2007. https://novaya gazeta.ru/articles/2007/09/10/32014-vybit-dur.

Lebedeva, Natalia. 2008. "Grazhdanskie braki v Rossii stanoviatsia normoi, no tol'ko do poiavleniia detei" [Civil marriages in Russia are becoming the norm, but only before children appear]. *Rossiiskaia Gazeta*, July 30, 2008. https://rg.ru/2008/07/30/brak.html.

Lebina, Natalia. 2019. *Passazhiry kolbasnogo poezda: Etiudy k kartine byta rossiiskogo goroda: 1917–1991*. Moskva: Novoe literaturnoe obozrenie.

———. 2024. *Khrushchevka: Sovetskoe i nesovetskoe v prostanstve povsednevnosti* [Khrushchevka: Soviet and non-Soviet in the space of everyday life]. Moscow: Novoe

literaturnoe obozrenie. http://www.nlobooks.ru/books/kultura_povsednevnosti
/26823/.

Ledeneva, Alena V. 1998. *Russia's Economy of Favours: Blat, Networking, and Informal
Exchange.* Cambridge Russian, Soviet and Post-Soviet Studies. Cambridge: Cambridge
University Press.

Leinaweaver, Jessaca B. 2008. *The Circulation of Children: Kinship, Mobility, and Morality in
Ayacucho.* Durham, NC: Duke University Press.

———. 2010. "Outsourcing Care: How Peruvian Migrants Meet Transnational Family Obligations." *Latin American Perspectives* 37 (5): 67–87.

———. 2013. "Toward an Anthropology of Ingratitude: Notes from Andean Kinship."
Comparative Studies in Society and History 55 (3): 554–78. https://doi.org/10.1017/S0010
417513000248.

Lenta.ru. 2012a. "Gosduma otkazalas' snimat' s povestki otvet na 'zakon Magnitskogo.'"
Lenta.ru, December 21, 2012. https://lenta.ru/news/2012/12/21/refuse/.

———. 2012b. "Naval'ny i Udal'tsov arestovany na 15 sutok." *Lenta.ru*, May 9, 2012. https://
lenta.ru/news/2012/05/09/naval/.

Leon, David A., Vladimir M. Shkolnikov, and Martin McKee. 2009. "Alcohol and Russian
Mortality: A Continuing Crisis." *Addiction* 104 (10): 1630–36. https://doi.org/10.1111
/j.1360–0443.2009.02655.x.

Lerner, Julia, and Claudia Zbenovich. 2013. "Adapting the Therapeutic Discourse to Post-
Soviet Media Culture: The Case of Modnyi Prigovor." *Slavic Review* 72 (4): 828–49.

Levada Center. 2014. "Vladimir Putin: Udachi i neudachi, sila" [Vladimir Putin: Successes
and failures, strength]. *levada.ru* (blog). September 9, 2014. https://www.levada.ru
/2014/09/09/vladimir-putin-udachi-i-neudachi-sila/.

Levitt, Peggy, and Sally Merry. 2009. "Vernacularization on the Ground: Local Uses of
Global Women's Rights in Peru, China, India and the United States." *Global Networks*
9 (4): 441–61.

Leykin, Inna. 2015. "Rodologia: Genealogy as Therapy in Post-Soviet Russia." *Ethos* 43 (2):
135–64. https://doi.org/10.1111/etho.12078.

———. 2019. "The History and Afterlife of Soviet Demography: The Socialist Roots of Post-
Soviet Neoliberalism." *Slavic Review* 78 (1): 149–72. https://doi.org/10.1017/slr.2019.12.

———. 2020. "Uneasy Translations: Vernacularizing Demography for Post-Soviet Statecraft."
Journal of the Royal Anthropological Institute 26 (1): 86–104.

———. 2022. "Toxic Memories and Amateur Genealogy in Contemporary Russia." *Rural History Yearbook/Jahrbuch für Geschichte des Ländlichen Raumes* 18:67–83. https://doi
.org/10.25365/rhy-2021-5.

Leykin, Inna, and Anastasia Gorodzeisky. 2024. "Post-Soviet Russia: Anti-immigrant Sentiment and Discourses of National Identity." In *Migration and Nationalism: Theoretical and Empirical Perspectives*, edited by Michael Samers and Jens Rydgren, 88–113.
Northampton, MA: Edward Elgar.

Leykin, Inna, and Michele Rivkin-Fish. 2022. "Politicized Demography and Biomedical
Authority in Post-Soviet Russia." *Medical Anthropology* 41 (6–7): 702–17. https://doi.org
/10.1080/01459740.2021.1987897.

Lialenkova, Tamara. 2007. "Muzhchina i zhenshchina. Obraz teshchi" [A man and a woman.
An image of a mother-in-law (woman's mother)]. *Radio Liberty*, September 23, 2007,
sec. Svobodnyi den. https://www.svoboda.org/a/413478.html.

Lifshitz, Feodor. 1990. "Perepis' naseleniia 1937 goda" [1937 census]. In *Demograficheskie protsessy v SSSR* [Demographic processes in the USSR], edited by Andrey Volkov, 174–207. Moskva: Nauka.

Light, Felix. 2022. "Desperation on Russia's Borders as Draft-Eligible Men Flee." *Reuters*, September 27, 2022, sec. Europe. https://www.reuters.com/world/europe/desperation -russias-borders-draft-eligible-men-flee-2022-09-27/.

Limaye, Yogita. 2023. "Ukraine War: Defying Russian Onslaught in City 'at the End of the World.'" *BBC News*, January 4, 2023, sec. Europe. https://www.bbc.com/news/world -europe-64153581.

Lincoln, Bruce. 2007. *The Conquest of a Continent: Siberia and the Russians*. Ithaca, NY: Cornell University Press. https://www.cornellpress.cornell.edu/book/9780801489228/the -conquest-of-a-continent/.

Lipman, Masha, and Michael McFaul. 2001. "'Managed Democracy' in Russia: Putin and the Press." *Harvard International Journal of Press/Politics* 6 (3): 116–27. https://doi.org/10 .1177/1081180001129172260.

Lipsky, Michael. 1980. *Street-Level Bureaucracy: Dilemmas of the Individual in Public Services*. New York: Russell Sage Foundation.

Litvinova, Galina I. 1981. *Pravo i demograficheskie protsessy v SSSR* [Law and demographic processes in the USSR]. Moskva: Nauka.

———. 1989. "Nado li povyshat' rozhdaemost'?" In *Svet i teni progressa (Sotsial'no-demograficheskie problemy SSSR)*, 63–142. Moskva: Sovetskaia Rossiia.

Loshak, Andrey. 2010. "Zakorotilo." *OpenSpace.Ru* (blog). May 3, 2010. http://os.colta.ru /society/projects/201/details/16563/.

Lovett, Jessica. 2023. "'The Fate of the Nation': Population Politics in a Changing Soviet Union (1964–1991)." *Nationalities Papers* 51 (4): 888–907. https://doi.org/10.1017/nps.2022.27.

———. 2024. "Turning Science into Fiction? Censoring Population Research in the Soviet Union, 1964–1982." *Contemporary European History* 33 (1): 192–211. https://doi.org /10.1017/S0960777322000054.

Luehrmann, Sonja. 2011. *Secularism Soviet Style: Teaching Atheism and Religion in a Volga Republic*. New Anthropologies of Europe. Bloomington: Indiana University Press.

———. 2016. "Innocence and Demographic Crisis: Transporting Post-abortion Syndrome into a Russian Orthodox Key." In *A Fragmented Landscape: Abortion Governance and Protest Logics in Europe*, edited by Silvia De Zordo, Joanna Mishtal, and Lorena Anton, 103–22. New York: Berghahn.

———. 2019. "'Everything New That Life Gives Birth To': Family Values and Kinship Practices in Russian Orthodox Antiabortion Activism." *Signs: Journal of Women in Culture and Society* 44 (3): 771–95. https://doi.org/10.1086/701160.

Mair, Jonathan, Ann H. Kelly, and Casey High. 2012. "Introduction: Making Ignorance an Ethnographic Object." In *The Anthropology of Ignorance*, edited by Casey High, Ann H. Kelly, and Jonathan Mair, 1–32. Culture, Mind, and Society. New York: Palgrave Macmillan. https://doi.org/10.1057/9781137033123_1.

Makovicky, Nicolette. 2010. "'Something to Talk About': Notation and Knowledge-Making among Central Slovak Lace-Makers." *Journal of the Royal Anthropological Institute* 16 (s1): S80–99. https://doi.org/10.1111/j.1467-9655.2010.01611.x.

Malinova, Olga. 2014. "'Dukhovnye skrepy' kak gosudarstvennaia ideologiia" ["Spiritual bonds" as state ideology]. *Russia in Global Affairs* 12 (5): 113–22.

Malthus, Thomas Robert. 1798. *An Essay on the Principle of Population, as It Affects the Future Improvement of Society: With Remarks on the Speculations of Mr. Godwin, M. Condorcet, and Other Writers*. London: J. Johnson.

Malyutin, Alexei. 2022. "Samochinnyi muchenik 'SVO.'" *Novaya Gazeta Evropa*, November 8, 2022. https://novayagazeta.eu/articles/2022/11/08/samochinnyi-muchenik-svo.

Mamdani, Mahmood. 1996. *Citizen and Subject: Contemporary Africa and the Legacy of Late Colonialism*. Princeton, NJ: Princeton University Press.

Markowitz, Lawrence P., and Vera Peshkova. 2016. "Anti-immigrant Mobilization in Russia's Regions: Local Movements and Framing Processes." *Post-Soviet Affairs* 32 (3): 272–98. https://doi.org/10.1080/1060586X.2015.1035526.

Martin, Aryn, Natasha Myers, and Ana Viseu. 2015. "The Politics of Care in Technoscience." *Social Studies of Science* 45 (5): 625–41.

Matskovsky, Mikhail. 1985. "Demograficheskoe povedenie" [Demographic Behavior]. In *Demograficheskii entsiklopedicheskii slovar'*, edited by Dmitry Valentei, 330. Moskva: Sovetskaia Entsiklopediia.

Matveev, Ilya. 2021. "Between Political and Economic Imperialism: Russia's Shifting Global Strategy." *Journal of Labor and Society* 25 (2): 198–219. https://doi.org/10.1163/24714607-bja10043.

———. 2023. "Postup' krizisa: Sotsial'nye problemy v Rossii posle 24 fevralia 2022 goda" [Pace of crisis: Social problems in Russia after February 24, 2022]. "The Russian Crisis." Report no. 3. Bonn: Friedrich-Ebert-Stiftung. https://russia.fes.de/meroprijatija/russian-crisis-4.html.

Matveev, Maksim, and Lilia Salikhova. 2016. "Otdavaia rebenka v kottedzhnyi ili kvartirnyi detskii sadik, roditeli ochen' riskuiut." *Real'noe vremia*, July 4, 2016. https://realnoevremya.ru/articles/34265.

Matyshin, Valery. 2017. "Kak v regionakh reshaiut problemu s nekhvatkoi mest v detskikh sadakh." *TASS*, August 30, 2017. https://tass.ru/v-strane/4518870.

Matza, Tomas. 2012. "'Good Individualism'? Psychology, Ethics, and Neoliberalism in Postsocialist Russia." *American Ethnologist* 39 (4): 804–18. https://doi.org/10.1111/j.1548-1425.2012.01396.x.

———. 2018. *Shock Therapy: Psychology, Precarity, and Well-Being in Postsocialist Russia*. Durham, NC: Duke University Press.

Maysuryan, Alexander. 2022. "A baby novykh narozhaiut, uspokoil sviashchennik." *Maysuryan* (blog). October 29, 2022. https://maysuryan.livejournal.com/1945941.html.

McKinnon, Susan, and Fenella Cannell, eds. 2013. *Vital Relations: Modernity and the Persistent Life of Kinship*. 1st ed. Santa Fe, NM: School for Advanced Research Press.

Meadows, Donella H., Jorgen Randers, and Dennis L. Meadows. 1972. *The Limits to Growth*. Washington, DC: Potomac.

Mediazona. 2023a. "Poteri Rossii v voine s Ukrainoi. Svodka 'Mediazony.'" *Mediazona*, February 24, 2023. https://zona.media/casualties.

———. 2023b. "V Mordovii vveli shtrafy za 'sklonenie' zhenshchin k abortu" [Mordovia has introduced fines for 'inciting' women to have abortions]. *Mediazona*, August 3, 2023. https://virgins-honorably-895956.appspot.com/news/2023/08/03/abortion.

Meduza. 2022a. "Detskii ombudsmen rasskazala, kak u vyvezennykh iz Mariupolia detei 'negativ preobrazuetsia v liubov k Rossii.'" *Meduza*, September 28, 2022. https://meduza.io/news/2022/09/28/detskiy-ombudsmen-rasskazala-kak-u-vyvezennyh-iz-mariupolya-detey-negativ-preobrazuetsya-v-lyubov-k-rossii.

———. 2022b. "Putin: Petr I ne ottorgal zemli—on ikh vozvrashchal. Na nashu doliu tozhe vypalo vozvrashchat'." *Meduza*, June 9, 2022. https://meduza.io/news/2022/06/09/putin-petr-i-ne-ottorgal-zemli-on-ih-vozvraschal-na-nashu-dolyu-tozhe-vypalo-vozvraschat.

———. 2024a. "75 tysiach pogibshikh rossiiskikh soldat: 120 smertei v den'—vot tsena, kotoruiu platit Rossiia za napadenie na sosedniuiu stranu" [75 thousand dead Russian soldiers: 120 deaths per day—this is the price that Russia pays for attacking a neighboring country]. *Meduza*, February 24, 2024. https://meduza.io/feature/2024/02/24/75-tysyach-pogibshih-rossiyskih-soldat.

———. 2024b. "Rosstat zakryl statistiku smertnosti ot vneshnikh prichin. Nezavisimye zhurnalisty ispol'zovali ee v raschetakh chisla pogibshikh na voine rossiian" [Rosstat hid statistics on the external causes of mortality. Independent journalists used it in calculating the number of Russians killed in the war]. *Meduza*, July 16, 2024. https://meduza.io/news/2024/07/16/rosstat-zakryl-statistiku-smertnosti-ot-vneshnih-prichin-nezavisimye-zhurnalisty-ispolzovali-ee-v-raschetah-chisla-pogibshih-na-voyne-rossiyan.

———. 2024c. "Smertnost' molodykh muzhchin v Rossii rezko vyrosla v 2023-m—pochti vdvoe dazhe po sravneniiu s 2022-m. Za dva goda na voine pogiblo ne menee 64 tysiach rossiian. Eto sleduet iz dannykh Rosstata, issledovannykh uchenym Dmitriem Kobakom" [The mortality rate of young men in Russia increased sharply in 2023—almost doubling even compared to 2022. Over two years, at least 64 thousand Russians died in the war. This follows from Rosstat data, studied by scientist Dmitry Kobak]. *Meduza*, June 27, 2024. https://meduza.io/feature/2024/06/27/smertnost-molodyh-muzhchin-v-rossii-rezko-vyrosla-v-2023-m-pochti-vdvoe-dazhe-po-sravneniyu-s-2022-m-za-dva-goda-na-voyne-pogiblo-ne-menee-64-tysyach-rossiyan.

Meduza and *Mediazona*. 2023. "Bring Out Your Dead: A Joint Investigation by Meduza and Mediazona Reveals the True Number of Russian Soldiers Killed so Far in the Invasion of Ukraine." *Meduza*, June 10, 2023. https://meduza.io/en/feature/2023/07/10/bring-out-your-dead.

Medvedev, Yuri. 2020. "Fantomnye strakhi. Valerii Fal'kov: Ob"ediniat' vuzy i NII ne budut" [Phantom fears. Valerii Fal'kov: Universities and research institutes won't be merged]. *Rossiiskaia Gazeta*, December 20, 2020, 287 (8341) ed., sec. Obshestvo. https://rg.ru/2020/12/19/valerij-falkov-prokommentiroval-obedinenie-vuzov-i-nauchnyh-institutov.html.

Meerovich, Mark. 2008. *Nakazanie zhilishchem: Zhilishchnaia politika v SSSR kak sredstvo upravleniia liud'mi 1917–1937*. Moskva: ROSSPEN.

———. 2018. "SSSR kak megaproekt." In *Sovetskii proekt. 1917–1930 gg.: Etapy i mekhanizmy realizatsii*, edited by Ludmila Mazur, 28–39. Yekaterinburg: Ural'skii federal'nyi universitet imeni pervogo Presidenta Rossii B. N. Yeltsina.

Merry, Sally Engle. 2006. "Transnational Human Rights and Local Activism: Mapping the Middle." *American Anthropologist* 108 (1): 38–51.

Mertz, Elizabeth. 2007. *The Language of Law School: Learning to "Think Like a Lawyer."* Oxford: Oxford University Press.

Meshkov, Alexander. 2008. "My stremitel'no teriaem stranu." *Stoletie*, December 26, 2008. http://www.stoletie.ru/russkiiy_proekt/anatoliy_antonov_mi_stremitelno_teryaem_stranu_2008-12-26.htm.

Michelutti, Lucia. 2007. "The Vernacularization of Democracy: Political Participation and Popular Politics in North India." *Journal of the Royal Anthropological Institute* 13 (3): 639–56.

Mody, Perveez. 2020. "Kinship Care." In *Spaces of Care*, edited by Loraine Gelsthorpe, Perveez Mody, and Brian Sloan, 183–200. Oxford: Hart.

Molodikova, Irina. 2007. "Transformation of Migration Patterns in Post-Soviet Space: Russian New Migration Policy of 'Open Doors' and Its Effect on European Migration Flows." *Review of Sociology* 13 (2): 57–76. https://doi.org/10.1556/revsoc.13.2007.2.4.

Morgan, Mary S., and Margaret Morrison, eds. 1999. *Models as Mediators: Perspectives on Natural and Social Science.* Cambridge: Cambridge University Press. https://doi.org/10.1017/CBO9780511660108.

Morozov, Sergey. 2009. "Medvedev predstavil 'strategiiu sberezheniia naroda.'" *RIA Novosti*, September 10, 2009, sec. Novosti. https://ria.ru/20090910/184531073.html.

Morris, Jeremy. 2015. "Notes on the 'Worthless Dowry' of Soviet Industrial Modernity: Making Working-Class Russia Habitable." *Laboratorium Russian Review of Social Research* 7 (3): 25–48.

———. 2016. *Everyday Post-Socialism: Working-Class Communities in the Russian Margins.* London: Palgrave Macmillan.

———. 2021. "From Prefix Capitalism to Neoliberal Economism: Russia as a Laboratory in Capitalist Realism." *Sociology of Power* 33 (1): 193–221. https://doi.org/10.22394/2074-0492-2021-1-193-221.

———. 2022. "Russians in Wartime and Defensive Consolidation." *Current History* 121 (837): 258–63. https://doi.org/10.1525/curh.2022.121.837.258.

Moscow Times. 2022. "Putin Signs Expanded 'Foreign Agents' Law." *Moscow Times*, July 14, 2022, sec. news. https://www.themoscowtimes.com/2022/07/14/putin-signs-expanded-foreign-agents-law-a78298.

———. 2023. "Rosstat otchitalsia o sokrashchenii naseleniia Rossii piatyi god podriad." *Moscow Times*, February 1, 2023, sec. news. https://www.moscowtimes.io/2022/12/11/rosstat-konstatiroval-obval-rozhdaemosti-v-rossii-a28119.

———. 2024a. "Putin vpervye dal otsenku poter' v Ukraine—chislo pogibshikh mozhet prevyshat' 130 000 soldat" [Putin for the first time gave an estimate of losses in Ukraine—the death toll could exceed 130,000 soldiers]. *Moscow Times*, June 6, 2024, sec. news. https://www.moscowtimes.ru/2024/06/06/putin-vpervie-dal-otsenku-poter-vukraine-chislo-pogibshih-mozhet-previshat-130-000-soldat-a133166.

———. 2024b. "Putin zaiavil o 'vazhnosti' sem'i posle otpravki milliona rossiian na voinu" [Putin speaks about the 'importance' of family after sending a million Russians to war]. *Moscow Times*, July 8, 2024, sec. news. https://www.moscowtimes.ru/2024/07/08/putin-zayavil-ovazhnosti-semi-posle-otpravki-milliona-rossiyan-navoinu-a136174.

———. 2024c. "Rosstat konstatiroval sokrashchenie naseleniia Rossii shestoi god podriad" [Rosstat noted a decline in Russia's population for the sixth year in a row]. *Moscow Times*, January 26, 2024, sec. news. https://www.moscowtimes.ru/2024/01/26/rosstat-konstatiroval-sokraschenie-naseleniya-rossii-shestoi-god-podryad-a119663.

Moser, Evelyn, and Anna Skripchenko. 2018. "Russian NGOs and Their Struggle for Legitimacy in the Face of the 'Foreign Agents' Law: Surviving in Small Ecologies." *Europe-Asia Studies* 70 (4): 591–614. https://doi.org/10.1080/09668136.2018.1444145.

Mukhametshina, Elena. 2023. "V Gosdume sozdali gruppu po sokhraneniiu traditsionnykh tsennostei." *Vedomosti*, January 19, 2023. https://www.vedomosti.ru/politics/articles/2023/01/19/959601-sozdali-gruppu-po-realizatsii-gospolitiki.

Mukhametshina, Elena, and Svetlana Bocharova. 2019. "'Kraine strannaia priamaia liniia.' Politologi ob itogakh obshcheniia Putina s narodom." *Vedomosti*, June 20, 2019. https://www.vedomosti.ru/politics/articles/2019/06/20/804682-pryamaya-liniya.

Mukhametshina, Elena, and Ekaterina Grobman. 2022. "Vladimir Putin postavil tochku v voprose o prinadlezhnosti Donbassa Ukraine." *Vedomosti*, February 21, 2022. https://www.vedomosti.ru/politics/articles/2022/02/21/910355-putin-obyavil-o-priznanii.

Myhre, Marthe Handå. 2017. "The State Program for Voluntary Resettlement of Compatriots: Ideals of Citizenship, Membership, and Statehood in the Russian Federation." *Russian Review* 76 (4): 690–712.

Nabatkina, Ksenia. 2023. "Papkam za detok: v Rossii predlagaiut vvesti 'ottsovskii' kapital" [To dads for babies: 'Paternal' capital has been introduced in Russia]. *Izvestiia*, November 2, 2023. https://iz.ru/1598800/kseniia-nabatkina/papkam-za-detok-v-rossii-predlagaiut-vvesti-ottcovskii-kapital.

Nakachi, Mie. 2016. "Liberation without Contraception: The Rise of the Abortion Empire and Pronatalism in Socialist and Postsocialist Russia." In *Reproductive States: Global Perspectives on the Invention and Implementation of Population Policy*, edited by Rickie Solinger and Mie Nakachi, 290–328. Oxford: Oxford University Press.

———. 2021. *Replacing the Dead: The Politics of Reproduction in the Postwar Soviet Union*. Oxford: Oxford University Press.

Nazarova, Nina. 2023. "Vyvoz detei iz Ukrainy v Rossiiu: Otvechaem na vse glavnye voprosy." *BBC News Russian*, March 28, 2023. https://www.bbc.com/russian/features-64954599.

Neef, Christian, and Matthias Schepp. 2007. "Interview with Alexander Solzhenitsyn 'I Am Not Afraid of Death.'" *Der Spiegel*, July 23, 2007, sec. international. https://www.spiegel.de/international/world/spiegel-interview-with-alexander-solzhenitsyn-i-am-not-afraid-of-death-a-496003.html.

Nevinnaya, Irina. 2007. "Liubov' Glebova: 'Zastavit'' semeinuiu paru poiti na rozhdenie vtorogo rebenka – ochen' slozhnaia zadacha." *Rossiiskaia Gazeta*, September 5, 2007. https://rg.ru/2007/09/05/rojdaemost.html.

Newslab. 2019. "Pochemu kazhdaia piataia sem'ia v Krasnoiarske otkazyvaetsia ot mesta v detskom sadu." *Newslab.ru*, September 12, 2019. https://newslab.ru/article/920167.

Newsru. 2016. "Obama podpisal initsiativu, pridaiushchuiu 'zakonu Magnitskogo' global'nyi status." *NEWSru.com*, December 24, 2016. https://www.newsru.com/world/24dec2016/obamalaw.html.

Nezavisimaia Gazeta. 2022. "Telegram stal dlia rossiian i gazetoi i televizorom." *Nezavisimaia Gazeta*, December 24, 2022. http://www.ng.ru/society/2022-12-24/05_8623_04.html.

Ninetto, Amy. 2005. "'An Island of Socialism in a Capitalist Country': Postsocialist Russian Science and the Culture of the State." *Ethnos: Journal of Anthropology* 70 (4): 443–64. https://doi.org/Article.

Noddings, Nel. 2013. *Caring a Relational Approach to Ethics & Moral Education*. Berkeley: University of California Press.

Notestein, Frank W. 1945. "Population: The Long View." In *Food for the World*, edited by Theodore Schultz, 36–57. Chicago: University of Chicago Press.

Novaya Gazeta. 2024. "S fevralia 2022 goda iz Rossii emigrirovali bolee 666 tysiach grazh-dan" [Since February 2022, more than 666 thousand citizens have emigrated from Russia]. *Novaya Gazeta*, July 16, 2024. https://novayagazeta.ru/articles/2024/07/16/s -fevralia-2022-goda-iz-rossii-emigrirovali-bolee-666-tysiach-grazhdan-issledovanie -the-bell-news.

OHCHR. 2023. "Ukraine: Civilian Casualty Update 6 February 2023." United Nations Office of the High Commissioner for Human Rights. February 6, 2023. https://www.ohchr .org/en/news/2023/02/ukraine-civilian-casualty-update-6-february-2023.

Osipov, Gennadii. 2004. "Vozrozhdenie rossiiskoi sotsiologii (60–90-e gody XX veka): Stranitsy istorii" [The revival of Russian sociology (1960s–1990s)]. *Sotsiologicheskie issledovaniia* 2 (238): 24–30.

Otte, Jedidajah. 2022. "'We're Scared, We Want to Run': The Russian Men Fleeing Conscrip-tion." *The Guardian*, September 27, 2022, sec. world news. https://www.theguardian .com/world/2022/sep/27/we-want-to-run-russian-men-fleeing-conscription.

Oushakine, Serguei Alex, ed. 2004. *Semeinye uzy: Modeli dlia sborki*. Moskva: Novoe liter-aturnoe obozrenie.

———. 2009a. "'Stop the Invasion!': Money, Patriotism, and Conspiracy in Russia." *Social Research* 76 (1): 71–116.

———. 2009b. *The Patriotism of Despair: Nation, War, and Loss in Russia*. Ithaca, NY: Cornell University Press.

———. 2010. "Somatic Nationalism: Theorizing Post-Soviet Ethnicity in Russia." In *In Marx's Shadow: Knowledge, Power, and Intellectuals in Eastern Europe and Russia*, edited by Costica Bradatan and Serguei Alex Oushakine, 155–73. Lanham, MD: Lexington Books.

———. 2014. "'Against the Cult of Things': On Soviet Productivism, Storage Economy, and Commodities with No Destination." *Russian Review* 73 (2): 198–236. https://doi.org/10 .1111/russ.10727.

———. 2019. "Second-Hand Nostalgia: On Charms and Spells of the Soviet Trukhlia-shechka." In *Post-Soviet Nostalgia: Confronting the Empire's Legacies*, edited by Otto Boele, Boris Noordenbos, and Ksenia Robbe, 38–69. New York and London: Routledge.

Ovcharova, Lilia, and Alina Pishnyak. 2005. "Sotsial'nye l'goty: Chto poluchilos' v resul'tate monetizatsii" [Social benefits: Monetization's results]. *SPERO. Sotsial'naia politika: Ekspertiza, rekomendatsii, obzory* 3:5–24.

OVD-Info. 2022. "Timeline of Russian Anti-war Protests." OVD-Info. November 28, 2022. https://en.ovdinfo.org/timeline-russian-anti-war-protests.

Pain, Emil, Tatiana Poloskova, and Zhanna Zaionchkovskaia. 2004. "Sposobstvuet li mi-gratsiia rostu etnofobii?" [Does migration increase ethnophobia?]. *Demoscope Weekly*, December 5, 2004. http://www.demoscope.ru/weekly/2004/0179/analit02.php.

Parsons, Michelle. 2014. *Dying Unneeded: The Cultural Context of the Russian Mortality Crisis*. Nashville, TN: Vanderbilt University Press.

Pashenko, Valeria. 2017. "Tiumenskie roditeli bol'she doveriaiut gosudarstvennym detskim sadam." *AiF*, July 22, 2017. https://tmn.aif.ru/society/family/tyumenskie_roditeli _bolshe_doveryayut_gosudarstvennym_detskim_sadam.

Pavlov, Boris. 1989. *Iz shkol'nogo v rabochii klass*. Moskva: Sovetskaia Rossiia.

Pechenkin, Gennady. 2010. "Rossiia nezdorova i teriaet zhiznesposobnost'." *MKRU*, August 19, 2010. https://www.mk.ru/social/article/2010/08/19/524137-rossiya-nezdorova-i -teryaet-zhiznesposobnost.html.

Peremitin, Georgy. 2015. "Putin podpisal zakon o nezhelatelnykh inostrannykh organizatsiiakh." *RBC*, May 23, 2015. https://www.rbc.ru/politics/23/05/2015/55609f719a794774b30bd2a7.

Perevedentzev, Victor. 1966. "O probleme rozhdaemosti i demograficheskom nevedenii" [On the problem of fertility and demographic illiteracy]. *Literaturnaia Gazeta*, August 13, 1966.

———. 1968. "Beregite drug druga!" [Protect each other!]. *Literaturnaia Gazeta*, November 13, 1968.

———. 1983. *Plachu dolgi, daiu vzaimy. Aktual'nye problemy demografii* [Paying dues, giving a loan: Current demographic problems]. Moskva: Sovetskaia Rossiia.

Perrot, Michelle. 1983. "Malthusianism and Socialism." In *Malthus Past and Present*, edited by Jacques Dupâquier, 257–74. London: Academic Press.

Pike, Ivy L. 2019. "Intersections of Insecurity, Nurturing, and Resilience: A Case Study of Turkana Women of Kenya." *American Anthropologist* 121 (1): 126–37. https://doi.org/10.1111/aman.13153.

Pilkington, Hilary. 1998. *Migration, Displacement and Identity in Post-Soviet Russia*. London: Routledge.

Pine, Frances. 2002. "Retreat to the Household?: Gendered Domains in Postsocialist Poland." In *Postsocialism: Ideals, Ideologies, and Practices in Eurasia*, edited by C. M. Hann, 95–113. London: Routledge.

Pirogov, Ivan. 2012. "Za gran'iu nakazannosti." *Kommersant*, August 17, 2012. https://www.kommersant.ru/doc/2004683.

Podrabinek, Alexandr. 2010. "Oleg Orlov: 'V Chechne pravozashchitniki priravneny k terroristam'" [Oleg Orlov: 'In Chechnya, human rights activists are equated to terrorists']. *RFI*, July 7, 2010, sec. Rossiia. https://www.rfi.fr/ru/rossiya/20100707-oleg-orlov-v-chechne-pravozashchitniki-priravneny-k-terroristam.

Pokshishevsky, Vadim V. 1966. "Naselenie mira i budushchego" [World population and the future]. *Novyi Mir* 1:200–13.

Pollock, Ethan. 2006. *Stalin and the Soviet Science Wars*. Princeton, NJ: Princeton University Press.

Polnomochnyi predstavitel' Prezidenta v Tsentral'nom federal'nom okruge. 2022. "V TsFO sozdaetsia Institut demograficheskoi politiki." Polnomochnyi predstavitel' Prezidenta v Tsentral'nom federal'nom okruge. April 15, 2022. http://cfo.gov.ru/demografia/51266/.

Popova, Larissa A. 2016. "Changing Trends in Quantitative and Qualitative Characteristics of the Birthrate in Russia and the Komi Republic." *Anthropology & Archeology of Eurasia* 55 (2): 131–52. https://doi.org/10.1080/10611959.2016.1302201.

Porter, Theodore. 1986. *The Rise of Statistical Thinking, 1820–1900*. Princeton, NJ: Princeton University Press.

———. 1995. *Trust in Numbers: The Pursuit of Objectivity in Science and Public Life*. Princeton, NJ: Princeton University Press.

———. 2009. "How Science Became Technical." *Isis* 100 (2): 292–309. https://doi.org/10.1086/599552.

Portisch, Anna Odland. 2010. "The Craft of Skillful Learning: Kazakh Women's Everyday Craft Practices in Western Mongolia." *Journal of the Royal Anthropological Institute* 16 (2010): S62–79. https://doi.org/10.1111/j.1467-9655.2010.01610.x.

Preobrazhensky, Ivan. 2023. "Kampaniia protiv abortov v Rossii i voina – gde sviaz'?" [The anti-abortion campaign in Russia and the war – what's the connection?]. *Dw.com*,

November 2023. https://www.dw.com/ru/kommentarij-kampania-protiv-abortov-v
-rossii-i-vojna-gde-svaz/a-67541958.

President of Russia. 2013. "Zasedanie Soveta po realizatsii prioritetnykh natsproektov i demograficheskoi politike." *Prezident Rossii.* February 26, 2013. http://kremlin.ru/events
/president/news/17586.

———. 2021. "Stat'ia Vladimira Putina 'Ob istoricheskom edinstve russkikh i ukraintsev.'"
Prezident Rossii. July 12, 2021. http://kremlin.ru/events/president/news/66181.

———. 2022a. "Plenarnoe zasedanie Peterburgskogo mezhdunarodnogo ekonomicheskogo fo-
ruma." *Prezident Rossii.* June 17, 2022. http://kremlin.ru/events/president/news/68669.

———. 2022b. "Podpisanie dogovorov o priniatii DNR, LNR, Zaporozhskoi i Khersonskoi
oblastei v sostav Rossii." *Prezident Rossii.* September 30, 2022. http://kremlin.ru/events
/president/news/69465.

———. 2022c. "Soveshchanie o merakh sotsial'no-ekonomicheskoi podderzhki regionov."
Prezident Rossii. March 16, 2022. http://kremlin.ru/events/president/news/67996.

———. 2022d. "Ukaz ob utverzhdenii osnov gosudarstvennoi politiki po sokhraneniiu i ukre-
pleniiu traditsionnykh rossiiskikh dukhovno-nravstvennykh tsennostei." *Prezident
Rossii.* November 9, 2022. http://kremlin.ru/acts/news/69810. http://static.kremlin.ru
/media/events/files/ru/qcDRpNRKdqbKAX8mD0TP9z02hAhAJAT4.pdf.

Prilepin, Zakhar. 2012. "Pis'mo Tovarishchu Stalinu." *Svobodnaia Pressa*, July 30, 2012. http://
svpressa.ru/society/article/57411/.

Pugacheva, Marina. 1994. "Institut konkretnykh sotsial'nykh issledovanii Akademii Nauk
SSSR, 1968–1972" [The institute of applied social research of the USSR Academy of Sciences, 1968–1972]. *Sotsiologicheskii zhurnal* 2:158–72.

Pyatigorskaya, Alina. 2019. "Bezuslovnyi prioritet poslaniia prezidenta – sberezhenie natsii."
Parlamentskaia Gazeta, February 20, 2019. https://www.pnp.ru/social/vladimir
-kruglyy-bezuslovnyy-prioritet-poslaniya-prezidenta-sberezhenie-nacii.html.

Quine, Maria Sophia. 1996. *Population Politics in Twentieth-Century Europe: Fascist Dictator-
ships and Liberal Democracies.* London: Routledge.

RBC. 2023. "Gosduma razreshila pravitel'stvu ne raskryvat' statistiku." *RBC*, February 22,
2023. https://www.rbc.ru/rbcfreenews/63f5eb2c9a79474bcd973dd8.

———. 2024. "Minfin predlozhil uvelichit' poshlinu za razvod v 8 raz" [The Ministry of Finance proposed to increase the fee for divorce by 8 times]. *RBC*, June 26, 2024. https://
www.rbc.ru/economics/26/06/2024/667afd269a794734119f705d.

RBK Life. 2023. "Matkapital razreshat tratit' na oplatu uslug ZHKKH. Kak eto budet rabotat'"
[Maternity Capital will be allowed to be spent on paying for housing and communal
services. How will it work]. *RBK Life*, January 16, 2023. https://www.rbc
.ru/life/news/63c4f56a9a7947bc2e8f964e.

Re: Russia. 2023a. "Begstvo ot voiny: Novye dannye pozvoliaiut otsenit' chislo uekhavshikh
rossiian v bolee chem 800 tysiach chelovek" [Fleeing from war: New data estimate the
number of Russians who left the country at more than 800 thousand people]. *Re: Russia* (blog). July 28, 2023. https://re-russia.net/review/347/.

———. 2023b. "Civil Society: One in Five Rubles Allocated by Presidential Grants Is Spent on
Pro-war Projects, While Socially Oriented NGOs Face Financial Hardship." *Re: Russia*
(blog). January 31, 2023. https://re-russia.net/en/review/172/.

———. 2023c. "Frustratsii neprotivleniia: Tipichnyi rossiianin podderzhivaet i ne podderzhivaet voinu odnovremenno, no ne khochet vygliadet' ee protivnikom" [Frustrations of

non-resistance: A typical Russian supports and does not support the war at the same time, but does not want to be seen as its opponent]. *Re: Russia* (blog). May 17, 2023. https://re-russia.net/review/269/.

———. 2023d. "Voina i mir rossiiskoi Demografii: Demograficheskii trend uluchshilsia, a shok voiny i emigratsii sebia eshche ne proiavil" [War and peace of Russian demography: The demographic trend is improving, but the shock of war and emigration has not yet manifested itself in statistics]. *Re: Russia* (blog). September 28, 2023. https://re-russia .net/review/376/.

Read, Rosie, and Tatjana Thelen. 2007. "Social Security and Care after Socialism: Reconfigurations of Public and Private." *Focaal* 2007 (50): 3–18.

Reece, Koreen M. 2020. "Home and Away: Mobility and Care in Botswana's Time of AIDS." In *Spaces of Care*, edited by Loraine Gelsthorpe, Perveez Mody, and Brian Sloan, 201–18. Oxford: Hart.

Reuters. 2022a. "Anti-War Protests Held in Cities across Russia, 2,000 People Arrested." *Reuters*, February 27, 2022, sec. Europe. https://www.reuters.com/world/europe /police-detain-more-than-900-people-anti-war-protests-across-russia-monitoring -2022-02-27/.

———. 2022b. "Factbox: Where Have Russians Been Fleeing to since Mobilisation Began?" *Reuters*, October 6, 2022, sec. Europe. https://www.reuters.com/world/europe /where-have-russians-been-fleeing-since-mobilisation-began-2022-10-06/.

———. 2022c. "Liberal Russian Radio Station Closes after Pressure over Ukraine." *Reuters*, March 3, 2022, sec. Europe. https://www.reuters.com/world/europe /liberal-russian-radio-station-dissolved-editor-2022-03-03/.

———. 2022d. "Novaya Gazeta, One of Russia's Last Independent Media, Banned by Court." *Reuters*, September 5, 2022, sec. media & telecom. https://www.reuters.com/business /media-telecom/russian-court-revokes-newspaper-novaya-gazetas -license-2022-09-05/.

———. 2022e. "Russian TV Channel Says It Is Temporarily Halting Work." *Reuters*, March 3, 2022, sec. retail & consumer. https://www.reuters.com/business/retail-consumer /russian-tv-channel-says-it-is-temporarily-halting-work-2022-03-03/.

RIA. 2021. "Pensionnyi vozrast v 2023—kogda vykhodiat na pensiiu muzhchiny i zhenshchiny." *RIA Novosti*, April 9, 2021, sec. Novosti. https://ria.ru/20210409/pensiya-1727617636.html.

Richmond, Yale. 2004. *Cultural Exchange and the Cold War: Raising the Iron Curtain*. University Park: Pennsylvania State University Press.

Rimashevskya, Natalia. 1999. "Russkii krest" [The Russian cross]. *Priroda* 6:3–10.

Rindzevičiūtė, Eglė. 2015. "Toward a Joint Future beyond the Iron Curtain: East–West Politics of Global Modelling." In *The Struggle for the Long Term in Transnational Science and Politics: Forging the Future*, edited by Jenny Andersson and Eglė Rindzevičiūtė, 115–43. London: Routledge. http://www.jstor.org/stable/10.5612/slavicreview.75.1.52.

Rivkin-Fish, Michele. 2003. "Anthropology, Demography, and the Search for a Critical Analysis of Fertility: Insights from Russia." *American Anthropologist* 105 (2): 289–301. https://doi.org/doi:10.1525/aa.2003.105.2.289.

———. 2005. *Women's Health in Post-Soviet Russia: The Politics of Intervention*. Bloomington: Indiana University Press.

———. 2006. "From 'Demographic Crisis' to 'Dying Nation'—The Politics of Language and Reproduction in Russia." In *Gender and National Identity in Twentieth-Century*

Russian Culture, edited by Helena Goscilo and Andrea Lanoux, 151–73. DeKalb: Northern Illinois University Press.

———. 2009. "Tracing Landscapes of the Past in Class Subjectivity: Practices of Memory and Distinction in Marketizing Russia." *American Ethnologist* 36 (1): 79–95.

———. 2010. "Pronatalism, Gender Politics, and the Renewal of Family Support in Russia: Toward a Feminist Anthropology of 'Maternity Capital.'" *Slavic Review* 69 (3): 701–24.

———. 2024. *Unmaking Russia's Abortion Culture: Family Planning and the Struggle for a Liberal Biopolitics*. Nashville, TN: Vanderbilt University Press.

Rogacheva, Sofia. 2009. "Pochemu v Rossii vse bol'she i bol'she grazhdanskikh brakov?" [Why are there more and more civil marriages in Russia?]. *Radio Liberty*, April 29, 2009. https://www.svoboda.org/a/1618261.html.

Rogers, Douglas. 2005. "Moonshine, Money, and the Politics of Liquidity in Rural Russia." *American Ethnologist* 32 (1): 63–81. https://doi.org/10.1525/ae.2005.32.1.63.

———. 2006. "How to Be a Khoziain in a Transforming State: State Formation and the Ethics of Governance in Post-Soviet Russia." *Comparative Studies in Society and History* 48 (4): 915–45. https://doi.org/10.1017/S001041750600034X.

Rosefielde, Steven. 1986. "Demographic Analysis and Population Catastrophes in the USSR: A Rejoinder to Barbara Anderson and Brian Silver." *Slavic Review* 45 (2): 300–306.

Rosenholm, Arja, and Irina Savkina. 2008. "'Rodi patriota—Spasi Rossiiu!' Natsiia i gender v demograficheskom diskurse rossiiskikh pechatnykh SMI, kommentirovavshikh 'Demograficheskoe poslanie' V.V. Putina" [Save Russia by giving a birth to a patriot: Nation and gender in the discourse on demography by printed media, which commented on V.V. Putin's 'Demographic State of the Union']. *Gendernye issledovaniia* 18 (2): 266–82.

Rosstat. 2010. *Demograficheskii ezhegodnik Rossii Rosstat*. Moskva: Rosstat.

———. 2011a. "Life Expectancy at Birth." Russia in Figures. 2011. https://www.gks.ru/bgd /regl/b11_12/IssWWW.exe/Stg/d01/05-07.htm.

———. 2011b. "Resident Population." Russia in Figures. 2011. https://www.gks.ru/bgd/regl /b11_12/IssWWW.exe/Stg/d01/05-01.htm.

———. 2011c. "Russia in Figures." Russian Federation Federal State Statistics Service. 2011. http://www.gks.ru/bgd/regl/b11_12/Main.htm.

———. 2011d. "Total Vital Statistics Rates." Russia in Figures. 2011. https://www.gks.ru/bgd /regl/b11_12/IssWWW.exe/Stg/d01/05-04.htm.

———. 2019. "Rosstat predstavil utochnennyi demograficheskii prognoz do 2035 goda." December 28, 2019. https://rosstat.gov.ru/folder/313/document/72529.

———. 2020. *Rossiia v tsifrakh. 2020: Kratkii statisticheskii sbornik*. Moskva: Rosstat.

———. 2022a. "Demografiia." 2022. https://rosstat.gov.ru/folder/12781#.

———. 2022b. *Sotsial'no-ekonomicheskoe polozhenie Rossii*. Moskva: Federal'naia sluzhba gosudarstvennoi statistiki.

Rostova, Natalia. 1996. "'Rossiiskaia gazeta' ob"iavliaet konkurs na natsional'nuiu ideiu" [Rossiiskaia Gazeta announces a competition for a national idea]. *Rastsvet rossiiskikh SMI* (blog). July 30, 1996. http://www.yeltsinmedia.com/events/july-30-1996/.

Rotkirch, Anna, Olga Tkach, and Elena Zdravomyslova. 2012. "Making and Managing Class: Employment of Paid Domestic Workers in Russia." In *Rethinking Class in Russia*, edited by Suvi Salmenniemi, 129–48. London: Ashgate.

Rotova, Raisa S., and Mikhail B. Denisenko, eds. 2006. *D. I. Valentei v vospominaniiakh kolleg i uchenikov* [D. I. Valentei as remembered by his colleagues and students]. Moskva: MAKS Press.

Roudakova, Natalia. 2017. *Losing Pravda*. Cambridge: Cambridge University Press.

Rybakovsky, Leonid. 2016. "Rezul'tativnost' kak osnovnoi pokazatel' otsenki sostoianiia i tendentsii rozhdaemosti" [Effectiveness as the main indicator of fertility trends]. *Sotsiologicheskie Issledovaniia* 4:23–30.

Sahlins, Marshall. 2011a. "What Kinship Is (Part One)." *Journal of the Royal Anthropological Institute* 17 (1): 2–19. https://doi.org/10.1111/j.1467-9655.2010.01666.x.

———. 2011b. "What Kinship Is (Part Two)." *Journal of the Royal Anthropological Institute* 17 (2): 227–42. https://doi.org/10.1111/j.1467-9655.2011.01677.x.

Sakwa, Richard. 2014. *Putin and the Oligarch: The Khodorkovsky-Yukos Affair*. New York: Bloomsbury.

Sauer, Pjotr. 2022a. "Putin Announces Partial Mobilisation and Threatens Nuclear Retaliation in Escalation of Ukraine War." *The Guardian*, September 21, 2022, sec. world news. https://www.theguardian.com/world/2022/sep/21/putin-announces-partial-mobilisation-in-russia-in-escalation-of-ukraine-war.

———. 2022b. "Russia Bans Facebook and Instagram under 'Extremism' Law." *The Guardian*, March 21, 2022, sec. world news. https://www.theguardian.com/world/2022/mar/21/russia-bans-facebook-and-instagram-under-extremism-law.

Savinskaya, Olga, ed. 2008. *Rabota i sem'ia v zhizni zhenshchin s det'mi-doshkol'nikami: Opyt goroda Moskvy* [Work and family in the lives of women with preschool children: Moscow-based experience]. Moskva: Variant.

Saxer, Martin, and Ruben Andersson. 2019. "The Return of Remoteness: Insecurity, Isolation and Connectivity in the New World Disorder." *Social Anthropology/Anthropologie Sociale* 27 (2): 140–55. https://doi.org/10.1111/1469-8676.12652.

Schenk, Caress. 2018. *Why Control Immigration?: Strategic Uses of Migration Management in Russia*. Toronto: University of Toronto Press.

Scherbov, Sergei, Stuart Gietel-Basten, Dalkhat Ediev, Sergey Shulgin, and Warren Sanderson. 2022. "COVID-19 and Excess Mortality in Russia: Regional Estimates of Life Expectancy Losses in 2020 and Excess Deaths in 2021." *PLOS ONE* 17 (11): e0275967. https://doi.org/10.1371/journal.pone.0275967.

Schweber, Libby. 2006. *Disciplining Statistics: Demography and Vital Statistics in France and England, 1830–1885*. Durham, NC: Duke University Press.

Scott, James C. 1998. *Seeing Like a State: How Certain Schemes to Improve the Human Condition Have Failed*. New Haven, CT: Yale University Press.

Scott, Mark. 2022. "Telegram Bans Russian State Media after Pressure from Europe." *POLITICO* (blog). March 4, 2022. https://www.politico.eu/article/russia-rt-media-telegram-ukraine/.

Seccombe, Wally. 1983. "Marxism and Demography." *New Left Review* I (137): 23–47.

Seddon, Max. 2023. "Russia Bans Largest Independent News Website Meduza." *Financial Times*, January 26, 2023, sec. war in Ukraine. https://www.ft.com/content/bae1d751-f032-4662-a346-873c91740472.

Sergeev, Mikhail. 2024. "V Rossiiskikh gorodakh podnimaetsia novaia volna demograficheskogo krizisa" [A new wave of demographic crisis is rising in Russian cities]. *Nezavisimaia Gazeta*, July 22, 2024. https://www.ng.ru/economics/2024-07-22/1_9054_crisis.html.

Sharafutdinova, Gulnaz. 2020. *The Red Mirror: Putin's Leadership and Russia's Insecure Identity*. New York: Oxford University Press.

Sharpless, John. 1997. "Population Science, Private Foundations, and Development Aid: The Transformation of Demographic Knowledge in the United States, 1945–1965." In

International Development and the Social Sciences: Essays on the History and Politics of Knowledge, edited by Frederick Cooper and Randall Packard, 176–200. Berkeley: University of California Press.

Shchipkov, Aleksandr. 2022. "Samootchishchenie. O chem govoril Vladimir Putin." *Parlamentskaia Gazeta*, April 11, 2022. https://www.pnp.ru/social/samoochishhenie-o-chem-govoril-vladimir-putin.html.

Shepelin, Ilya. 2013. "Kak kuiutsia dukhovnye skrepy." *Slon*, November 14, 2013. https://republic.ru/posts/35324.

Sherbakova, Ekaterina. 2020. "Demograficheskie itogi I polugodiia 2020 goda v Rossii (Chast' I)" [Demographic results of the first half of 2020 in Russia (Part I)]. *Demoscope Weekly*, September 13, 2020. http://www.demoscope.ru/weekly/2020/0867/barom03.php.

Shevchenko, Olga. 2009. *Crisis and the Everyday in Postsocialist Moscow*. Bloomington: Indiana University Press.

Shevel, Oxana. 2011. "Russian Nation-Building from Yel'tsin to Medvedev: Ethnic, Civic or Purposefully Ambiguous?" *Europe-Asia Studies* 63 (2): 179–202. https://doi.org/10.1080/09668136.2011.547693.

Shkel, Tamara. 2006. "Liubov' Sliska: 'Zabotu o "sberezhenii" naroda nel'zia svalivat' na odnu meditsinu'." *Rossiiskaia Gazeta*, June 29, 2006. https://rg.ru/2006/06/29/slisca.html.

Shkolnikov, Vladimir M., and Alexander Nemtsov. 1997. "The Anti-alcohol Campaign and Variations in Russian Mortality." In *Premature Death in the New Independent States*, edited by Jose Luis Bodadilla, Christine A. Costello, and Faith Mitchell, 239–61. Washington, DC: National Academy Press.

Shlapentokh, Dmitry. 2007. "Dugin Eurasianism: A Window on the Minds of the Russian Elite or an Intellectual Ploy?" *Studies in East European Thought* 59 (3): 215–36.

Shohet, Merav. 2021. *Silence and Sacrifice: Family Stories of Care and the Limits of Love in Vietnam*. Oakland: University of California Press.

Shore, Cris. 2008. "Audit Culture and Illiberal Governance: Universities and the Politics of Accountability." *Anthropological Theory* 8 (3): 278–98. https://doi.org/10.1177/1463499608093815.

Shore, Cris, and Susan Wright. 1997. *Anthropology of Policy: Critical Perspectives on Governance and Power*. London: Routledge.

Shpakovskaya, Larisa, and Zhanna Chernova. 2022. "How the Everyday Logic of Pragmatic Individualism Undermines Russian State Pronatalism." *Social Inclusion* 10 (3): 184–93. https://doi.org/10.17645/si.v10i3.5272.

Shriver, Lionel. 2003. "Population in Literature." *Population and Development Review* 29 (2): 153–62.

Shryock, Andrew. 2013. "It's This, Not That: How Marshall Sahlins Solves Kinship." *HAU: Journal of Ethnographic Theory* 3 (2): 271–79. https://doi.org/10.14318/hau3.2.015.

Shulman, Ekaterina. 2022. "Mobilizatsiia demobilizovannykh." *Re: Russia* (blog). September 16, 2022. https://re-russia.net/analytics/018/.

Sifman, Rosa I. 1974. *Dinamika rozhdaemosti v SSSR* [The dynamics of birthrates in the USSR]. Moskva: Statistika.

Signal. 2022. "Demshiza. I v chem ona byla ne prava?" [Demshiza. And what she was wrong about?]. *Signal, Meduza* (blog). November 21, 2022. https://us10.campaign-archive.com/?u=ff4a009ba1f59d865f0301f85&id=f071ffe2f7.

Simonov, Aleksander. 2011. "Roditeli protestuiut protiv nekhvatki mest v detskikh sadakh." *Uchitel'skaia Gazeta*, October 17, 2011. https://ug.ru/roditeli-protestuyut-protiv-nehvatki-mest-v-detskih-sadah/.

Sinel'nikov, Alexandr. 2016. "Vliianie razvodov i otkazov ot registratsii braka na rozh-daemost'" [The impact of divorces and unregistered marriages on fertility]. *Psikho-logicheskaia Gazeta*, December 13, 2016. https://psy.su/feed/5794/.

———. 2018. "Sem'ia i brak: Krizis ili modernizatsiia" [Family and divorce: Crisis or modernization]. *Sotsiologicheskii zhurnal* 24 (1): 95–113.

———. 2019. "Transformatsiia braka i rozhdaemosti v Rossii" [Transformation of marriage and fertility in Russia]. *Narodonaselenie* 22 (2): 26–39.

Slezkine, Yuri. 1994. "The USSR as a Communal Apartment, or How a Socialist State Promoted Ethnic Particularism." *Slavic Review* 53 (2): 414–52.

———. 2017. *The House of Government: A Saga of the Russian Revolution*. Princeton, NJ: Princeton University Press.

Smallwood, Steve, and Jessica Chamberlain. 2005. "Replacement Fertility, What Has It Been and What Does It Mean?" *Population Trends* 119 (119): 16–27.

Smirnov, Sergey. 2022. "RF kontraliruet 78% ploshchadi anneksirovannykh oblastei." *Aussiedlerbote.de* (blog). October 4, 2022. https://aussiedlerbote.de/2022/10/rf-kontroliruet-78-ploshhadi-anneksirovannyx-oblastej/.

Smith, Mark B. 2010. *Property of Communists: The Urban Housing Program from Stalin to Khrushchev*. DeKalb: Northern Illinois University Press.

Smolkin, Victoria. 2019. *A Sacred Space Is Never Empty: A History of Soviet Atheism*. Princeton, NJ: Princeton University Press.

Sokolov, Mikhail. 2022. "Faculty Self-Governance, Professorial Power, and Academic Freedom in Russia." *Demokratizatsiya: The Journal of Post-Soviet Democratization* 30 (1): 59–83.

Stanziani, Alessandro. 2017. "European Statistics, Russian Numbers, and Social Dynamics, 1861–1914." *Slavic Review* 76 (1): 1–23. https://doi.org/10.1017/slr.2017.3.

Starostina, Yulia. 2022. "Mozhno li vse-taki vyiasnit', skol'ko rossiian pogiblo na voine? A k chemu privedet emigratsiia iz Rossii—i byla li ona po-nastoiashchemu massovoi?" *Meduza*, December 13, 2022. https://meduza.io/feature/2022/12/13/mozhno-li-vse-taki-kak-to-vyyasnit-skolko-rossiyan-pogiblo-na-voyne-a-k-chemu-privedet-emigratsiya-iz-rossii-i-byla-li-ona-po-nastoyaschemu-massovoy.

Steshenko, Valentina. 2001. "Mikhail Vasilievich Ptukha kak demograf 1884-1961" [Mikhail Vasilievich Ptukha as a demographer 1884-1961]. *Demoscope Weekly*, October 7, 2001. https://www.demoscope.ru/weekly/035/nauka03.php.

Stevenson, Lisa. 2014. *Life beside Itself: Imagining Care in the Canadian Arctic*. Berkeley: University of California Press.

Strathern, Marilyn. 2003. *Commons and Borderlands: Working Papers on Interdisciplinarity, Accountability and the Flow of Knowledge*. Oxon: Sean Kingston.

Strel'nikov, Alexei. 2023. "Aborty v Rossii. V chastnykh klinikakh uzhe vveden zapret?" [Abortion in Russia. Has a ban already been introduced in private clinics?]. *Dw.com*, November 16, 2023. https://www.dw.com/ru/aborty-v-rossii-v-castnyh-klinikah-uze-vveden-zapret/a-67418676.

Sudoplatov, Anatoly. 2006. "Politicheskie kulisy razvitiia demografii v MGU" [Behind the political curtains of the development of demography at the Moscow State University]. In *D. I. Valentei v vospominaniiakh kolleg i uchenikov* [D. I. Valentei as remembered by his colleagues and students], edited by Raisa S. Rotova and Mikhail B. Denisenko, 6–14. Moskva: MAKS Press.

Sulashkin, S., ed. 2008. *Natsional'naia identichnost' Rossii i demograficheskii krizis: Materialy II Vserossiiskoi nauchnoi konferentsii* [Russia's national identity and the demographic crisis: Proceedings of the II All-Russian Scientific Conference]. Moskva: Nauchnii Ekspert.

Super, Roman. 2022. "Rvite povestki." *Super* (blog). September 24, 2022. https://t.me /romasuperromasuper.

Surinov, Aleksander. 2009. "Chislennost' naseleniia Rossii v blizhaishie gody budet padat'— Rosstat." *RIA Novosti*, November 26, 2009. https://ria.ru/society/20091126/195646195.html.

———. 2014. *Itogi perepisi Naseleniia 2014 goda v Krymskom Federal'nom Okruge*. Moskva: Rosstat.

Surnacheva, Elizaveta, and Aleksander Gabuev. 2012. "Kremlevskie sovetologi." *Kommersant" Vlast'*, June 18, 2012. http://www.kommersant.ru/doc/1958059.

Suslov, Mikhail. 2018. "'Russian World' Concept: Post-Soviet Geopolitical Ideology and the Logic of 'Spheres of Influence.'" *Geopolitics* 23 (2): 330–53. https://doi.org/10.1080 /14650045.2017.1407921.

Syrokomsky, Vitaly. 2001. "Zagadka patriarkha" [The patriarch's riddle]. *Znamia* 4:161.

TASS. 2018. "Putin obnovil strategiiu gosudarstvennoi natsional'noi politiki na period do 2025 goda." *TASS*, December 7, 2018. https://tass.ru/politika/5884170.

———. 2022a. "Putin podpisal ukaz ob uchrezhdenii zvaniia 'Mat'-Geroinia.'" *TASS*, August 15, 2022. https://tass.ru/obschestvo/15477923.

———. 2022b. "Putin utverdil osnovy gospolitiki po sokhraneniiu dukhovno-nravstvennykh tsennostei." *TASS*, November 9, 2022. https://tass.ru/obschestvo/16283057.

———. 2023. "Inostrannye agenty v rossiiskom zakonodatel'stve. Istoriia statusa i ego prim- enenie" [Foreign agents in Russian legislation: History of the status and its applica- tion]. *TASS*, September 12, 2023. https://tass.ru/info/18731205.

———. 2024a. "Putin nazval narodosberezhenie i ekonomiku glavnymi v programme razvitiia strany" [Putin named population care and economy the most important pro- grams of the country's development]. *TASS*, March 19, 2024. https://tass.ru /politika/20289187.

———. 2024b. "VTSIOM: Vosem' iz desiati brakov v RF v 2024 godu raspadalis'" [VTSIOM: Eight out of ten marriages ended in divorce in 2024]. *TASS*, December 18, 2024. https:// tass.ru/obschestvo/22702277?ysclid=m4tqwg0d3q370636877.

Thelen, Tatjana. 2015. "Care of the Elderly, Migration, Community: Explorations from Rural Romania." In *Anthropological Perspectives on Care*, edited by Erdmute Alber and Heike Drotbohm, 137–55. New York: Palgrave Macmillan.

Thelen, Tatjana, and Cati Coe. 2019. "Political Belonging through Elderly Care: Temporali- ties, Representations and Mutuality." *Anthropological Theory* 19 (2): 279–99. https://doi .org/10.1177/1463499617742833.

Thelen, Tatjana, and Carolin Leutloff-Grandits. 2010. "Self-Sacrifice or Natural Donation? A Life Course Perspective on Grandmothering in New Zagreb (Croatia) and East Berlin (Germany)." *Horizontes Antropologicos* 16 (34): 427–52.

Thelen, Tatjana, André Thiemann, and Duška Roth. 2014. "State Kinning and Kinning the State in Serbian Elder Care Programs." *Social Analysis* 58 (3): 107–23.

Ticktin, Miriam Iris. 2011. *Casualties of Care: Immigration and the Politics of Humanitarian- ism in France*. Berkeley: University of California Press.

Timakov, Vladimir, and Aleksey Tokarev. 2014. "Istoriia s demografiei." *Kommersant" Vlast'*, October 13, 2014. https://www.kommersant.ru/doc/2584425.

Tkach, Olga. 2015. "Zabotlivyi dom: Ukhod za pozhilymi rodstvennikami i sovmestnoe prozhivanie" [A caring home: Caring for aging relatives and co-residence]. *Sotsio- logicheskie issledovaniia* 10:94–102.

Todes, Daniel Philip. 1989. *Darwin without Malthus: The Struggle for Existence in Russian Evolutionary Thought*. New York: Oxford University Press.

Toepler, Stefan, Ulla Pape, and Vladimir Benevolenski. 2020. "Subnational Variations in Government-Nonprofit Relations: A Comparative Analysis of Regional Differences within Russia." *Journal of Comparative Policy Analysis: Research and Practice* 22 (1): 47–65. https://doi.org/10.1080/13876988.2019.1584446.

Tolts, Mark. 1987. "Skol'ko zhe nas togda bylo?" [How many of us were there then?]. *Ogonek* 51:10–11.

———. 1989. "Nedostupnoe izmerenie." In *V chelovecheskom izmerenii*, edited by Anatoly Vishnevsky, 325–42. Moskva: Progress.

———. 1991. "Perepis', prigovorennaia k zabveniiu" [Census condemned to oblivion]. In *Sem'ia i semeinaia politika*, edited by Anatoly Vishnevsky, 161–78. Moskva: Institut Sotsial'no-ekonomicheskikh problem narodonaseleniia.

———. 2001. "The Failure of Demographic Statistics: A Soviet Response to Population Troubles." Paper presented at the IUSSP XXIVth General Population Conference, Salvador-Bahia, Brazil, August 2001.

———. 2004. "Tainy sovetskoi demografii" [The Secrets of Soviet Demography]. *Demoscope Weekly*, October 10, 2004. http://demoscope.ru/weekly/2004/0171/analit06.php.

———. 2008. "Population Trends in the Russian Federation: Reflections on the Legacy of Soviet Censorship and Distortions of Demographic Statistics." *Eurasian Geography and Economics* 49 (1): 87–98.

Travkin, Nikolai. 2023. "Molodykh zhalko." *NTravkin* (blog). March 7, 2023. https://t.me/NTravkin/2661.

———. 2024. "I sozdal On mir . . ." [Then he created the world . . .]. *NTravkin* (blog). January 2, 2024. https://t.me/NTravkin/3488.

Traynor, Ian. 2001. "Kremlin Silences Its Main Media Critic." *The Guardian*, April 4, 2001, sec. world news. https://www.theguardian.com/world/2001/apr/04/russia.iantraynor.

Treshchanin, Dmitry. 2024. "Tsena Bakhmuta. My poluchili dokumenty 'CHVK Vagnera' o 'proekte K'—i znaem vse o pogibshikh i zaverbovannykh zakluchennykh" [Bakhmut price. We received documents from the Wagner PMC about 'Project K' and we know everything about the dead and recruited prisoners]. *Mediazona*, June 10, 2024. https://zona.media/article/2024/06/10/42174.

Tretyakov, Vitaly. 2006. "Sberezhenie naroda—vysshaia izo vsekh nashikh gosudarstvennykh zadach." *Russkaia Liniia*, April 28, 2006. https://rusk.ru/st.php?idar=17024.

Troianovski, Anton, and Valeriya Safronova. 2022. "Russia Takes Censorship to New Extremes, Stifling War Coverage." *New York Times*, March 4, 2022, sec. world. https://www.nytimes.com/2022/03/04/world/europe/russia-censorship-media-crackdown.html.

Trudovoi kodeks RF. 2014. "Stat'ia 256. Otpuska po ukhodu za rebenkom." Trudovoi kodeks RF. August 17, 2014. https://www.trudkod.ru/chast-4/razdel-12/glava-41/st-256-tk-rf.

Turner, Victor Witter. 1967. *The Forest of Symbols: Aspects of Ndembu Ritual*. Ithaca, NY: Cornell University Press.

Unger, Corinna R., and Heinrich Hartmann. 2014. "Counting, Constructing, and Controlling Populations: The Histrory of Demography, Population Studies, and Family Planning in the Twentieth Century." In *A World of Populations: Transnational Perspectives on Demography in the Twentieth Century*, edited by Heinrich Hartmann and Corinna R. Unger, 1–15. New York and Oxford: Berghahn Books.

UNHCR. 2023. "Situation Ukraine Refugee Situation." Operational Data Portal. UNHCR. February 28, 2023. https://data.unhcr.org/en/situations/ukraine.

United Nations, Department of Economic and Social Affairs, Population Division. 2015. *World Population Prospects: The 2015 Revision, Volume I: Comprehensive Tables*. ST/ESA/SER.A/379. New York: United Nations.

URBC.RU. 2015. "Deputaty EGD utverdili aktualizirovannyi Genplan razvitiia Ekaterinburga do 2025" [Yekaterinburg parliament approved the city general plan until 2025]. *URBC.RU—Novosti Ekonomiki*. November 24, 2015. https://urbc.ru/1068049542-deputaty-egd-utverdili-aktualizirovannyy-genplan-razvitiya-ekaterinburga-do-2025-goda.html.

Urlanis, Boris. 1968. "Beregite muzhchin!" [Protect the men!]. *Literaturnaia Gazeta*, July 24, 1968.

———. 1974. *Problemy dinamiki naseleniia SSSR* [Problems of the population dynamics in the USSR]. Moskva: Nauka.

———. 1975. "Demograficheskaia politika v sovremennom mire" [Demographic policy in the contemporary world]. *Mirovaia ekonomika i mezhdunarodnye otnosheniia* [World economy and international relations] 5:106–12.

Utekhin, Ilya. 2004. *Ocherki kommunal'nogo byta*. Moskva: OGI.

Utrata, Jennifer. 2011. "Youth Privilege: Doing Age and Gender in Russia's Single-Mother Families." *Gender & Society* 25 (5): 616–41. https://doi.org/10.1177/0891243211421781.

———. 2015. *Women without Men: Single Mothers and Family Change in the New Russia*. Ithaca, NY: Cornell University Press.

———. 2017. "Grandmothers in Russia's Matrifocal Families: Shoring up Family Life." In *Grandparents in Cultural Context*, edited by David W. Shwalb and Ziarat Hossain, 133–56. New York: Routledge.

Valentei, Dmitry, ed. 1980. *Upravlenie demograficheskimi protsessami* [The regulation of demographic processes]. Moskva: Statistika.

Valentei, Dmitry, and Anatoly Sudoplatov, eds. 1982. *Problemy narodonaseleniia: Sovremennaia demograficheskaia situatsiia v razvivaiushchikhsia stranakh* [Population problems: Contemporary demographic situation in developing countries]. Moskva: Progress.

Varga-Harris, Christine. 2015. *Stories of House and Home: Soviet Apartment Life during the Khrushchev Years*. Ithaca, NY: Cornell University Press.

VCIOM. 2019. "Otnoshenie k brakam i razvodam: Monitoring" [Attitudes toward marriage and divorce: Monitoring]. VCIOM Novosti. July 8, 2019. https://wciom.ru/analytical-reviews/analiticheskii-obzor/otnoshenie-k-brakam-i-razvodam-monitoring?ysclid=lxo6ivaphc715131947.

———. 2022. "Spetsial'naia voennaia operatsiia: Monitoring" [Special military operation: Monitoring]. VCIOM Novosti. June 30, 2022. https://wciom.ru/analytical-reviews/analiticheskii-obzor/specialnaja-voennaja-operacija-monitoring-20223006?utm_source=yxnews&utm_medium=desktop.

Vedomosti. 2022. "Putin nazval preemstvennost' pokolenii osnovoi natsional'noi identichnosti Rossii." *Vedomosti*, November 15, 2022. https://www.vedomosti.ru/society/news/2022/11/15/950410-putin-nazval-preemstvennost-pokolenii.

Vepreva, Anastasia, and Roman Osminkin. 2022. *Kommunalka na Petrogradke*. Moskva: Novoe literaturnoe obozrenie.

Verdery, Katherine. 1994. "From Parent-State to Family Patriarchs: Gender and Nation in Contemporary Eastern Europe." *East European Politics and Societies* 8 (2): 225–55.

———. 1996. "The 'Etatization' of Time in Ceausescu's Romania." In *What Was Socialism, and What Comes Next?*, 39–57. Princeton, NJ: Princeton University Press.

Villadsen, Kaspar, and Ayo Wahlberg. 2015. "The Government of Life: Managing Populations, Health and Scarcity." *Economy and Society* 44 (1): 1–17. https://doi.org/10.1080/03085147.2014.983831.

Vilquin, Eric. 2005. "History of Population Thought." In *Demography: Analysis and Synthesis: A Treatise in Population*, edited by Graziella Caselli, Jacques Vallin, and Guillaume Wunsch, IV:5–26. New York: Academic Press.

Vishnevsky, Anatoly, ed. 1977. *Brach'nost', rozhdaemost', smertnost' v Rossii i v SSSR* [Nuptiality, fertility, mortality in Russia and USSR]. Moskva: Statistika.

———. 1979. "Demograficheskaia revoliutsiia i budushchee rozhdaemosti i smertnosti v SSSR" [The demographic revolution and the future trends of fertility and mortality in the USSR]. In *Nashe budushchee glazami demografa* [Our future in the eyes of the demographer], edited by Dmitry Valentei, 27–43. Moskva: Statistika.

———. 1993. "Sud'ba odnogo demografa: Portret na fone epokhi. Vospominaniia M.V. Kurmana" [The fate of one demographer: A portrait against the backdrop of the era. M.V. Kurman's Memoirs]. *Cahiers Du Monde Russe et Soviétique* 34 (4): 589–629.

———. 1996. "Trudnoe vozrozhdenie demografii" [The difficult resurgence of demography]. *Sotsiologicheskii Zhurnal* 1–2:93–116.

———. 2005. "Demograficheskaia revoliutsiia." In *Izbrannye demograficheskie trudy: Demograficheskaia teoriia i demograficheskaia istoriia* [Selected publications in demography: Demographic theory and demographic history], I:5–214. Moskva: Nauka.

———. 2007. *Rossiia pered demographicheskim vyborom.* Moskva: GU VSHE.

———. 2010. *Sberezhenie naseleniia ili depopuliatsiia Rossii.* Moskva: Gosudarstvennyi universitet vysshei shkoly ekonomiki.

———. 2014. "Demograficheskaia revoliutsiia meniaet reproduktivnuiu strategiiu vida Homo sapiens" [Demographic revolution changes reproductive strategies of Homo sapiens]. *Demograficheskoe Obozrenie* 1 (1): 6–33.

Vishnevsky, Anatoly, and Igor Kon, eds. 1979. *Brachnost', rozhdaemost', sem'ia za tri veka (Novoe v zarubezhnoi demografii)* [Nuptiality, fertility and family in the last three centuries]. Moskva: Statistika.

Volkov, Andrey, ed. 1971. *Faktory rozhdaemosti* [Indicators of fertility trends]. Moskva: Statistika.

———. 1976. "O neobkhodimosti vozdeistviia na rozhdaemost'." In *Rozhdaemost'*, edited by Leonid E. Darsky, 35–61. Moskva: Statistika.

———. 1981. "Sem'ia kak faktor iIzmeneniia demograficheskoi situatsii" [Family as a factor of the transformation in the demographic situation]. *Sotsiologicheskie issledovaniia* 1:34–42.

———. 1986. *Sem'ia—ob"ekt demografii.* Moskva: Mysl'.

———. 1990. *Perepis' naseleniia SSSR 1937 g.: Istoriia i materialy* [1937 census of the USSR: History and materials]. Moskva: Muzei Goskomstata SSSR.

———. 1993. "Po sledam perecherknutoi perepesi" [Following the erased census]. In *Naselenie Sovetskogo Soiuza. 1922–1991* [Population of the Soviet Union. 1922–1991], edited by E. M. Andreev, L. E. Darsky, and T. L. Kharkova, 23–29. Moskva: Nauka.

———. 1997. "Kak stalo krivym zerkalo obshchestva: K 60-letiiu perepisi 1937 goda" [How the mirror of society became warped: Towards the 60th anniversary of the 1937 census]. *Voprosy statistiki* 3:14–21.

———. 2001. "Sushchestvuet li nauka demografiia?" [Does demography as a science exist?]. *Demoscope Weekly*, November 18, 2001. http://www.demoscope.ru/weekly/041 /nauka01.php.

———. 2003. "My sdelali, chto smogli. . ." [We did what we could. . .]. *Demoscope Weekly*, September 21, 2003. https://www.demoscope.ru/weekly/2003/0125/nauka01.php.

———. 2014. "Perepis' naseleniia 1937 goda: Vymysly i pravda" [1937 census: Myths and truth]. In *Izbrannye demograficheskie trudy* [Selection of work in demography], 121–67. Moskva: Gosudarstvennyi Universitet Vysshei Shkoly Ekonomiki.

Volkov, Andrey, and Leonid E. Darsky, eds. 1975. *Brak i sem'ia: Demograficheskii aspekt (Novoe v zarubezhnoi demografii)* [Marriage and family: A demographic perspective (new in foreign demography)]. Moskva: Statistika.

———, eds. 1979. *Razvod. Demograficheskii aspekt (Novoe v zarubezhnoii demografii)* [Divorce: A demographic perspective (new in foreign demography)]. Moskva: Statistika.

Vorobyova, Maria. 2015. "Kommunal'naia kvartira v sovetskikh kinofil'makh i anekdotakh: Popytka ob"emnogo portreta." *Labirint* 2:19–31.

Vucinich, Alexander. 1984. *Empire of Knowledge: The Academy of Sciences of the USSR (1917–1970)*. Berkeley: University of California Press.

Vyzhutovich, Valery. 2007. "Valery Tishkov: Rossii ne ugrozhaet demograficheskaia katastrofa." *Rossiiskaia Gazeta*, January 24, 2007, 4276 ed. http://www.rg.ru/2007 /01/24/demografia.html.

———. 2017. "Anatoly Vishnevsky: Rossii nuzhny vysokokvalifitsirovannye migranty." *Rossiiskaia Gazeta*, January 24, 2017. https://rg.ru/2017/01/24/anatolij-vishnevskij-rossii -nuzhny-vysokokvalificirovannye-migranty.html.

Wedel, Janine R. 1998. *Collision and Collusion: The Strange Case of Western Aid to Eastern Europe, 1989–1998*. New York: St. Martin's Press.

———. 2005. "U.S. Foreign Aid and Foreign Policy: Building Strong Relationships by Doing It Right!" *International Studies Perspectives* 6 (1): 35–50.

Weismantel, Mary. 1995. "Making Kin: Kinship Theory and Zumbagua Adoptions." *American Ethnologist* 22 (4): 685–704. https://doi.org/10.1525/ae.1995.22.4.02a00010.

Weston, Kath. 1991. *Families We Choose: Lesbians, Gays, Kinship*. Between Men—Between Women. New York: Columbia University Press.

Whittaker, Andrea. 2022. "Demodystopias: Narratives of Ultra-low Fertility in Asia." *Economy and Society* 51 (1): 116–37. https://doi.org/10.1080/03085147.2021.1968672.

World Bank Indicators. 2022a. "Death Rate, Crude (per 1,000 People) - Russian Federation | Data." World Bank. 2022. https://data.worldbank.org/indicator/SP.DYN.CDRT .IN?locations=RU.

———. 2022b. "Fertility Rate, Total (Births per Woman) – Russian Federation | Data." World Bank. 2022. https://data.worldbank.org/indicator/SP.DYN.TFRT.IN?locations=RU.

———. 2022c. "Life Expectancy at Birth, Male (Years) – Russian Federation and Eurasia." World Bank Open Data. 2022. https://data.worldbank.org.

———. 2022d. "Life Expectancy at Birth, Total (Years) – Russian Federation | Data." World Bank. 2022. https://data.worldbank.org/indicator/SP.DYN.LE00.IN?locations=RU.

World Health Organization. 1966. "World Health Assembly Resolution 19.43." World Health Organization Handbook of Resolutions and Decisions. Geneva: World Health Organization. http://apps.who.int/iris/bitstream/10665/85788/1/Official_record151_eng .pdf.

Yaffa, Joshua. 2023. "The Quiescent Russians." *Foreign Affairs*, February 23, 2023. https://www.foreignaffairs.com/ukraine/quiescent-russians.

Yakunin, Vladimir, Vardan Bagdasaryan, and Stepan Sulakshin. 2007. *Gosudarstvennaia politika vyvoda Rossii iz demograficheskogo krizisa*. Moskva: Nauchnyi Ekspert, Ekonomika.

Yapparova, Lilia. 2024. "'Oni mogut nachat' protivodeistvovat': Rossiiskie vlasti boiatsia detei, nasil'no vyvezennykh iz Ukrainy. Ikh pytaiutsia 'perevospitat'' i postavit' pod zhestkii tsifrovoi kontrol'" ['They may begin to resist': Russian authorities are afraid of children forcibly taken from Ukraine. They are trying to 're-educate' them and put them under strict digital control]. *Meduza*, March 11, 2024. https://meduza.io/feature/2024/03/11/oni-mogut-nachat-protivodeystvovat.

Yarris, Kristin E. 2020. *Care Across Generations: Solidarity and Sacrifice in Transnational Families*. Stanford, CA: Stanford University Press.

Yudin, Greg. 2017. "Passivnyi grazhdanin." *Vedomosti*, May 14, 2017. https://www.vedomosti.ru/opinion/articles/2017/05/14/689725-passivnii-grazhdanin.

———. 2020. "Governing through Polls: Politics of Representation and Presidential Support in Putin's Russia." *Javnost – The Public* 27 (1): 2–16. https://doi.org/10.1080/13183222.2020.1675434.

———. 2022a. "Sotsiolog Gregory Yudin pro fatalizm rossiian." *Polit.ru* (blog). July 14, 2022. https://m.polit.ru/news/2022/07/14/yudin/.

———. 2022b. "The War in Ukraine: Do Russians Support Putin?" *Journal of Democracy* 33 (3): 31–37.

Yurchak, Alexei. 2005. *Everything Was Forever, Until It Was No More: The Last Soviet Generation*. Princeton, NJ: Princeton University Press.

Yuriev, Evgenii. 2007. "O realizatsii natsional'noi programmy demograficheskogo razvitiia Rossii" [On the realization of the national program of Russia's demographic evolvement]. In *Natsional'naia identichnost' Rossii i demograficheskii krizis*, edited by S. Sulashkin, V. Bagdasarian, M. Vilisov, Yu. Zachesova, N. Pak, O. Seredkina, and A. Chirva, 282–9. Moskva: Nauchnii Ekspert.

Zabelin, Igor M. 1977. "My i mir, kotoryi nas okruzhaet" [We and the world surrounding us]. *Novyi Mir* 5:207–22.

Zagovora, Maxim. 2022. "'Delai vid, chto vse v poriadke, a zaodno bud' gotov umirat': Sotsiolog Grigory Yudin—o tom, kak eskalatsiia voiny vliiaet na rossiiskoe obshchestvo." *Zhurnal Kholod*, October 15, 2022. https://holod.media/2022/10/15/yudin-interview/.

Zaitzev, Nikolay. 2022. "Za i protiv: Stoit li otdavat' rebenka v chastnyi detskii sad." *Tinkoff Zhurnal*, October 11, 2022. https://journal.tinkoff.ru/private-kindergarten-pros-cons/.

Zakharov, Sergei. 2008. "Russian Federation: From the First to Second Demographic Transition." *Demographic Research* 19 (July): 907–72. https://doi.org/10.4054/DemRes.2008.19.24.

Zasn.ru. 2009. "Missiia dvizheniia 'Za sberezhenie naroda.'" Zasn.ru. 2009. https://zasn.ru/documents/missiya.

Zavrazhin, Konstantin, Sergey Kuksin, and Vladimir Kuzmin. 2017. "Putin: Vsia nasha rabota dolzhna byt' natselena na sberezhenie natsii." *Rossiiskaia Gazeta*, December 23, 2017. https://rg.ru/2017/12/23/putin-vsia-nasha-rabota-dolzhna-byt-nacelena-na-sberezhenie-nacii.html.

Zdravomyslova, Elena. 2010. "Working Mothers and Nannies: Commercialization of Childcare and Modifications in the Gender Contract (A Sociological Essay)." *Anthropology of East Europe Review* 28 (2): 200–225.

Zdravomyslova, Elena, Anna Temkina, and Anna Rotkirch. 2007. "Who Helps the Degraded Housewife?: Comments on Vladimir Putin's Demographic Speech." *European Journal of Women's Studies* 14 (4): 349–57.

Zhegulev, Ilya. 2019. "'I Want to Feel Like I'm in Russia, and That's How I Feel' Opposition Leader Mikhail Khodorkovksy Talks Putin, Navalny, Prigozhin, and More Five Years after His Release from Prison." *Meduza*, February 1, 2019. https://meduza.io/en/feature/2019/02/01/i-want-to-feel-like-i-m-in-russia-and-that-s-how-i-feel.

Zhvanetsky, Mikhail. 2018. "Naselenie i narod: Iazyk chinovnikov kak osobyi fenomen" [Population and people: Bureaucratic language as a unique phenomenon]. *Ogonek* 49 (December): 8.

Zlobin, Andrey. 2022. "V Mintruda zaiavili o slozhnoi demograficheskoi situatsii v Rossii" [The Ministry of Labor acknowledged the difficult demographic situation in Russia]. *Forbes*, December 6, 2022. https://www.forbes.ru/society/482104-v-mintruda-zaavili-o-sloznoj-demograficeskoj-situacii-v-rossii.

Zvereva, Natalia. 1980. "Ob"ektivnaia neobkhodimost' planomernogo upravleniia razvitiem narodonaseleniia pri sotsializme" [Objective necessity in the planned regulation of population development in socialism]. In *Upravlenie demograficheskimi protsessami* [The regulation of demographic processes], edited by Dmitry Valentei, 3–20. Moskva: Statistika.

INDEX

INNA LEYKIN is Senior Lecturer at the Department of Sociology,
Political Science and Communication at the Open University of Israel.

For Indiana University Press

Sabrina Black, *Editorial Assistant*
Tony Brewer, *Artist and Book Designer*
Anna Garnai, *Production Coordinator*
Sophia Hebert, *Assistant Acquisitions Editor*
Samantha Heffner, *Marketing and Publicity Manager*
Katie Huggins, *Production Manager*
Gigi Lamm, *Director of Sales and Marketing*
Nancy Lightfoot, *Project Manager/Editor*
Annie L. Martin, *Editorial Director*
Bethany Mowry, *Acquisitions Editor*
Dan Pyle, *Online Publishing Manager*
Michael Regoli, *Director of Publishing Operations*
Jennifer L. Wilder, *Senior Artist and Book Designer*